The Party Line

The Party Line

How the Media Dictates Public Opinion in Modern China

Doug Young

WILEY

John Wiley & Sons Singapore Pte. Ltd.

Other Wiley Editorial Offices
John Wiley & Sons, 111 River Street, Hoboken, NJ 07030, USA
John Wiley & Sons, The Atrium, Southern Gate, Chichester, West Sussex, P019 8SQ, United Kingdom
John Wiley & Sons (Canada) Ltd., 5353 Dundas Street West, Suite 400, Toronto, Ontario, M9B 6HB, Canada
John Wiley & Sons Australia Ltd., 42 McDougall Street, Milton, Queensland 4064, Australia
Wiley-VCH, Boschstrasse 12, D-69469 Weinheim, Germany

ISBN 978-0-470-82853-3 (Cloth)
ISBN 978-0-470-82855-7 (ePDF)
ISBN 978-0-470-82854-0 (Mobi)
ISBN 978-0-470-82856-4 (ePub)

Typeset in 11.5/14pt, Bembo by MPS Limited, Chennai, India.

10 9 8 7 6 5 4 3 2 1

I would like to dedicate this book to my parents, Bernard and Ellen Young, who have patiently put up with all my China fixations over the years.

Contents

Acknowledgments

Tackling such a broad and complex subject as the media in China has been a challenge that I never could have undertaken without the help of many people, both inside and outside the country. First and foremost, I would like to thank the many people who provided me with insight on the workings of the Chinese media and the broader context of events described in this book, including Dou Fengchang, Paul Pickowicz, Shen Yachuan, Sun Qian, Tu Yan, B.Y. Wong, Xiao Jiansheng, William Zhang, Zhang Zhi'an, Zheng Zhong, and Zuo Zhijian. I'd also like to thank Gao Qi and the Universities Services Centre for Chinese Studies at the Chinese University of Hong Kong, where I spent many happy hours poring over old copies of Chinese newspapers for my research. I would also like to acknowledge the book *Marketing Dictatorship*, and thank its author, Anne-Marie Brady, for providing me with insight on many of the finer points about how the Chinese media machine operates.

Readers are also critical to improving any manuscript, especially when the writer is someone like myself, who has spent way too much time working in the subject area and may lose perspective on some of the issues that might not be so familiar to others. In that regard, I'd like to thank Bill Berkeley, John Brill, Renee Chiang, Emily Rourke, and

Gina Keating for their feedback, and especially Josephine Khu and my sister, Margo Young, for making it through the entire manuscript.

At Wiley, special thanks are due to Nick Melchior for helping me to develop my idea into a real book, and I'd also like to thank Gemma Rosey, who helped me see the project through to completion. Much of my knowledge of the Chinese media comes from nearly a decade working as a journalist in Asia, and for that I'd like to thank Reuters for giving me the opportunity to report from a wide range of positions and locations over that time. Also at Reuters, I'd like to thank Don Durfee for introducing me to Wiley, and for his additional support in my endeavor.

Finally, I'd like to thank a woman who probably doesn't even remember me, my graduate school historiography teacher at Columbia University, Madeleine Zelin, who unknowingly helped to set me on my current course in life through one of her class assignments. That assignment, which asked us to compare a historical event as detailed in the press versus how it was later recorded by historians, helped me to see how I could join my passions for writing and history through a journalism career, with the realization that journalists really are the first recorders of history.

Introduction

Imagine this: You wake up one morning, roll out of bed, and turn on your radio to hear the morning drive-to-work show as you get ready to go to the office. Mike, Harold, and Samantha are going through their usual banter when the news announcer breaks in: "This just in," he says. "We're getting word that Clinksburg Mayor Tom Whitfield has been arrested as an accessory to murder. There are no further details at this time, but we'll be back with more on this breaking story when we have new information."

The show returns to Mike, Harold, and Samantha, who instantly jump on this breaking story by cracking jokes about Whitfield, the mayor of Clinksburg, who was elected two years ago on a campaign of toughness on crime. You wonder how the very man you voted for could have been busted for such a serious offense, even though you're not really sure what the crime actually is.

After dressing, you turn on your laptop and go to the *Clinksburg Chronicle* homepage. Sure enough, under the "breaking news" section is an article accompanied by an unrelated photo of Mayor Whitfield at a recent event. It offers several new details beyond the original bulletin without citing any sources. "Mayor Whitfield Arrested in Murder

Cover-Up" reads the headline in bold, followed by the lead: "Clinksburg Mayor Tom Whitfield has been arrested and charged as an accessory to murder. The mayor was taken into custody this morning at his home in suburban Clinksburg." You want to know more, but you really need to leave for work.

You pull out of your driveway and quickly tune to the local radio news station. You learn that Mayor Whitfield's wife is the one actually accused of murder. The report adds that the mayor found out about the crime and tried to hide it, but again no further details are given.

You soon arrive at work, where the story is already the talk of the office. Everyone is generally as surprised as you are, but no one ever stops to question where the accusations are coming from, despite the lack of details and attributions. What's more, the story so far has been devoid of images, with no news conferences, video, or photos of the mayor or his wife being led away in handcuffs, or anyone making statements. It's all been text on the page and announcers stating facts with no sources.

You check the *Chronicle* and several other web sites throughout the morning for updates, and are also in regular touch with friends and close colleagues via e-mail and instant messaging to stay on top of the story. You have a few more details by lunchtime, but you're no longer sure what is coming from where and how reliable the sources are. According to various reports you've received, the mayor's wife fell out with one of her business associates, an unnamed Kenyan man, whom she is now suspected of having killed. There are still no names of accusers behind the allegations, but the *Chronicle* is now saying that Mayor Whitfield was believed to have known about the murder just a few days after it occurred but failed to go to the police.

Minor details trickle in through the rest of the day. Oddly enough, there are no comments from the mayor or any member of his staff, from the district attorney, or from anyone else, for that matter. After work, you skip the usual drink with your colleagues and drive straight home to catch the evening news on TV.

The mayor's arrest is at the top of the broadcast, and by now the report is probably as close to complete as it's going to get today. The announcer rehashes the details you've already heard, with yet another old photo of Whitfield. She says the mayor was arrested at about six-thirty this morning at his suburban home, and is being charged as an

accessory to murder. He reportedly learned about the crime committed by his wife a couple of days after the Kenyan man died in a mysterious auto accident. But he failed to go to the police for at least the
next week, leading to his arrest this morning.

The whole story has a certain strangeness—not so much the
actual facts, but the lack of attribution. You expected the usual multi-
media circus, which should have included TV footage and photos of
the mayor and possibly his wife being led away in handcuffs from their
home, press conferences by his lawyer and the district attorney, and
possibly even written statements from the family of the Kenyan man.
Instead, all the reports and images have a kind of flatness to them.

The next morning, the newspapers mostly rehash accounts from
the previous day. On your way to the kitchen you notice someone
has slipped a manila envelope under your front door with the words
"strictly confidential" written in heavy black marker on the front. Upon
opening it, at the top left of the document inside you see "Official,
Final Version," and below that "For Immediate Release." Then two lines
down, at the center of the page, comes the headline: "Clinksburg Mayor
Tom Whitfield Guilty of Murder Cover-Up." As you read down the
page you realize that the document you are now holding is the sole
source of information for all the facts you heard yesterday, containing
everything from the auto accident that killed the Kenyan man to the
fact that the mayor knew about his wife's involvement in the case for at
least two weeks without going to the police. Nowhere on the sheet is
there any indication of who is accusing the mayor, what evidence there
is against him, where he is now, or how he or anyone else in the case
has responded to the allegations. And yet, he was arrested anyway—and
the media reported it all as if it were fact without noting any sources.

Welcome to news reporting as experienced in China. While the
following story may sound strange, it closely mirrors a case that cap-
tivated much of China in the spring of 2012. That case saw a former
Communist Party high-flier named Bo Xilai arrested for serious breach
of discipline after his wife allegedly had a British business associate
murdered when their relationship soured. No stories appeared in the
Chinese media for several weeks after Bo's disappearance from public view, despite widespread rumors. When the media finally reported
on the matter, all stories came from a single source: the official Xinhua

News Agency, with editors and reporters throughout the country understanding that this was the truth of the matter as decided by the highest ranks of the Communist Party.

The following pages will explore how the Party has used its tight control of the media over the past six decades to publicize news and win over public opinion for its agenda, first for building a socialist state and later for its current plan to build a market-oriented economy with "Chinese characteristics." They will also explore how that media message gets cast, by examining the vast bureaucracy that news stories must pass through before being published to make sure they conform to the message of the day.

There is one overriding theme that holds just as true today as it did in 1949 when the People's Republic of China was founded: On major issues, the Chinese media speak with a single voice, which is that of the Communist Party. Any semblance of many voices created by the nation's wide and varied range of newspapers and TV and radio stations is mostly an illusion. Yet at the same time, this book will also explore how China's media are far from a stagnant force and have undergone a steady process of change over the years. Perhaps nowhere is that change more apparent than in the current era, when the Party is having to rethink its approach in response to the rapid rise of the Internet, which now allows millions of Chinese to voice their views on current events alongside official versions in the state-owned media.

In the course of my survey, I will examine several major events and how the Chinese media reported on them, from the 1950–1953 Korean War, to the Tiananmen Square crackdown of 1989, to the 2008 Beijing Olympics. In exploring these events, my purpose is not to critique how closely Chinese media accounts conformed to reality, but rather to provide some insight into why the Chinese media reported on those events the way they did, and what their approach said about the Communist Party's agenda at the time. At the same time, I also hope to show how the government has modified its approach over the years in response to new proprieties and challenges of the times.

After more than a decade of working as a reporter in China, I find the Chinese media especially fascinating for their remarkable focus and ability to stay on message. In many ways, my interest in this subject dates back to a project in my graduate school days when we were asked to compare newspaper accounts of a historical event with later accounts in history books. My fascination with the idea of journalists and newspapers as the first recorders of history quickly grew, and was one of the reasons I became a reporter.

A key misconception among Westerners about the Chinese media is their assumption that, as with Western media, the ultimate goal is to report a story as objectively and truthfully as possible. Whereas the Western media are interested in presenting developments as they appear to reporters on the ground, China, through its media, is more interested in reporting a version of the truth that it wants its own people to believe, a sort of idealized image of itself.

From the Western perspective, the depiction of events in the Chinese media is often considered highly flawed—painting an overly simplistic view of the world where everything is black and white: white if the matter is in line with Party objectives and priorities, and black if it is not. From the Communist Party's perspective, this all makes perfect sense. To quote Party doctrine, the media are simply the "Voice of the Party."

Chapter 1

The Agenda

Telling the Party's Story

Locals read Chinese newspapers displayed on a public notice board in central Beijing March 23, 2011. The practice of displaying newspapers on public bulletin boards for all to read dates back to the earliest days of the founding of the People's Republic of China in 1949.

Photo Credit: Reuters/OTHK

A helpful metaphor to understand the world as depicted by China's media is the classic family portrait. This highly choreographed photo has mother and father at the center surrounded by their sons and daughters, everyone cheerful and smiling. Nowhere is there any sign of the many conflicts that most such families have, from minor issues like everyday fights between siblings to deeper resentments due to different priorities. All of those negative elements have been left out of the portrait, even though they exist and are very real factors for everyone within.

As head of the Chinese "family," the Communist Party uses China's media to show the world a harmonious place—one where farmers and factory workers smile and whistle while they work, where scientific and economic achievements abound, and where the Party is a source of comfort and assistance in times of trouble. Seldom is there mention of the constant power struggles taking place behind the scenes, or of smaller embarrassments like the naming in 2010 of a jailed dissident as China's first Nobel Peace Prize winner, to say nothing of major screw-ups like the Great Leap Forward—an agricultural fiasco of the 1950s that saw as many as 40 million people die of starvation during one of Mao's many disastrous initiatives under the country's centrally planned economy.

China's media are a sort of window on the soul of the Communist Party. They present the Party's message of the day, its broader agenda, and information on how it aims to achieve its goals. They also contain messages—some straightforward and others more veiled—of what is and is not acceptable, and what happens to those who make trouble. Equally important is what's *not* reported, be it an event that's considered taboo or an official who has fallen out of favor. By understanding

China's media, and how and what they choose to report, one can start to understand not only the Communist Party's agenda, but also its hopes and insecurities, what it sees as its accomplishments and short-comings, and how it plans to lead the world's most populous nation and second-largest economy through the 21st century en route to becoming the next global superpower.

The mandate of China's media is to tell China and the world about the Communist Party's agenda. While that agenda has changed over time, several major themes and tools in the media's tool kit have remained surprisingly constant in the more than six decades since the Communist Party founded the People's Republic of China in 1949. These include such tactics as emphasis on the actions of Party leaders, and a focus on positive news and achievements, all aimed at raising the government's prestige and legitimacy in the eyes of the Chinese people.

While most reports they carry tend to have an element of truth at their center, the Chinese media have never worried about massaging that truth to make it better fit the government's agenda. A poignant example occurred in 2003, when Yang Liwei became China's first man in space. Millions of Chinese watched on China Central Television, the country's largest broadcaster and one of the Party's main mouthpieces, as the Shenzhou 5 capsule blasted off on October 15 for the historic mission, as China became only the third country in the world to send a man into space. Later reports suggested that broadcast of the launch, which was billed as live, was actually delayed by several minutes to give officials time to disrupt the program in the event of any disaster or unforeseen problems.

While that precaution proved unnecessary, excessive G-forces on the capsule's reentry caused Yang's lip to split and start bleeding, leaving his face covered with blood when the hatch was opened with cameras rolling outside. Officials quickly determined that such an image wasn't the triumphant one that they wanted the world to see. So they quickly cleaned up the blood, sent Yang back into the capsule, and had him reemerge for a second, more befitting "first time," flashing a victory sign to the delight of proud Chinese viewers. This "touchup" of the truth came to light only many years later when an official from Xinhua, China's official news agency, told the story to a group of journalism students to illustrate when prettying up the truth was necessary to make sure the public got the right message.

Stories incapable of such "touching up" because they simply have no positive side are often just excluded from media coverage altogether. Such selective "editing" of entire events from the record books was more common in the 1950s and 1960s, when China was still a closed society and most media worked hand in hand with local propaganda departments. One old-time reporter I talked to recalled one such instance of selective "non-reporting" during the Cultural Revolution, the 1966–1976 mass movement that saw Mao throw China into chaos as he tried to rekindle the nation's Communist revolution and attack his critics.

In one of Mao's campaigns at the time, the nation's communes were called upon to introduce double planting seasons to increase yields. But as was often the case with many of Mao's campaigns, this one had no scientific foundation, and many regions where the growing season was simply too short for two plantings saw their net harvests dive from previous levels, leaving many hungry.

The reporter, working in a rural radio station at the time, wrote an article implicitly criticizing the policy based on his observations at many of the surrounding communes he had visited. He mailed the piece to his provincial newspaper and the *People's Daily*, the official Communist Party newspaper, without informing his editor. Such unsolicited submissions from rurally based reporters were common at the time, as even the biggest publications lacked the resources to do much reporting outside their immediate home bases. The *People's Daily* editors were less than pleased to receive the editorial, and informed the reporter's provincial propaganda department. Not only did the article never see the light of day, but the reporter's hometown police department issued a warrant for his arrest. Throughout the crisis, the media carried no reports about the policy's disastrous fallout, opting instead for locally written accounts singing the praises of its wisdom and effectiveness.

A more recent example came in 2010 when Liu Shaobo, an outspoken critic of the Communist Party and author of an open doctrine calling for democracy in China, won the Nobel Peace Prize. Despite frequent denunciations of the award by Chinese officials, whose remarks were meant for foreign consumption, the matter received little or no mention in domestic Chinese-language publications. One reporter I spoke with remarked that the more daring newspapers today will often take chances and write about controversial news where an official line has yet to be firmly established, reflecting the central government's loosening oversight on less-sensitive issues in recent years. But in Liu's case, he said, there was no gray area whatsoever: The news was not to be reported, and the media acted as if the event had simply never happened.

Another reporter noted that Liu's name was absent from the Chinese media throughout the entire nominating and selection process. There were no veiled threats in the media when it was widely believed that Liu was a front-runner for the prize, and no condemnations when he received the award. The reporter speculated, based on previous experience, that while many in the media were probably aware of developments by word of mouth, Communist Party propaganda officials had most likely talked to top editors in advance, a common practice in today's China, and instructed them not to print any news on Liu, as if the matter didn't exist. Reflecting a cynicism held by many Chinese reporters in the current climate due to limits on what they can report, he added that if a top Chinese government or Party official had received the prize, it would have been the leading news item in all the domestic media for at least several days.

The occasional maverick newspaper that does try to carry reports out of line with the official agenda can face major consequences, as I learned from one reporter whose newspaper dared to publish such an article.

It was 2002, and the reporter had interviewed Li Rui, a former secretary of Mao Zedong, on the sidelines of the National People's Congress, China's annual gathering of top government, business, and social leaders in Beijing. Negative news during this period is strictly prohibited. Rather, during the many policy speeches, press conferences, and photo opportunities open to reporters, the focus is on government achievements over the past year and on the agenda for the year ahead.

Li, who was around 85 at the time, used the interview to call for political reform—a topic strictly forbidden by the economically liberal but politically conservative Communist Party. During the interview an outspoken Li spoke critically not only of the current administration, but also of his former boss, Mao, and Deng Xiaoping, architect of China's economic reform. Despite the sensitive nature of the topic, the reporter's paper went ahead and published an article. One month later, the paper was shut down. The Li article was perhaps the final straw for the paper, which had angered propaganda officials with a steady stream of investigative-style profiles of Party officials that went beyond the usual puffery and tried to present their subjects as real people with strengths and weaknesses.

Specific agenda items have come and gone over the years, but one thing has remained constant: The Party is always front-page news. A quick look at any established Chinese newspaper, from the biggest city dailies to the smallest provincial papers, quickly reveals a surprisingly uniform set of images and stories across the spectrum on any given day. A closer examination of many of these papers further reveals that most of their top stories are identical, taken directly from Xinhua reports featuring the latest comings and goings of top officials and accompanying photos. Even articles from day to day start to look the same, describing which meetings top leaders attended, whom they met, what was discussed, and even the occasional text of a speech, all accompanied by photos of handshakes, people at meetings, welcoming banquets, and so forth.

China watchers take delight in "reading the tea leaves" by observing front pages of domestic newspapers, noting who is in and out of favor by looking at the order of names in articles and who appears in stories at the top of the front page, who appears at the bottom, and who doesn't appear at all. The average Chinese often simply skips these front-page stories and goes straight to the inside pages where more conventional news is placed. One reporter told me that monikers used for top leaders in their obituaries are particularly revealing, reflecting the current state of politics as much as the stature of the person who died. The most important leaders are remembered as "Great Revolutionaries of the Classless Society." Next down the pecking order are "Loyal Communist Warriors," followed by "Outstanding Revolutionaries of the Classless Society." Past leaders who have fallen out of favor often get no moniker at all, and their deaths may be carried as simple four- or five-line announcements with few or no details beyond the fact that they died.

One reporter at a provincial newspaper told me that the rules at his paper were quite straightforward: The front page was reserved for the province's two top officials—the governor and the Party secretary. As a general rule, no other government official could appear as the lead of page one, he said. To fill so much space with the comings and goings of just two people, the newspaper had a dedicated team of about a half-dozen reporters who, each evening, would receive the two men's schedules for the next day, and then follow them around and take copious notes on all of their meetings and events.

I got an interesting taste of this mindset while teaching journalism at one of Shanghai's top universities. For one of their weekly assignments, I asked my students to write about an emergency meeting of the United Nations Security Council after Israel had attacked a flotilla of Turkish ships carrying aid supplies to the Gaza Strip in 2010. To my surprise, quite a few of my students' papers came back with simple leads that said "The United Nations Security Council met after Israel attacked a flotilla of Turkish aid ships." Nowhere was there any mention of what action the Security Council took—just the fact that they met. I explained to the class that what happened at the meeting was the news, and not the meeting itself. In response, one of the bolder students raised her hand and quietly pointed out that in the Chinese media it is just the opposite: The fact of the meeting and details like who attended are always the news, and substance is strictly secondary.

The Party's iron grip over the nation's front pages has persisted to this day and is still evident in most media, which are nearly all state-owned at some level. But at the same time, the Party, as part of its move toward a more market-oriented economy, has also encouraged the media to sink or swim on their own, cutting off most of the government funding they received in the past and making them rely on advertising and other market-oriented revenue sources to fund their operations. This shift has produced an interesting new dichotomy over the past decade between official Party newspapers, which still rely on the state for much of their funding, and a new generation of newspapers and magazines carrying more consumer-friendly fare.

Such a split actually dates back as far as the 1950s and early 1960s, when most papers were categorized as either Party papers, such as the *People's Daily* in Beijing and *Liberation Daily* in Shanghai, which devoted most of their ink to the latest Party news, or more commercial populist papers, such as Shanghai's *Wenhui Bao*, which had its roots as a real commercial paper in pre-Communist China. The Party papers, most of them formed around or after 1949, got a big chunk of their news directly from Xinhua, China's official news agency, whose stories were the closest thing to official Party news releases. The populist papers were separate from these official Party mouthpieces, and usually contained more features and locally based reporting.

The more consumer-oriented papers were largely forced to toe the Party line for much of the 1960s and 1970s, during the Cultural Revolution, but have gravitated back to their commercial roots in the current Reform era. In addition, a new generation of consumer-oriented papers has sprung up since the 1990s, many founded by the older stalwart publications but quickly supplanting their parent papers to become bigger breadwinners. This new generation of more commercial papers, while still avoiding taboo subjects like Tibetan and Taiwanese independence, look more like Western newspapers, carrying a wide array of articles on sports and entertainment, local news, and healthy doses of international stories on subjects that are less politically sensitive in China. Even the stalwarts have joined the populist movement, devoting their front pages to Party politics but then leaving the rest of the paper for more popular material. Many Chinese will say that anyone who buys one of these papers won't even bother looking at the front page, but instead will skip straight to the inside for more interesting fare.

Tool for Social Stability

The media's function as a tool for social stability has been another major theme over the past 30 years, especially in the current Reform era, when massive changes have drastically altered millions of lives in a very short time with the elimination of many socialist-era safety nets. Top officials can be quite frank on this topic. One top Chinese official in Hong Kong, Hao Tiechuan, caused a commotion in 2010 when he told a local association of journalists that maintaining social order was one of the Chinese media's main roles in society. Regular readers of

Chinese newspapers and magazines will be quick to note they seldom carry reports of unrest of any kind, be it labor unrest due to low or unpaid wages, or protests over cronyism and corrupt local officials. Such reports, so the thinking goes, could incite others to take similar action. On the other hand, reports detailing the arrest of local officials for corruption or the settlement of a labor dispute are much more common, showing readers that their grievances are being heard without the threat of social upheaval.

I got a first hand look at this phenomenon while working in the Hong Kong bureau of Reuters in the spring of 2010 when a series of strikes broke out in the affluent Pearl River Delta, home to many of China's biggest exporters. The unrest began with a series of suicides at one major Taiwanese-run complex, as despondent young workers took their lives after working long hours for low pay, often in isolation designed to keep productivity high. The unrest later spread to Japanese-invested factories making parts for big automakers like Honda and Toyota, with workers going on strike over low pay and long working hours.

Chinese media are sometimes allowed to report such problems if they occur at foreign-owned factories, and many wholeheartedly jumped on the bandwagon by sending their own reporters to cover the first wave of suicides. They later flocked to the auto parts makers to cover the latest developments. But several weeks into both cases, the government clearly started to worry that all the reports were having a contagious effect, leading more unhappy workers to consider the possibility of staging their own strikes. Concern over this potential for growing unrest resulted in a crackdown that saw the number of reports drop off sharply and in some papers disappear completely. Reporters at those papers later said that propaganda officials banned them from writing their own reports, and that only the official reports from Xinhua, which were often brief and thin on details, could be carried on either subject. One reporter at a newspaper in the region later told me that reporters are generally conditioned to be careful when reporting on matters that can influence public order or create social instability, or to simply avoid such topics altogether.

Another reporter commented that strikes are a sensitive matter in China, as are suicides, and that an understanding exists between propaganda officials and journalists to generally avoid reporting on such matters or to exercise caution when doing so.

More progressive publications print stories on labor unrest and other social problems at their peril, as they run the risk of being severely censured or even closed down by having their licenses revoked if they upset the wrong people. A textbook example is a case involving a progressive publication in the southern city of Guangzhou that ran a story about an out-of-towner waiting to have a grievance heard who died of a suspected police beating while in custody. That article exposed an underground system of informal detention centers in many of China's major cities used to confine "undesirables." Such centers, while not officially authorized, had become a useful tool for local police to deal with large numbers of similar petitioners who often came from the countryside to lodge protests on anything from local corruption to dissatisfaction over terms of compensation for confiscated land, and who loitered around without any real hope of having their grievances heard. The story caused an uproar when published, and led to calls for reform—clearly one of the newspaper's goals in printing it. It also resulted in the detention and later arrest of three of the newspaper group's top officials.

Others run a similar risk. One reporter I interviewed from another progressive publication told me of an instance in 2005 when farmers in the central province of Hebei clashed with a local steel factory that wanted their land in order to expand its operations. The farmers were resisting the local government's attempt to confiscate the land, and so the publication sent several reporters to cover the conflict. On learning that reporters were talking to the farmers, local police went to the scene and roughed up the reporters, seizing their notes and film. The publication's headquarters later got a call from propaganda officials informing them they didn't have the authority to report on the matter. Despite that warning, they went ahead and published a story on the conflict, complete with photos smuggled from the scene, leading to the resignation of the head of the township's news and propaganda department.

While such news with the power to fan discontent is clearly off limits, just the opposite is true for "happy news," which is always welcome and has been a staple of the Communist Party's media agenda, especially in the post-Mao era. Most Chinese reporters have numerous tales about stories they pitched that were ultimately shot down for lack of a positive message. Writers of downbeat stories are often asked to rewrite them with a more positive spin if they want their work to see the light of day, with the result that many Chinese papers often exude a surrealistic Pollyana-esque glow.

One former Xinhua reporter I talked with said his editors would often ask him to tone down his stories if they sounded too liberal, or to remove facts that sounded too negative. Stories of discontent in any form or about people who had died in conflicts were generally discouraged, he said, as were taboo topics like crime and prostitution. The main mission was to show society in a positive light. Another reporter said that any rookie reporter writing in the 1960s, 1970s, and even into the 1980s quickly realized that the media were the "Party's tongue and throat," to quote a popular slogan coined early on and still in use today. Reporting positive news is especially important during high-profile events like the 2008 Beijing Olympics, the 2010 Shanghai World Expo, or just about any major Party gathering—especially the annual National People's Congress held every March.

A former reporter for China Central Television (CCTV), the country's main national broadcaster and one of the Communist Party's main mouthpieces, described a particular experience that highlights the extreme difficulties that reporters face in trying to tell a negative story. In that instance the reporter traveled from Beijing to a village in eastern China's Anhui province to visit a school for poverty-stricken children set up by a former law student. The school had previously received national media attention and was constantly being praised for its good work. But the purpose of his trip wasn't to write yet another feel-good story, but rather to explore allegations that the law student was also a pedophile who had sexually abused boys at his school.

Despite receiving the go-ahead from his editors, the reporter was discouraged before even leaving by a local education minister in Anhui, who made it clear that this kind of report would tarnish the school and all its good work. But the minister was powerless to stop the story since CCTV, as a national broadcaster and an official voice of the Communist Party, had the authority to pick and choose its own stories without local interference. Undeterred by the local minister's words, the reporter traveled to the school to interview its founder and some alleged victims.

Things went relatively smoothly until the reporter returned to Beijing to produce his final story. It was then that the problems began. His first attempt at a story consisted of two parts, each 25 minutes long, set to air on a CCTV investigative news magazine show. That version got the green light from his supervisor and was set to air the next day. But that evening, while the reporter and his assistant were out celebrating, he received a call saying that the following day was China's officially designated Teachers Day, and that it would be inappropriate to broadcast the story then. Later that night he got another call and learned that a more senior editor had seen the piece and thought it too long and negative to be released—the first signs of major resistance to the story.

After a heavy round of cutting, which saw the piece trimmed by half to a single 25-minute segment that included a toning down of the more negative elements, the story was again approved for broadcast. The reporter was out celebrating once again when he got another call, this time saying the story was still too negative and asking him to add a few more positive elements. Ultimately he had to recast the story eight times and spent two months working on it. In the end, it was never even broadcast, costing him a big part of his salary in an industry where reporters are paid partly based on the number of their pieces that are aired.

While negative news is generally discouraged, propaganda officials have begun to make a subtle distinction in the past decade between two kinds of such news, namely problems that can be solved with relative ease and those that have no easy answer. One-off problems, such as a gas explosion or a coal mining disaster, have become relatively regular fodder in today's Chinese media, as they are both sensational enough to appeal to broader audiences and acceptable to propaganda officials because they don't tend to dwell on deeper social issues. Some say that the 2003 outbreak of SARS (severe acute respiratory syndrome) marked a watershed in allowing certain types of negative news because a disease of this sort, while negative and potentially devastating, didn't reflect badly on the Party itself or any of its policies. Such a problem was instead an act of nature in which the Party could actually boost its public image by showcasing its efforts to fight the deadly disease and save lives.

Media are also allowed to report on select, more endemic, problems if such reports dovetail with the government's latest agenda. A good case in point is reporting on corruption, which has risen sharply in recent years. Seldom does a week go by without a report about an official in one province or another detained for accepting bribes or for other corrupt acts. However, the reports nearly always involve low-level officials, and the stories they tell fit neatly with the government's narrative that the Party is heeding the call of a frustrated public by diligently weeding out the bad apples within its ranks. One editor I spoke with noted that official sources like Xinhua or other major Party publications are nearly always the ones to "break" news of official corruption cases, as smaller papers often lack the resources and audacity to pursue such news. In such cases, the announcement by Xinhua or another official source of an arrest is a signal to the broader media that they can report on the matter, using both the official accounts as well as accounts based on their own work.

Reporters have also been given free rein to discuss other, less-sensitive issues like pollution and workplace accidents, as the government realizes that stories on these troublesome issues can advance its agenda of trying to stem these problems that have accompanied China's rapid modernization. Barely a day goes by in most major cities without a report of a factory dumping illegal waste into a nearby waterway, or an explosion in a poorly run private coal mine that has left dozens of people dead. Such reports often lead local police, environmental, and other officials to spring into action, again helping the government to meet its objective of showing it is actively addressing these troublesome issues.

One area that is becoming more open but still remains quite sensitive is economic and financial news. After the global financial crisis of 2008 led to some of the worst inflation to hit the country in recent years, many media were initially barred from reporting on the phenomenon to keep from exacerbating consumer discontent. The strategy seemed to be that by keeping big-picture inflation stories out of the media, consumers would assume the problem wasn't so bad. But as inflation became too obvious to ignore, the blackout was lifted and stories on rising prices soon became a staple in many daily news reports. Even in this case, reports were often quick to point out the inflation was largely imported, created by loose monetary policies in the West. Thus, angry consumers could hardly blame the Communist Party, which itself was a victim of irresponsible Western behavior.

Negative economic news is also permissible if given the right spin to teach people a proper lesson that the Party wants to convey, such as the negative consequences of irrational consumer behavior. One such case occurred in the spring of 2011 after a huge earthquake hit northern Japan, causing a major radiation leak at a nuclear power plant. As concern started to grow about radioactive water dumped into the sea reaching China, word started to spread that iodine could ward off radiation poisoning and that salt was a readily available source of iodine. A huge run on salt followed, leaving store shelves empty of all salt products after a wave of panic buying.

Seeking to halt the panic, China quickly mobilized the media to dispel the rumors by putting out reports citing officials and scientists declaring that salt contained far too little iodine to counter the effects of radiation, and that radiation poisoning from Japan was highly unlikely in any event. Reporters then went on a sort of witch hunt, most likely encouraged by central propaganda officials, for people who had stocked up during the panic buying. One of those, a man from western China who had purchased 6.5 tons of the product at inflated black-market prices, only to discover he had spent much of his life savings on something that was worthless to stop a threat that didn't exist, became a national pariah overnight. The reports about the man were generally derisive, simultaneously warning and mocking anyone foolish enough to think that China was under threat from radiation, or that salt could lower the risk.

Many reporters will say that financial news in general has become much less sensitive in recent years, and that this is one of the few areas where the government has let the media adopt a more Western-style role of watchdog to help keep China's freewheeling corporate world from becoming too unruly. Before 2000, one reporter told me that bosses at big state-run companies would often complain to local propaganda departments when newspapers carried unflattering stories about them, resulting in the customary "courtesy call" that nearly every editor in China has received from either a company or propaganda official when one of his reporters wrote something politically incorrect. But nowadays such complaints to propaganda departments often fall on deaf ears, as the Party allows the media to help police an increasingly affluent and powerful corporate sector. In one instance, the reporter said, he wrote an article about the embarrassing failure of a merger between two state-run companies, and received a call from an official at one of the firms berating him for his audacity and reminding him he could have the reporter arrested. Later, the official's superior called to apologize for the earlier exchange, in a quiet acknowledgment that such reporting, if done responsibly and accurately, was acceptable.

In terms of the Party's own agenda, the media have always been and remain a steadfast tool for the government to show its people who is in charge. On the international front, most major daily newspapers still feature prominent pictures and stories on their front and international pages any time a head of state visits China. Such reports seldom discuss what was said or done at those meetings, probably because very little of major substance occurred. Instead, these kinds of reports are designed to show Chinese officials simply looking like leaders. Most Chinese readers will tell you they don't bother to look at such reports, but certainly the images of their top officials shaking hands with other global leaders must leave at least some kind of impression that, consciously or not, adds to the credibility of these leaders.

The Party also uses the media to make its views known on international incidents that directly or tangentially involve China, many of which will be discussed in more detail in the later chapters of this book. Such use of the media can appear somewhat whimsical to the outside observer, with reports suddenly changing tenor midway through the course of a story, or even disappearing from the media altogether. One recent case occurred in 2010, when a former Filipino police officer took a bus full of Hong Kong tourists hostage in Manila. The incident ended with eight of the hostages killed in a bungled rescue attempt by the Filipino authorities. Initial Chinese media reports on the incident were largely indignant over the poor handling of the situation, creating friction in Sino-Philippine affairs that soon threatened to spiral out of control. Sensing this, propaganda officials stepped in and ordered local papers to keep the tone of their stories in line with official foreign ministry statements, to report more positively on the rescue effort, and not to link the case with Sino-Philippine relations.

While most negative news is discouraged, other sensitive topics are explicitly off limits and are never featured in the local media. These include most religious matters and conflicts between the Han Chinese majority and the country's many ethnic minorities, as well as anything critical of China's human rights record. Another topic off the agenda is the Falun Gong spiritual movement, a broad-based, well-organized group that burst on the scene in the 1990s, and later was outlawed and deemed an "evil cult."

Another interesting case along these lines occurred during the Jasmine Revolution of early 2011, also called the "Arab Spring," which saw a series of uprisings destabilize and unseat longstanding govern-ments in the Middle East and North Africa, starting in Tunisia and then spreading as far and wide as Egypt, Libya, and Syria. As the unrest spread, China's leaders and propaganda officials worried that the protests might inspire the same in their own country, and ordered a sudden ban in the media on the use of many of the words related to the movement. In the weeks that followed, most news reports on the subject were outlawed, and "Egypt," "Tunisia," and other related words were expunged from most of the nation's major news and social media web sites. All pho-tos and video of the protests were also banned, amid concerns that they might remind some of similar images from China's own Tiananmen stu-dent movement of 1989, which ended in a bloody crackdown.

The only news about the Jasmine Revolution allowed were reports from Xinhua and other official outlets, which usually focused on China-related elements of the unrest, such as spotlighting how the government was helping to evacuate Chinese nationals trapped in the region. When Egyptian President Hosni Mubarak finally stepped down, the news got little play in the Chinese media. One editorial, playing to a broader fear of national civil unrest, even warned that China could plunge into chaos if the country wasn't careful and tried to stage its own similar movement.

Changing with the Times

While certain elements have remained on the agenda in the Party's more than six decades in power, many other items have come and gone depending on who was running the show. The biggest divide was between the Mao era from 1949 to 1976, and the post-Mao era that now accounts for more than half of Chinese history under Communist

Party rule. Whereas the earlier period was filled with revolutionary messages as Mao and his Party consolidated power and set up their vision of a socialist state, the post-Mao era has been characterized by greater pragmatism on the part of the Party, with messages aimed at demonstrating the government's dedication to improving the lot of more than a billion Chinese through the adoption of a more market-oriented economy.

The early era saw the media singing the praises of the Communist Party and Mao Zedong. During that time, when literacy and newspaper distribution were still low and TV nearly nonexistent, easy-to-remember slogans were often the most effective way of conveying the Party's latest message to the hundreds of millions of Chinese farmers who still lived in the countryside, and whose main access to the media came through loudspeaker systems set up throughout their villages, through radios played during meals at communal mess halls, and from newspapers posted on communal bulletin boards. Each slogan was part of a broader campaign, and reporters often traveled to the countryside both to spread those messages and to report back on how campaigns were being carried out at the grassroots level.

One reporter I talked to worked for a rural broadcaster in central China in the 1960s and early 1970s. He recalled a series of slogans that typified the messages of the day, all employing simple concepts aimed at making the average rural Chinese understand and appreciate the Party's efforts at building a more just socialist state. One, *Nongye xue Dazhai*, called on farmers to "learn agriculture from Dazhai," a rural village in western Shanxi province set up as a model agricultural area. A companion slogan, *Gongye xue Daqing*, called on factory workers to "learn industry from Daqing," an oil-rich area in northeastern Heilongjiang province. Two other popular slogans of the day were for everyone to "Learn from the People's Liberation Army" and "Engage in class struggle," messages that were clearly close to Mao's heart as he tried to push socialist reforms in cities and the countryside in the early days, and to turn class struggle and worship of the nation's military into pillars of the national consciousness.

In those days, reporters, many of them recruited from smaller villages and towns, were generally encouraged to travel back to their hometowns and other remote areas to report on the changes that were happening in those places as Mao and the Communists sought to transform both agriculture and industry. First drafts of all stories went through a heavy-handed editing process, which often included the addition of language praising Mao, the Communists, and socialism. Typically the final stories bore little or no resemblance to the original drafts.

The reporter I talked to recalled submitting one article with another reporter about the improving situation in an area inhabited by the Miao minority, where many young people were starting to get a basic education, a step up from the illiteracy and hand-to-mouth existence of the previous generations. Their story included references to the difficulties of life without education and culture. These references were quickly cut by the editors for being too negative and not in keeping with the message from Mao, and replaced with language blasting the tyranny of the previous regime under the Nationalists, whom the Communists had defeated in 1949 after a prolonged civil war.

In many instances from that era, the media engaged in outright lies, painting beautiful pictures of how the latest Mao campaign had improved the life of millions of peasants when just the opposite was true. In one instance, villages all over China were set to literally digging away hills and knolls to create new farmland, in response to a tale popularized by the government about how people from one village had literally moved a mountain to create new fields. During that campaign, one reporter recalled how his office was inundated with heavily edited reports from village communes throughout the area on how they were digging up earth, specifying how many tons of dirt they had moved to create new fields. But when the spring rains came the following planting season and created a huge muddy mess, no one wrote in telling of major disruptions caused by the ill-conceived policy, and the media carried no reports on these events.

In the post-Mao era, the agenda shifted from a focus on class struggle, which had plunged the country into a decade of chaos during the Cultural Revolution of 1966–1976, to an economic agenda of building a more market-oriented economy while maintaining the Party's grip on power. The Chinese media began portraying China as a country of laws, as the Party sought to convince outside investors who were crucial to its economic development that they would be treated fairly and not be subject to the whims of local officials. One reporter used the following metaphor to describe this turning point: Before the shift at the beginning of the Reform era in 1979, the media were like someone tied to a chair and locked in a room—it didn't matter whether the person was dead or alive. After the shift, the media became more like someone still locked in the room, but no longer tied to the chair. Suddenly he has a little freedom to do his job, though still within a highly restrictive environment. Whereas even the smallest things like socializing with foreigners had been strictly taboo for reporters and raised suspicion in the period of class struggle, many of those things became acceptable in the newer climate.

During this time, especially in the early Reform era, reporters were still often assigned to write stories with messages that the government wanted to publicize. One reporter said he was once assigned to report a "story" in the early Reform era with the prewritten headline "China Sticks to Socialism." In effect, the story was an unsubtle message telling both the Chinese people and the world that China was practicing market economics but was still sticking to the core socialist values that gave the Communist Party its legitimacy.

The post-Mao Communist Party emphasis on economics was clearly demonstrated in the media following the bloody government crackdown on a student movement at Tiananmen Square in 1989 that called for democratic reforms. After the crackdown, which saw hundreds of people killed by tanks and troops advancing into the city, Party officials, using the media as their voice, went on their own assault to assure both domestic and foreign audiences that the country was still on an unstoppable road to economic reform, even if it had rejected the kind of political reform sought by the Tiananmen students. During this period, the media also went to great pains to carry a detailed "explanation" of why the government had launched the crackdown. A host of catchphrases came into the media lexicon, calling the movement an "antigovernment rebellion" and saying it had been orchestrated by a small number of antigovernment "black hands" manipulating a well-intentioned general public.

Immediately after the crackdown, the media were also awash with comments from the handful of stalwart Chinese allies who voiced support for the use of military force, saying it was understandable and necessary. Nowhere was there mention of the far more numerous statements from other nations condemning the crackdown. This tactic, whereby the media carry a carefully filtered selection of standalone stories, each showing support from a different global leader, is commonly used by the media to this day. In some cases the aim is to justify government actions like the Tiananmen crackdown, while in others the goal is to show indignation over acts like NATO's accidental bombing of the Chinese embassy in Belgrade during NATO's bombing of Yugoslavia in 1999.

As economic achievements have become the message of the day, showcasing government accomplishments has also moved to the center of the Party's agenda, providing justification for its continued leadership after the abandonment of its socialist agenda. In this more recent period, we see a big increase in reporting on natural disasters such as earthquakes and floods, which provide strong opportunities to show the government hard at work assisting and rescuing victims of such acts of nature. A nonstop stream of articles and photos filled the national media after a huge earthquake struck Sichuan province in 2008, leaving tens of thousands of people dead. And during a particularly harsh drought in the spring of 2011, barely a day went by without mention in the media of how the controversial Three Gorges Dam on the Yangtze River, built during the Reform era in the 1990s, had helped to alleviate suffering by releasing extra water into drought-stricken regions.

In recent years, China has also discovered that "big events," most notably sporting events, are an effective means of showcasing its new economic prosperity. Since the Beijing Olympics of 2008, barely a year has gone by without China hosting one kind of major sporting event or another that inevitably gets huge coverage from the domestic media, which report on every detail, from elaborately choreographed opening ceremonies to the actual events and finally the equally elaborate closing ceremonies. During such big events, all negative news is banned from the media.

During one such pageant, the Asian Games of October 2010, held in Guangzhou, a huge fire broke out in an apartment building under renovation thousands of kilometers away in Shanghai, leaving more than 50 people dead and exposing the broader issue of shoddy practices throughout China's construction industry. One reporter recalled how his publication was banned from carrying anything on the story besides the short, official Xinhua reports while the Asian Games were still in progress. In that instance, his paper adopted a tactic that has become increasingly common among progressive media: that of using the Xinhua report as the foundation of the article, but then adding liberal amounts of the paper's own reporting. By taking this approach, papers have found they can get around bans on reporting of certain negative stories, since anything from Xinhua is officially allowed to appear in local media. And by adding in their own reporting, which often goes beyond Xinhua's more superficial treatment, they also give readers a more in-depth view of the issues.

Interestingly, times of political turbulence are among the few exceptions when control from the center is jettisoned and most decision making happens locally in terms of what to report. The two most famous periods in that regard are the decade-long Cultural Revolution and the Tiananmen Square student movement of 1989. The former saw many newsrooms become camps divided between those loyal to Mao's ideas preaching a return to class struggle and more moderate leaders, who advocated a less-radical approach and more focus on economic development, with different groups prevailing at different times and in different publications despite all the dogma that filled the media during those times. Despite the relative freedom to take sides, the media in this period were ironically largely devoid of real news, and instead were filled with vacuous slogans and editorials calling on people to follow the thinking of whatever camp had the upper hand at the time. During the Tiananmen Student Movement, the reporting became much more varied as the center again lost control, with many major newspapers sending reporters to Beijing to file their own stories—something that would have been unthinkable under normal circumstances when most media would simply use reports from either Xinhua or China Central Television.

On more local issues that fall off the central government's radar screen, internal debates about government policymaking still take place, with the potential to produce bold and innovative reporting. One such case occurred in 2006, when Shanghai's local Communist Party boss, a man named Chen Liangyu, and those around him came under fire for allegedly misspending city funds in a scandal that eventually resulted in his ouster. Throughout the scandal, it was clear that a branch of the Party, probably with strong support from central leaders in Beijing, was trying to remove Chen and that no one was in clear control. As a result, the media both in Shanghai and throughout China were relatively free to write whatever they wanted about the situation. One Shanghai-based reporter recalled receiving a steady string of scoops during that time from anti-Chen forces, and feeling confident enough to publish them despite the risk of backlash from Chen's allies.

Agendas may come and go over the years, but at the end of the day the Communist Party really has one main goal that never changes: staying in power. Even top Chinese leaders are subject to this one major tenet, and talk of plurality from them or anyone else is strictly banned from publication. Premier Wen Jiabao commented on the need for political reform in several high-profile speeches during the closing years of his tenure from 2002 to 2012, which many took to refer to a stronger separation of the Communist Party from the government, perhaps even to allowing non-Party members into top government posts. Yet despite wide coverage of his remarks in foreign media, domestic publications blacked out his comments under strict orders from central propaganda officials. That blatant ban led 23 prominent leaders from across the political and cultural spectrum to sign a rare open letter calling for an end to such censorship, which, ironically, was itself censored from all domestic media. During a 2011 visit to the United States, President Hu Jintao's remarks on China's human rights record, made in response to a reporter's question, met with a similar fate, receiving zero coverage in the Chinese media, which otherwise provided nonstop coverage of the trip.

Clearly, when any leader or group wants to stay in power, it will tend to stifle any talk of political plurality or giving voice to dissenters, even when such talk comes from within the top echelons of its own ranks. Viewed from this perspective, the vast majority of what appears in China's media, both the actual content and the packaging, all has a common aim. When there's good news, it's there to show off the Party's accomplishments. When there's bad news, it's there to let the public know that the problem is being tackled. On the broadest basis it's all about using the media to show a picture of a China that may be less than perfect, but one that is still presenting its best face to both its own people and the rest of the world.

Chapter 2

Spreading the Word

The Machinery

To make sure its media message is properly and uniformly delivered, Beijing has developed a well-oiled machine to craft and control that message by making decisions at the top and letting those coverage guidelines filter down to the provinces with ever-increasing speed. Cogs in the machine are many and varied, ranging from placement of a Communist Party secretary in the top ranks of most major media, to frequent phone calls and memos sent by the Propaganda Ministry to senior editors at those same media. The message-crafting machinery has moved in step with the media's own changing role over time, ebbing and flowing with the level of central control in the 60 years since the founding of the People's Republic.

In its very early days, the Communist Party took a surprisingly relaxed view toward the media, from both political and commercial standpoints. Immediately after 1949, a large number of smaller political parties, many sympathetic to the Communists, were allowed to keep publishing their own newspapers and magazines with their own political views. The two sides had an understanding: The smaller parties had no designs on power or governing, which would be the exclusive terrain of the Communist Party. Instead, the smaller parties reserved the right to constructively criticize the government's policies, acting as a benign watchdog to keep the Party honest and moving in the right direction.

That relatively enlightened situation lasted for only a few years into the 1950s, when Mao discovered he wasn't as fond of criticism as he had previously thought, especially when the criticism was directed at some of his pet projects, like the collectivization of farms that would ultimately lead to the catastrophic Great Leap Forward of 1958–1961, which saw millions die of starvation. As Mao and the Communists became increasingly uneasy with the criticism and plurality of the earliest media landscape, most of the smaller Party papers were either gradually shut down or gutted of their critical voices and replaced with the centrally controlled system that came to characterize China for much of the 1960s and 1970s, where all media, regardless of their stated political affiliation, became little more than bullhorns to tout the Communist Party's latest accomplishments and promote its initiatives.

From a populist standpoint, the media in the earliest days of the People's Republic were also expected to serve a dual purpose for their readers. They were expected to spread the Party's message, acting as a propaganda tool. But in a more idealistic time, when the Party had just come into power, it also encouraged the media to carry a more commercial form of news that would appeal to the ordinary person rather than just the same old news about the government and its latest accomplishments.

One reporter I interviewed attended journalism school and started his reporting career during this interesting time in the 1950s. In the early days from 1949 to 1956, the media reported on a wide range of issues of general interest and also kept in line with the Party's aim of rapid modernization. The reporter recalled how, during his days as a journalism student in Shanghai, one professor espoused this dual role of the media as both a propaganda and a populist force, only to be attacked as an antirevolutionary for those same views under an anti-rightist campaign in 1957.

This was one of many such campaigns under Mao, who loved to float new ideas but then would quickly become incensed at any consequences or feedback he disliked.

After seeing their professors attacked for their more liberal views in the late 1950s, most reporters began to realize the media were strictly meant to be the voice of the Party, or the Party's "tongue and throat," as the popular expression went. The initial atmosphere of optimism and idealism quickly faded to fear and disappointment, and many journalism departments and newspapers soon became hotbeds for criticism sessions—another tactic used by Mao to attack people and issues he didn't like. In 1958, this reporter recalled, his university's entire journalism department, one of the leading such schools in China, was sent to the countryside for a year to learn first hand about the poverty-stricken proletarian masses that made up most of China's population at that time. Such mass deportations of academics and other city folk to the countryside to "learn from the masses" became a staple under Mao Zedong's rule, culminating with the displacement of millions of people for years and even decades during the Cultural Revolution of 1966–1976. Rather than hone their journalism skills during their time in the countryside, the group of young students instead spent much of their time in group sessions criticizing many of their former teachers for their rightist views. They were rewarded the next year by being sent to work at an iron factory as part of their "education through labor"—a favorite tactic of Mao, who believed that such educated elite lacked understanding of lower-class, blue-collar, and rural workers.

The years after the Great Leap Forward of 1958 to 1961 saw a return to a more tolerant view toward the media, as Mao retreated in the face of the agricultural fiasco that left as many 40 million dead by letting other, more pragmatic leaders take control of the economy and other organs govern the day-to-day running of the state. But the old dogma quickly returned a few years later in the mid-1960s under an even more determined Mao, who believed that class struggle was the only thing that mattered and had to be discussed on a daily basis. From this point on, the media became Mao's personal soapbox, leveling criticism at everything from leaders who had lost their revolutionary spirit to movies, books, or other cultural items deemed antirevolutionary or feudal. This period of dogma and intolerance would last all the way through Mao's death and the end of the Cultural Revolution in 1976. This cycle of openness followed by clampdowns has been a recurring theme with the Chinese media in the Communist Party era, and continues to this day.

While the level of central control has ebbed and flowed, the types of media used in China over time have also changed continually, closely following trends in the developed world, albeit usually a few steps behind. From the founding of the People's Republic in 1949 through the early 1980s, radios and newspapers were the most common vehicles used to deliver the message of the day. In those days, only the most well-connected people owned radios, and even relatively affordable individual newspaper subscriptions were rare, while TV ownership was virtually nonexistent for the average Chinese, who lived at subsistence levels. When I first lived in China in the late 1980s, the average salary in Beijing was around 100 yuan per month, about $20 at that time, and even that was considered high. With incomes so low, people could barely afford most daily necessities, let alone such luxuries as a daily newspaper or a radio. Instead, newspapers were routinely available at people's work units, the large compounds of low-rise, brick office buildings managed as a single entity, often around production or provision of a specific product or service. Newspapers were also posted page-by-page on outdoor glass-cased bulletin boards that can still be seen in the older areas of many cities. This public posting of news reached a fever pitch during the Cultural Revolution, when a brand of soapbox journalism saw people from all backgrounds and walks of life, coaxed on by Mao to show their revolutionary spirit, spouting their views by plastering big-character posters on any sort of outdoor surface, be it a wall or a tree, denouncing anti-revolutionaries or praising the latest thoughts of Mao himself.

Listening to the news during this early period of Communist Chinese history was also a highly public affair, as most radios were available only at people's work units. Broadcasts carried not only the message of the day, but also a healthy dose of upbeat music, radio dramas with inspirational themes, and other revolutionary-themed work. Shortly after the founding of the People's Republic, the Communist Party issued directives requiring the installation of radios at all government offices, factories, and other large organizations to make sure that people stayed current with the latest Party messages. To ensure that people were paying attention, the Party also specified that every organization should designate a person to make certain that everyone listened to important broadcasts on a regular basis.

Most of the massive compounds where most people worked and lived from the 1950s through the 1990s were also outfitted with extensive speaker systems from the late 1950s that carried the latest radio broadcasts to anyone within earshot, which usually extended quite far. To this day, I can remember the mandatory wakeup calls these systems delivered to my Beijing apartment every morning in the late 1980s at 6 or 7 A.M., usually beginning with the latest headlines followed by some calisthenic-type music that was always a tad too peppy for someone who had just woken up. I honestly don't know what the purpose of waking everyone up so early was, but my cynical side always believed these harsh morning calls were meant to be an unsubtle reminder for everyone of the tight control the Party held over them.

A reporter I interviewed actually worked for one such radio station in his rural hometown in central China in the 1960s and 1970s. Chinese radio was typically run by the local propaganda ministry and, depending on the size of the market, employed a small squadron of editors and announcers who gathered all the latest news from nearby towns and villages, and compiled it into two daily broadcasts, one in the early morning and one in the evening. In those days, he recalled, much of the news came from citizen-written reports mailed in from nearby communes and other work units, often penned directly or approved by the local Party boss. Articles would typically detail the great work the commune was doing, including everything from how crop yields were improving thanks to new harvesting techniques, to soaring literacy rates thanks to the latest educational campaign.

In the early days, another form of truly grassroots communications was the mass rally, often organized by government-sponsored trade and social groups such as doctors' associations, women's advocacy organizations, and the like. The Party not only used these groups to deliver its messages to their members, but also allowed reporters to cover their rallies and other events as a source of news itself that could be spread more widely via the mass media. In newspapers from the

1950s through the 1970s, reports on rallies or meetings by one group or another were a regular staple, sometimes protesting a foreign country's aggression and other times voicing support for the latest Party initiative. These rallies were particularly common during times of unrest, such as during the Korean War and especially during the Cultural Revolution, as the leaders in charge often used them as platforms to express their own views on a subject.

Today the government still uses rallies to deliver its message, though much more sparingly as it has learned that such mass events, with the help of modern communications like cell phones and the Internet, can quickly cause situations to spiral out of control. This was the case with the anti–US and anti-Japan rallies of 1999 and 2005, respectively, the former after NATO accidentally bombed the Chinese embassy at the start of its war in Yugoslavia and the latter after Japan published some textbooks downplaying its role in World War II. In both instances, the resulting mass rallies quickly got out of hand, forcing the government to finally step in and crack down with draconian measures, including the arrest of anyone who defied orders to cease the demonstrations. Once the government decided to end the demonstrations, no mention of them appeared in the media again.

As the country began to embrace economic reform in the 1980s and people's incomes started to rise, many homes could afford TVs, which took over as the major medium of choice to influence public opinion. During my time as a reporter covering China's electronics industry in the 1980s and early 1990s, I paid several visits to some of the many factories churning out low-cost color TVs by the thousands, destined for homes from the biggest cities like Beijing and Shanghai to the smallest hillside hovels. The widespread ownership of television sets radically changed the country's media landscape in a very short time. To make reception easier, China underwent its own cable revolution in the 1990s, making a wide range of stations, all government owned, available virtually anywhere. At the top of the TV heap is China Central Television, or CCTV, which operates about two dozen channels, most of which enjoy national distribution, unlike most provincial stations, which are confined largely to their home markets. Like Xinhua, anything on CCTV is also generally regarded by editors at regional newspapers and TV stations as "Party approved."

Rise of the Internet as a New Major Force

Most recently, the Internet has become another major media force, with China officially surpassing the United States in 2008 to become the world's biggest online market based on the number of web surfers. In this new Internet age, Beijing has conceded some degree of control with the explosion of huge volumes of online content on blogs, message boards, and foreign web sites that are impossible to monitor closely. But the government hasn't completely relinquished its role as opinion leader, designating nine web sites in 2000 as flagships of China's official online news. In making that decision, it instructed newspaper editors nationwide to closely follow those nine, which included Xinhua, the English-language *China Daily*, and *People's Daily*, making them the Party's official online voices. It also still closely monitors the web and attempts to strategically "seed" online discussions that promote its agenda in various blogs and chat rooms. A typical case occurred in 2003, after the outbreak of severe acute respiratory syndrome (SARS), when central officials were particularly miffed by an article in *Time* magazine critical of China's handling of the outbreak. In response, propaganda officials quietly encouraged Chinese web surfers to criticize the report in online forums both at home and abroad to give the impression of widespread indignation. At the same time, the government also legally requires web hosts to actively police their sites and immediately pull down any content that is forbidden or off the agenda.

In today's wired age it's quite interesting to note that the "mass rally" technique of years past has effectively migrated to the Internet, with topics often taking on a life of their own as web surfers vent over one issue or another. A case in point illustrates at once how this phenomenon continues to thrive on the Internet, and also how such rallies are often truly born at the grassroots level, beyond the government's control. It came in 2011, after one of China's state-of-the-art high-speed rail trains rear-ended another one, killing more than 30 and injuring about 200. Online discussion of the topic quickly mushroomed out of control, to the point that nearly every major forum touched on the issue in some way. Most decried the country's rush to build its high-speed rail network so quickly, without enough regard for safety. Many speculated that corruption resulting in substandard construction had caused the accident.

Talk was also rife that corrupt officials were attempting to cover up the cause of the crash by quickly removing carriages and preparing to dispose of them almost immediately after the accident. Outrage also grew after railway officials decided to call off the search for survivors 20 hours after the crash, but continued at the insistence of a local officer, only to discover a 2-year-old girl still alive in the wreckage. The chatter soon became so vehement that the government cut most of it off, and blacked out all reports in newspapers and on TV except for those from Xinhua or CCTV.

The sprawling web of bureaucracy and interpersonal connections that has become China's media scene today may look vast and decentralized, but that appearance hides a level of central control that is still surprisingly efficient at keeping most of these disparate channels on message. The key is in ownership: All media in China, from the biggest TV station to the smallest provincial newspaper, and even most magazines with foreign-sounding names, are at some level owned by the state, which reserves the right to hire and fire publishers and editors, and even to shut down publications completely if their transgressions are big enough.

At the center of this bureaucratic web, waving the baton and calling the major shots, is the all-powerful but seldom-seen Propaganda Ministry in Beijing. In the course of doing interviews for this book, I was amused by how nearly every reporter recounted his or her own story about the classic, often anonymous, phone calls that arrive on a regular basis to nearly every publication where they've worked, instructing them on what to print or not to print, and how to spin major stories. The Ministry uses such calls, rather than sending out printed instructions, to leave as few traces of its activity as possible, avoiding "smoking guns" that could fuel public outrage if they fell into the hands of less-friendly people.

From a definitional point of view, the Propaganda Ministry now defines itself as a body that provides spiritual guidance for China's media and, by extension, for the broader population. It aims to propagate the government's latest thinking into society, seeking not only to inform but also to sway public opinion toward the Party's latest views. The Ministry's firm hand extends not only to the mass media, but also to most forms of popular culture, such as movies and popular music, all of which must be screened and approved by propaganda officials before it can be legally sold in China. In one notable case in 2006, propaganda officials made a splash when they forbade the Rolling Stones during their first-ever China tour from playing five of their songs, including "Honky Tonk Woman" and "Brown Sugar," because they were deemed politically incorrect. In typical fashion, the Propaganda Ministry never explained the reason for its decision, but simply left people guessing.

The Propaganda Ministry's tactics have a simple goal at their center: to create the impression of consensus and uniformity in an otherwise-fragmented society where large differences exist between rich and poor and urban and rural, and where those gaps are growing wider as the country embraces an open economic policy. The forging of such a consensus is crucial to maintaining social order and harmony, casting a real or imagined cloak of legitimacy around the Party's latest policies by showing how everyone agrees with them and how they benefit both the common person and broader society.

The Ministry achieves this impression of consensus in a number of ways, including through the previously mentioned phone calls and also other means such as broader bulletins, to ensure that all media outlets carry the same message. Such tactics create a sense of uniformity, as ordinary people reading the papers, watching TV, and surfing the Internet get basically the same message packaged in different ways. In reading old newspapers to research this book, I was amazed at how often the front pages of major daily newspapers from different cities often looked virtually identical, carrying the same Xinhua articles and photos in similar layouts on any given day, usually featuring the movements and words of the current leadership. Inside pages, while less uniform in actual content, were still remarkably similar in tone, digging down to a more grassroots level by showing how local people agreed with the latest government policies. It's not hard to see how so many voices complimenting government policies could easily sway individual readers, especially in the pre-Reform era when the state-run media were the sole source of information.

One reporter recalled how, during the administration of Jiang Zemin in the 1990s, the Propaganda Ministry would regularly send faxes to his paper, a major daily in central China, giving it specific headlines for the next day, along with an outline of what the accompanying story should contain. His editors would then assign the story to an individual reporter, who would be responsible for the actual writing.

Another popular tool in the Propaganda Ministry's kit is the op-ed—a far more prevalent form of writing in Chinese media than in the West, and one that overtook general news reporting during the Cultural Revolution, when propagating Mao Zedong's thought took precedence over everything else. One reporter noted that, ironically, the Cultural Revolution was one period where editorial writing became truly diverse and multifaceted, as the presence of so many competing factions during that politically turbulent time gave many papers the freedom to take their own stand on particular issues without fear of retribution from the Propaganda Ministry, or any other central or local officials, most of whom were too preoccupied with their own internal power struggles to have time for interference with what was being reported in the media.

Op-ed writing is one of the few places where the use of centrally produced articles, while still common, is not monolithic, and locally produced material is strongly encouraged. But local op-eds still take their cue from centrally produced works, giving the broader op-ed culture an oddly uniform sound despite the appearance of many voices. During times of friction with the United States, Japan, or any other major power, it's not at all uncommon to see locally penned editorials appear daily in major newspapers and on TV, all denouncing the offending nation for its latest transgression. During Google's high-profile spat with China in 2010 over censorship issues, Chinese newspapers were filled with a steady stream of derisive commentaries, mostly ridiculing Google for not being able to compete in the tough Chinese market and creating an impression that the world's leading search engine was suffering from a case of sour grapes. Such an approach gives the impression of a diverse range of views, even though most op-ed writers are acutely aware they can't stray too far from the Party line communicated internally through memos from Beijing and from official reports and editorials in Xinhua and the *People's Daily*.

In both op-eds and mainstream news, one of the most important tools in the Propaganda Ministry's kit for shaping national opinion and molding consensus is the repeated and consistent use of specified words and phrases when referring to a certain subject. The practice is actually common not only in China but among journalists worldwide, though in the latter case it is more out of laziness or conformity than due to any centrally coordinated effort. It's much easier to say *Y2K* than to explain each time the process whereby some predicted that a global computer meltdown would occur in the year 2000 due to the binary system of dates used in early machines. The big difference is that the use of such consistent phraseologies is mandatory in China, and any reporter or editor who strays even slightly from the Party-mandated terminology is likely to be censured or even fired.

Similar to this use of buzzwords is another device that sees Chinese newspapers often use sloganeering banners at the top of their pages as umbrellas for broader coverage of particular subjects featuring many articles. Such banners were common during the Cultural Revolution and other political movements in the early days, and often contained inflammatory jargon, providing an excuse for what I like to call "guerrilla coverage" on a subject. This rather crude tool is based on the thinking that readers who see enough articles, editorials, photos, and testimonials splashed across the papers under the same banner day after day are more likely to start believing what they see due to the sheer onslaught of material. One recent recipient of such guerilla coverage was the Falun Gong spiritual movement, a quasi-religious meditation group with a charismatic US–based leader. After the group surprised Chinese leaders with a secretly organized mass demonstration in Beijing in 1999 protesting their persecution, the *People's Daily*, the official newspaper of the Communist Party, went on a rampage, printing articles nonstop that denounced the group for days afterward under banners like "Worship Science" and "Oppose Superstition."

Such guerilla coverage is less common today, but the more subtle form of word control, called *tifa*, or designated ways of referring to particular events, issues, or groups, remains a powerful tool. The consistent use of words, especially across a wide range of media, helps to quietly build consensus over time as people unconsciously come to accept, for example, that the exiled Dalai Lama, often considered the spiritual leader of Tibet, is a "splittist" or that Falun Gong is an "evil cult," both standard phrases in the *tifa* lexicon.

Wordplay is also important for what's *not* included in the media, with a wide range of words, names, and other topics expressly banned from any state-owned publication. When political dissident and democracy activist Liu Xiabo won the Nobel Peace Prize in 2010, his name was absent from all domestic media, even though he was the first ethnic Chinese to have received the honor. Names of most dissidents and troublemakers in general are also banned from the domestic media, unless, of course, someone repents and realizes the error of his or her ways. In the more unruly Internet, web firms must self-police their own sites to make sure that such banned words never appear. In a case illustrating this point, a list of banned words uncovered by hackers from one site in 2004 revealed that two thirds were related to either sex or the Falun Gong spiritual movement. Most of the remainder were related to sensitive issues such as Tibetan or Taiwanese independence and the June 4, 1989 crackdown at Tiananmen Square. Another widely used device in this form of news-speak is the use of quotation marks, which indicate a putdown. Taiwan will never have a real president, but rather just a "president," according to the Chinese media, which use the quotes to stress the Party line that Taiwan is a province of China and thus cannot have a real president. One reporter told me that no one is ever formally schooled on banned and approved words and terminologies. Instead, people come into the system already knowing most of the ground rules based on their own exposure to the media, making most of the approved and banned phrases second nature for everyone.

Just as there are approved and banned words and phrases, so, too, are there approved and banned topics. On the bigger issues, the Propaganda Ministry often creates detailed guidelines on how to write about certain subjects and propagates them throughout the system to create a consistent tone in the national media. Numerous reporters told me how they and their newspapers or TV stations were told repeatedly in the run-up to the 2008 Beijing Olympics to write only positive stories about the event. With regard to Falun Gong, the opposite is true, and only negative stories are allowed. Topics that are generally off limits to almost everyone include sensitive areas such as the military, religion, or anything involving minorities, one reporter recalled, adding no one would even bother doing a story on any of those topics because it would never see the light of day.

Breaking News: An Uneasy Truce

Breaking news, when it's hard to know in advance what the Party line will be, is one area where the media and the Propaganda Ministry have reached an uneasy truce in recent years. Generally speaking, several reporters said, the media are free to report on breaking events like fires, earthquakes, or major violent crimes in whatever way they want immediately after it happens. But once Propaganda Ministry officials formulate and propagate a specific strategy on coverage, then everyone has to stick to that angle. In the 1980s and 1990s, the Ministry's decisions could often take days to come, as news traveled slowly and public opinion was slow to build. But in the current era when news travels almost instantaneously and public opinion can reach a crescendo just hours after an event, the Propaganda Ministry has also become much faster at formulating and implementing its positions.

One reporter illustrated the constant game of cat-and-mouse that goes on between the media and the Propaganda Ministry using the following tale. He recalled how his newspaper learned through the Internet one morning in 2011 that a disenchanted former bank employee in a small town in northwestern China had thrown a Molotov cocktail into a room where 50 of his former co-workers were meeting, seriously injuring 10 to 20. The newspaper's senior editors held a quick meeting and decided to send reporters to the town, even though it was thousands of kilometers from their home province. They decided which reporters would go, and arranged for them to take a 6:30 flight that evening. The reporters were on the plane, waiting to depart, when at 6 P.M. a call came from the Propaganda Ministry telling them not to report on the incident because it was too negative. The town, it turned out, was also full of ethnic minorities, and the ministry feared that the story could fan tensions between the different groups in the area. End of story. As a postscript, the reporters ended up flying to the town anyhow, since it was already too late for them to get off the plane when the Propaganda Ministry called. In the end they did the interviews and wrote their stories, none of which was ever published.

In a similar case, another reporter recalled how a new bridge in his home county collapsed due to shoddy construction before it was even opened to traffic in the mid-2000s, killing more than 100 people. Before any reports could come out, local propaganda officials had already instructed all provincial media outlets not to report on the collapse on their own, and instead to use the official Xinhua report that put the official number of dead at 86.

The Propaganda Ministry tries to maintain a low profile to avoid leaving any paper trails or other smoking guns by avoiding written documents and doing everything orally whenever possible, relying on a trickle-down effect as the latest agenda items get passed down the ranks from senior editors to more junior reporters, sometimes in casual conversation and often in more formal daily or weekly meetings where, again, there are no written records. One reporter said that he and his peers had to attend a weekly meeting at their publication where they were briefed on the latest Party agenda, including topics that had and had not been approved for writing. During those weekly sessions, reporters would also learn about the government's broader agenda, including what it was advocating and what it was discouraging. For example, he said, one week in the 1980s they were told to stress in their articles that China's economic liberalization was not the same as capitalism; instead they should refer to the process as "new socialism" or "socialism with Chinese characteristics." Reporters would also receive guidance at such meetings on how to report on specific events or issues, such as a strike at a factory or a movie that the government disliked. Reporters who wrote in accordance with the Party line were more quickly rewarded and promoted than those who showed more independence, he said.

Written records of these meetings are scarce, but the occasional memo that does find its way into public hands reveals a level of guidance and control that would seem almost surreal to the average Westerner. One memo that I saw many years after the fact, which was sent out to local government agencies in Beijing in 2002, seems to nicely characterize the broader approach to micromanaging the messages that make it into the media. Titled "Strengthening Management Interviews by Foreign Media," the memo was timed to head off any negative articles by foreign reporters in the run-up to the Chinese New Year, China's most important holiday and a time when negative news is severely discouraged. It was essentially a primer for government officials on how to behave at interviews with foreign reporters, and what to look out for. Among other things, the memo instructed any official being interviewed to find out as much as possible about the interviewer in advance, and to make sure the reporter had "proper thinking." It also cautioned any officials doing interviews not to give away any Party or state secrets, and to steer the conversation away from any sensitive subjects like Falun Gong, religion in general, human rights, and China's one-child policy. The memo also details what to do when reporters are "caught" doing interviews about "unforeseen matters," which seems to refer to the periodic street protest or demonstration that breaks out, often around Tiananmen Square and often during sensitive times like important anniversaries or in the run-up to a big holiday.

While the Propaganda Ministry aims for uniformity in the broadest sense, it realizes a certain level of localization is also necessary, especially in the current era, where newspapers have been ordered to sink or swim by becoming more commercial and less dependent on funding from the state. However, local reports are still closely monitored by propaganda officials, who are quick to make one of their anonymous calls to anyone who pushes the envelope too far.

The allowance for locally based reporting on regional issues actually dates back to the earliest days of the Communist era, when a new generation of reporters, many born and raised in the countryside, were urged to travel back to their roots to write about the Communist Party's modernization efforts. Workers at newly established agricultural communes and state-owned factories were also encouraged to write their own grassroots reports and mail them to newspapers for publication, telling the world about the latest positive developments in the new China being forged by the Communist Party.

Several reporters I interviewed came from this early new generation of journalists in the 1950s and 1960s, many handpicked from their villages for fast-track promotion on recommendations from their local teachers. They said that their rapid promotion was partly ideological, as Mao and the Communists believed in giving the common people a bigger voice in the nation's media. But their rise also had a more practical side, since the country faced a severe shortage of talent after many of its most educated young people either had fled to Taiwan or were blacklisted because of their previous "capitalist roots."

China suffered a similar brain-drain in the 1960s, when most schools and universities closed for at least two to three years, and sometimes for much longer, at the height of the Cultural Revolution that lasted from 1966 to 1976. During that time, Mao, seeking to rekindle the nation's revolutionary spirit, encouraged young people to go to the countryside, voluntarily or by force, with the result that many ended up spending years in remote areas to "learn the ways of the common people." As a result, the nation again had to look to the countryside and other sources, such as the military, for reporters to staff newspapers and other media in the 1970s and into the early 1980s.

The inclusion of so many grassroots reporters led to a blossoming of local reports during those periods, though all were carefully managed to stay on message. One reporter in central China recalled one article he wrote during the Cultural Revolution that was typical of the times. Headlined "The Iron Ox Tills the Mountain of the Miao," the article detailed how the Miao people, a minority group in the area, were using tractors to farm their land, saving them from the laborious and back-breaking ancient method of using oxen. The article was so well received that it was ultimately carried in the *People's Daily*, which often reprinted such locally generated, upbeat articles.

In more modern times, a wide range of local reports have become the norm in the drive to become more commercial, with minor negative news allowed on topics like traffic accidents, small-time robberies, and the occasional industrial conflict on approved topics like pollution. Editorial pages are also often highly localized, though writers and editors must be careful to stay on message with the Party line or at least not to stray too far.

The Propaganda Ministry also has a few other tricks that it uses to make sure people see issues in a certain way, or, in some cases, don't see them at all. When bad news happens at home that the Ministry wants to downplay or keep out of sight completely, one of its favorite tools is the distraction. Nationalism has become a powerful tool in this approach, as the sacredness of China and the Chinese people is one of the few things that most people can agree upon in this large and highly diverse society. The Chinese media also routinely bring up Japan and its atrocities during World War II as another distraction in times of stress. American hegemony and global bullying are also a favorite topic in similar situations.

In the distraction department, a favorite foreign whipping-boy for the Chinese media over the years has been the Voice of America (VOA), the US government–operated shortwave radio network that was a primary source of outside news for many Chinese in the pre-Internet era. In one typical case I came across during my research, the Chinese media blasted VOA for fanning the flames of conflict in early 1989, after local Chinese students in the city of Nanjing attacked African students over an interracial dating incident. One article published during the incident saw a top university official single out VOA for criticism, accusing the station of blowing the incident out of proportion by saying it reflected a broader racism in China against the many African students studying in its universities. Such comments, focusing on the US report rather than the actual conflict, look like an attempt to divert attention from the issue that very real tensions existed between Chinese students and the many African students on their campuses.

In recent years, propaganda officials have started using Chinese nationalism to discredit the West in general when they want to rein in an admiration for those societies' broader prosperity and openness that sometimes goes overboard. One such case in the mid-1990s saw a book titled *China Can Say No* become a national bestseller by discussing how China should stand up to the West. With the help of nonstop attention from the media, the book became all the rage for several months, feeding on a latent nationalism that saw Chinese people growing weary after years of being lectured by Westerners on subjects like human rights and the need for more transparent government.

Another key instrument in the Propaganda Ministry's kit for creating distractions is playing up the role of China as a victim. Since the earliest years, Chinese media have proven quite adept in times of trouble at casting the country as a victim. This kind of ploy appears almost from the start of the People's Republic, with China painting itself as victim of US aggression during the Korean War of 1950–1953. During that turbulent time, just a year after the Communists came into power, the domestic media were filled with howls of protest after the United States entered the war a week after North Korea invaded the South to start the conflict. No mention is made about North Korea's original aggression, China's support for the invasion, or China's initial entry into the war weeks after the United States sent in its first troops.

China's media repeatedly play up the victim mentality in major events such as the US entry into the Korean War, and even just before a string of national anti-Japanese protests of 2005, both of which will be examined more closely in future chapters.

At a broader level, this victim mentality comes from a very real sense among some top Chinese leaders, especially in earlier decades, that the world was out to get China and that China-bashing was at the top of the Western media agenda. Even today propaganda officials closely monitor the articles written by all foreign journalists living in China and zero in on reporters they view as overly negative. I personally had little trouble from officials during my days as a Reuters reporter in Shanghai, largely because I wrote about noncontroversial business topics. But some of my colleagues who reported on more sensitive political matters would get calls from time to time when they wrote negative stories, reminding them to behave in a manner consistent with Chinese reporting rules. In more severe cases, foreign reporters will even get called into government offices for similar reminders in person. But that said, few foreign correspondents these days are thrown out of the country due to their reporting, although sometimes their visas can be delayed or even rejected with little or no explanation.

A common refrain in the victim approach is the notion of "hurting the feelings of the Chinese people," a phrase often seen in the media and one that pops up regularly in talking with everyday Chinese. This expression usually finds its way into the national consciousness after another country does something to upset the government or after a face-losing incident. The words most often originate at the top in a Xinhua editorial or from a high official at a press conference, and then find their way into the media en masse. For example, the phrase almost inevitably comes up after any leader of a major nation meets with the Dalai Lama, the exiled spiritual leader of Tibet, whom China considers a "splittist" for his views that Tibet should have more autonomy or even become independent.

One recent case occurred before the 2008 Beijing Olympics, when the torch relay was disrupted while passing through Paris by thousands of pro-Tibet protesters in a noisy scene that made global headlines and even caused the torch to be extinguished. Afterward, China's domestic media were filled with reports of indignation, treating the disruption as a personal affront by France and one that hurt the feelings of the Chinese people. Large anti-France rallies broke out across the country and citizen groups organized boycotts of French goods and travel to France, all with at least implicit government backing. One of my journalism students even used the "hurt feelings" expression when discussing the incident several years later, underscoring just how effective the Chinese media have been at embedding this concept of China as a victim of bullying world powers into the broader national consciousness.

Another subset of the victim approach is to show a flood of support from foreign leaders, often after others do something to upset Beijing. In the early days of the Korean War, domestic newspapers were filled with a daily barrage of stories that contained little more than a quote from one Chinese ally or another condemning the US aggression. After the brutal crackdown of the student movement at Tiananmen Square in 1989, the Chinese media were also filled with a similar steady stream of one-quote articles from leaders expressing their understanding for China's actions, with no mention of all of the condemnation from the West.

As China's economic clout has grown in recent years, the country has also discovered "soft power" as an effective tool to enhance its image both at home and especially abroad. The desire to influence foreign opinion dates back more than 30 years to the Reform era that began in the 1980s, when China was establishing relations with many of the world's major countries and wanted to make a good impression. One reporter recalled how he was an early inductee into a Xinhua program aimed at cultivating reporters who could tell China's story to the world through Xinhua's then-nascent English-language service. To better appeal to foreigners, journalists from abroad were brought in to instruct trainees on how to write in a more Western style, rather than simply spouting the latest Party line.

The soft-power push has continued and even accelerated through the present, mirroring a global trend as governments try to make a good impression through more subtle methods. Around the year 2000, China reached a landmark agreement that gave wide access for its English-language TV channel to US viewers in exchange for giving foreign broadcasters limited access to the Chinese market. Since then CCTV has added channels in Spanish and French, in a bid to reach a bigger global audience and better shape foreign perceptions of China. More recently, China has also begun setting up Confucius Institutes in countries around the globe, all with funding from Beijing, where local people can come to learn Chinese and get other information about China. The first of those opened in 2004, with ambitious plans for around 100 institutes worldwide by 2010, mostly teaching written and spoken Chinese. As China's economic clout grows, so undoubtedly will its desire to influence how the world sees the country, which it will do increasingly by exporting not only its manufactured goods, but also its official media and culture through both traditional and newer, more subtle channels.

Chapter 3

Ultranetworked

Caught Up in Connections

T alk with any foreigner who has spent a significant amount of time in China, and one word almost inevitably comes up: *guanxi*. Literally meaning *connections* or *relationships*, *guanxi* is an intrinsic part of the fabric of Chinese society, so much so that Confucius, writing more than 2,000 years ago, tried to distill all the human relationships in the world into five basic types, each with its own set of norms, behaviors, forms of etiquette, and taboos.

It is impossible to overstate the importance of *guanxi*, which permeate every facet of life in China, from big matters like determining where your kid goes to college down to the most mundane details like booking a hotel room. Tales of how this or that person used his *guanxi* to perform anything from the most difficult to the simplest tasks are a staple in conversation for many Chinese, especially the older generation, who relied almost exclusively on such interpersonal connections to get anything done back in the socialist era of the 1950s through the 1980s.

In one conversation, a friend told me how his plane to Beijing was stuck on the tarmac in Shanghai for several hours, with no explanation for the cause of the delay or when the plane might take off. He finally grew impatient and used his cell phone to call a friend who worked for the local airport authority to complain of the situation. Lo and behold, the plane began taxiing and took off a short time later, he said. On another recent trip to southern China, another friend used his local business contact to help us rent a car, even though it would have been little or no problem to call a rental agency and book the car directly. And in yet another case, an older friend one evening boasted to a roomful of us over dinner that he never paid full fare for air tickets when he traveled, because his friends at the local airline could always get him a "special price."

All of these examples illustrate just how pervasive *guanxi* networks are in today's China and how they reach across boundaries, encompassing everything from family and personal networks to government and business organizations. Recognizing and appreciating the sprawling webs of bureaucratic and interpersonal networks that permeate modern China is critical to understanding the media, whose behavior often can otherwise look cryptic or even contradictory to outsiders due to the many interests pulling it in widely different directions.

Today's bureaucratic Communist Party has taken the *guanxi* model to new levels, creating a society where state and private sectors are inextricably intertwined, and a massive tangle of politicians, bureaucrats, and other officials all jostle for a say in just about everything. This sprawling network is the legacy of China's first 50 years under Communist rule, when the Party had an active hand in just about every aspect of life, from obvious areas like government and enterprise all the way down to other key elements of a modern society, like the healthcare, public security, and education systems. Caught in the middle of this tangle are the media, whose many masters constantly pull them in multiple directions at once, often resulting in far more intrigue behind the stories than in the news itself.

In the first few decades of Communist Party rule, government officials exercised a high degree of control over what was printed in the media, a tradition that continues to a lesser degree to this day—a connection that might seem counterintuitive to many Westerners. One of the Party's biggest tools in controlling what gets printed in the media is what I like to call "proofing rights," or the right to see just about any article a reporter writes before its actual publication, a strict taboo in most Western publications. In the nation's first four decades of Communist rule, when everything was owned by the state, the media were in many ways a purely promotional tool with extensive coverage of government activities and the latest public efforts to create a more just and affluent society. Most of the articles from that period were what we journalists like to call "single-source stories," or stories based on a single interview with little or no independent checking on the facts or truth of what was said. In the early days of China this kind of reporting was the overwhelming norm, with the added twist that interviewed officials got to review all articles before they went to press and make changes, or even kill stories altogether if they didn't like the tone or changed their mind about wanting to talk on a subject. This kind of pre-publication review is strictly forbidden in today's Western media, where the accepted norm is that no interview subject can see an article until after its publication. All of the reporters I interviewed who worked in the 1980s and earlier said their articles based on interviews with nearly all government and industry officials were routinely subjected to this kind of review, and a few younger reporters said that to this day they often avoid interviews with Party officials for this reason.

One Hong Kong–based reporter working for Xinhua in the 1970s and 1980s recalled how he was subjected to such proofing rights during the sensitive negotiations between Britain and China on the return of the colony to Chinese rule in 1997. When covering the latest developments in the widely watched negotiations, he would submit each of his articles to his editor, who in turn would hand them over to the actual Chinese negotiator for his personal review. The negotiator, a man named He Zaishuo, had the authority to change anything and everything in those reports, rewriting them in his own words if he wanted or deleting things he may have said at one point but that later should not appear in the Chinese media. Another Xinhua reporter in Beijing at around the same time described a similar pattern, where stories involving any kind of government spokesperson, no matter how high or low, would automatically get kicked back to the relevant ministry for review before publication. Articles involving high-ranking officials were subject to particular scrutiny, sometimes being sent as high as the Politburo for review.

Another reporter detailed the typical path most stories would take after submission at his regional newspaper in central China in the 1970s and 1980s, again reflecting the complex web of bureaucratic hurdles that all articles had to clear before publication. After writing the story, the reporter said he would typically give it to his editor, who would look it over and make his own changes and suggestions. If the article involved a Communist Party official, which was the case for many stories at the time, it would then get passed to the official for his or her approval, and then returned to the editor. It would then get passed to one of the newspaper's section editors for his review, before being passed up to the newspaper's deputy editor for yet another review. When all of those reviews were finished, it would finally travel to the office of the editor-in-chief, who was always a senior Communist Party member, for one last review before finally going to the layout editors for inclusion in an upcoming edition of the newspaper or broadcast.

This complex and time-consuming process, which often saw stories take days or even weeks to clear the editing process, was well suited for the Chinese media of the 1950s through the 1980s, when most news came through exclusive interviews between a reporter and a government official, and the idea of the modern press conference attended by many reporters was relatively uncommon. In that kind of environment it mattered little if an interview held on Monday was published on Friday, or even a month later, as long as it contained new material that was on the Party's agenda. In today's world where press conferences are increasingly the norm and news often appears in Internet chat rooms and blogs within minutes of happening, the old system of proofing rights has broken down to some extent in the past decade, with officials yielding control to locally based senior editors at most publications, especially in the case of breaking news. While the "proofing rights" concept was originally conceived as a means to control media coverage, particularly on matters that were sensitive or involved Party officials, this mentality worked its way down into the broader media culture to the point where it became an accepted practice.

In my experience as a business reporter in Shanghai and Hong Kong from 2002 to 2006, company officials whom I interviewed for stories seldom asked to see my articles before publication, and in the rare instance when they made such a request, they were quick to back down when I informed them such reviews were against the policy at most Western media. One case reflective of the older mindset saw me attend a telecommunications forum in 2005, where I struck up a conversation with a top official from the telecoms regulator's internal research arm. During our chat the official mentioned an interesting new line of thinking that his institute was proposing as part of China's plans to issue 3G wireless telecommunications licenses. Considering his comments interesting but certainly not major news, I quickly wrote up a short story and submitted it within the hour, and it appeared a short time later over the Reuters newswire. I thought nothing more of it until an hour or two later when I got a panicked call from the same official saying that domestic media were swamping him with queries about the story and asking if Reuters could withdraw it. The implication was that I should have shown him in advance any-thing that I intended to publish; clearly he never expected any story to come out without getting his nod of approval. Having miscalculated on that front, his next impulse was simply to strike both the interview and resulting story from the record, as if they had never happened. Needless to say, the story remained unchanged and I never heard from him again.

While many officials are learning that proofing rights are off limits at Western media, they often still try to exercise such rights on their own domestic reporters, although even that is starting to change some-what. One reporter at a progressive publication said that many of the government officials that he approaches won't consent to an interview unless he agrees to show them his articles before publication. In most of these instances, he said, officials understand that they no longer have the right to directly change articles, but are rather more interested in seeing how they will be presented, which at least gives them a chance to argue for changes. This reporter recalled that he agreed several times to such pre-publication reviews in the past, but that the back-and-forth exchanges that followed often led many stories to lose most of their news value by the time both sides could agree on the final form. As a result, he said, he rarely interviews government officials anymore, and that most market-oriented media will also avoid such interviews.

While government officials are a bureaucratic lot in general, company officials are more of a mixed bag, depending on whether they work for a private or a government-controlled entity. The former generally behave in a more Western style in their relationship to the media, while the latter often still try to exercise the old-style controls over how the media write about them. The same reporter who said that he avoids interviews with government officials added that his newspaper, which is financially focused, will often accept the condition of proofing rights in exchange for interviews with top officials from big state-run companies. Yielding to such conditions often results in the inevitable puzzled query as to why the final story isn't more positive, a natural reaction from this older generation of officials for whom propaganda and news were one and the same. Despite their puzzlement, many of those same people are slowly coming to realize that balanced reporting is generally more credible than the older generation of propaganda-style positive pieces, with the result that it is now easier to produce more balanced and even negative stories about major state companies.

Promoting the Party's Agenda

As with just about everything else in China, at the end of the day the *guanxi* networks that permeate modern society and have such a profound impact on the media are all about one thing: the Communist Party and promoting its agenda. Top officials throughout the media industry, including most editors-in-chief, publishers, and station managers, are all trusted Party members who have proven their loyalties over the years to do what's in the best interests of the Party. Every media organization—and indeed any major organization in general, be it a state-run business, an industry association, or even a sports federation—always has a Party secretary as one of its top officials, usually on par with the CEO or association president. It goes without saying that all top officials at the Propaganda Ministry are also Party members with solid loyalties proven over the years through their steadfast support of Party policies. In the early days and still today at many older publications, the Party members at the top echelons of every media outlet effectively act as a filter to ensure that everyone stays on message, and that bothersome or even counterproductive reports never make it into print, onto the airwaves, or into cyberspace. Even at more progressive publications the most senior editors are usually well-connected Party members, and while they may be willing to take more chances they are also keenly aware of what borders not to cross.

The presence of so many Party officials, especially in government offices and state-run enterprises, often makes reporting on such entities a minefield, especially when the news is anything other than a feel-good story. One reporter commented on the complexity of the issue, noting that the savvy interviewer needs to treat every person in a sprawling government office or big state-run enterprise as the end point in a vast web of *guanxi* that can ultimately come back to bite him. If a big shot at a company dislikes a reporter's article, he can call his friends in the government and complain, ultimately resulting in an anonymous Propaganda Ministry call back to the newspaper's editor or worse. The reporter recalled one such case involving an article he wrote about a failed merger between two state-run companies, one with ties to the police, that made both sides look sloppy and ineffectual. After the story came out, an official from one of the companies called to rant and complain, saying he could have the reporter thrown in jail. The unfazed reporter stayed calm and informed the irate official that he was tape-recording their conversation. The next day, the official's superior called back and offered an apology for the threat, showing at once not only the power that state officials still wield over the media, but also the media's growing willingness to fight back.

The power of *guanxi* comes into play most often when local officials want to keep negative stories about their districts out of the public eye. Such attempts to suppress negative news are hardly exclusive to China. I have faced several such efforts in my years as a reporter in the United States, including one by the Los Angeles mayor's office when I was writing a report critical of some of the city's policies. But whereas Western officials are careful to avoid appearing overly aggressive and intimidating, Chinese officials are much more likely to use such intimidation by turning to their *guanxi* networks to get stories modified or simply killed outright.

One editor said that the *guanxi* of local officials is always a major consideration when his paper decides whether to cover a story. In

making that decision, he said, his paper must guess in advance how
well connected local officials may be and the likelihood that those
officials may try to suppress a story. If a major accident occurs but no
one dies, for example, then local government officials may keep their
guanxi at bay and show more tolerance by not interfering with reporters
who come to cover the incident. But in cases of government corruption, wrongdoing, or negligence, local officials are more likely to use
their *guanxi* to keep the case out of the spotlight to protect their own
reputations. The editor recalled one case that illustrated this point.
A large number of children in a town in Shanxi, one of China's poorer
provinces, became sick after receiving a particular vaccination. The
media began reporting on the case when the news first broke, causing local leaders to panic that the wave of illnesses, which was clearly
due to quality issues, would reflect poorly on them. So they turned to
their personal *guanxi* networks, and a couple of days later Propaganda
Ministry calls went out to all major media telling them to cease their
reporting on the case.

The rise of the Internet, which makes big news spread almost
instantaneously, has created a new challenge for local officials, who are
becoming ever faster at stopping potentially embarrassing cases before
they incur the wrath of both the public and government leaders. In
one such case, traditional media and the Internet were buzzing—
mostly in outrage—for a day or two after the worst apartment blaze
in modern Shanghai history left 58 dead in 2010. But all of the talk
was suddenly snuffed out from both the media and the Internet when
lax government oversight of construction practices that led to the blaze
became the focus of the reports. One Shanghai-based reporter told me
it's not at all unusual for local officials to call major media every day to
ask them in advance what their top stories will be that day, and then
to quickly apply pressure, directly or through the Propaganda Ministry
and other channels, to get stories killed if they will cast local government in an unflattering light.

When it comes to big events, especially planned ones like the 2008
Beijing Olympics or the 2010 Asian Games in Guangzhou, the *guanxi*
web, with the Propaganda Ministry sitting at the center, is even more
adept at making sure that everyone toes the official Party line. One
reporter recalled his experiences during the Asian Games to show how

the process works. Months before the event, he said, propaganda bosses from Guangdong province, where Guangzhou is located, wined and dined top local media executives at a series of meetings and banquets, where they also explained the kind of coverage they expected out of the games. After that, the top editors, publishers, and station managers went back to their respective outlets and held meetings with other managers to explain how the event was to be covered. The message ultimately trickled down to rank-and-file reporters, who were charged with keeping it in mind when pitching any stories and filing on-site reports. In the case of the Asian Games, the main message was relatively straightforward: No negative news was allowed.

In an increasingly mobile age where long-distance travel is common, one entity that has proven more difficult for local *guanxi* networks to control is the out-of-town reporter, who is typically far removed from such local influences. In the first 50 years of the People's Republic of China, nearly all newspapers and TV stations were largely limited to reporting on their own turf, with only the largest outlets like Xinhua and the *People's Daily* staffing bureaus outside their home cities. Reporters rarely traveled to other provinces, and any news from those areas usually came from official reports written by Xinhua, the *People's Daily*, or CCTV. By limiting journalists to reporting only on events in their home regions, local officials conveniently had easy access to the hometown propaganda, police, and other government connections they needed to quickly nip any potentially embarrassing reports in the bud, ensuring they would never make it into either the local or national media.

Nowadays, most major Chinese media frequently send reporters to other regions when big news breaks. These reporters are a difficult force to control for propaganda officials in Beijing, to say nothing of the challenges they present for local government officials. A clear case of this growing clash came after the massive Sichuan earthquake of 2008, which had a magnitude of 8.0 and which ultimately left 68,000 dead. After the quake, all major media immediately told their reporters to get on planes or buses, or to use any other means of getting to Sichuan, to cover the disaster. Several journalists I interviewed said Propaganda Ministry officials in Sichuan initially tried to order all the out-of-town reporters to go home and leave the reporting work to Xinhua, arguing they would just get in the way and that the news

was outside their jurisdiction anyhow. But in the end the officials realized this was a hopeless effort and stood aside. They ultimately even
ended up supporting the huge influx of journalists when they realized
the positive propaganda value of the vast majority of reports, which
showed a caring government rushing to aid disaster victims.

An even more recent case reflecting the challenge of controlling the
media occurred in the summer of 2011, involving a man who kidnapped
six karaoke lounge singers and held them as sex slaves in his home, killing two when they tried to escape. The story was broken by a reporter
from the *Southern Metropolis Daily*, an aggressive newspaper based in the
southern city of Guangzhou, even though the kidnappings occurred
hundreds of kilometers away in the central Chinese city of Luoyang.
The news quickly spread over the Internet, prompting local officials in
Luoyang to resort to unusual action to deal with a reporter who clearly
fell outside the realm of control for their *guanxi* networks. In the days
after breaking the story, the reporter said he was followed by two men
claiming to be government officials, who openly confronted him with
the accusation that he had betrayed "state secrets," even though his
source for the stories was a local policeman in Luoyang. Use of the "state
secrets" excuse is an old socialist-era ploy that officials, both local and
national, fall back on from time to time when sensitive news is leaked, be
it economic data or crime-related matters that could cause public panic
or embarrass officials. The reporter, who wasn't harmed, later speculated
that perhaps the local officials had used this tactic because the city was
vying for the title of China's "most civilized city" and a public airing of
such dirty local laundry might have hurt its case.

In this kind of environment, it's not difficult to imagine the frequent emergence of power struggles to exercise influence, as people
with competing agendas vie to tell their version of the story in the
media or keep the story out of sight altogether. In the earlier days when
only the biggest media were allowed to report outside of their home
territory, the biggest power struggles typically occurred between the
center and the provinces, with central outlets like Xinhua or CCTV
often trying to get information for reports that could potentially
embarrass local officials, who would do their best to stop any such intelligence gathering. Such reports, usually for official use only, were often
actually commissioned by Beijing as part of the efforts by central leaders

to understand what was happening around the country—a process that will be further discussed in Chapter 4.

One tactic that officials often used in these turf wars to gain the upper hand against the media was intimidation. Several reporters from big national media organizations recalled the difficulty they faced when doing investigative-style work far from home after getting tips about local corruption or other unflattering things going on. One reporter recalled how, when traveling to distant regions for investigative reporting, local officials would regularly appoint people to "take care of" him, when the real purpose was to closely monitor the reporter's movements and quickly inform local officials when undesirable things happened, such as citizens on the street complaining about local corruption, pollution, or other negative issues. At the end of the day, the reporter said, such local "handlers" saw their main task as convincing the out-of-town reporter to squelch the story completely, sometimes resorting to threats but just as often using more sugar-coated tactics like offering gifts and lavish meals to achieve that aim. The reporter added that even in the most extreme cases, local officials would seldom resort to outright force or harm an out-of-town reporter, most often because they realize that their own locally based *guanxi* networks are far inferior to those of such big-city reporters, who are usually attached to a media organization with strong links to the central government.

That same reporter recalled a case that showed just how vast the web of connections is, and how it can straddle all kinds of lines when local officials choose to call in a favor. He had traveled to a small city in central China to interview its mayor after receiving a tip that the man was corrupt. After arriving in the town he went to city hall and demanded a meeting, only to be barred from the building. The reporter fired back that he was on assignment from CCTV, the country's biggest broadcaster, and demanded to be let in, saying local officials had no power to stop him and would have to resort to official channels if they wanted to keep him out. So the local officials did just that, calling in a favor to their local propaganda department, which in turn cashed a chip with one of its propaganda department connections in Beijing, who then called the reporter's editor at CCTV, who then called the reporter outside the city hall and told him to back down. All of that took place in the space of an hour, he added, demonstrating just how efficient the *guanxi* networks can be.

An interesting corollary of the growing power struggles between groups with competing agendas is that news that would sometimes never have gotten out in the first place actually makes it into the media or comes close due to competing agendas. This phenomenon was especially common in times of turbulence such as the Cultural Revolution or the Tiananmen Student Movement of 1989, both of which saw a flourishing of many voices in the media, most of which seized on power vacuums at the time to publish whatever they wanted with relative impunity. With the notable exception of the Tiananmen crackdown, much of the past 30 years has been characterized by a more unified Communist Party front, making it more difficult for the media to exploit competing agendas to get out the news they want to report. But some skillful reporters still find ways to play various factions against each other to get out news that might otherwise go unpublished.

One Shanghai-based reporter recalled one such instance in the 1970s when he learned about an explosion at a poppy seed processing factory in the city of Harbin in northeast China's Heilongjiang province. He went to the scene and gathered some facts, but was then quickly told by local officials that no media, local or out of town, could report on the story. After everyone had left, the reporter secretly stayed behind at a disease prevention center, where he met another official who wanted the story told. That official gave him a doctor's uniform and smuggled him back to the factory where the explosion had occurred. He personally witnessed a scene of mass devastation there that no reporter had seen thus far.

He quickly learned that the factory actually manufactured textiles and not foodstuffs, that 180 people had been killed or injured, and that the cause of the blast was negligence. Through talking with people on the scene, he also figured out where many of the injured had been hospitalized, and went to interview them. Among other things, he learned that no factory officials had been killed or injured in the blast, mostly because none were present at the time because they were all off the job—a fact that would prove embarrassing not only for the factory if it got out, but also for local officials, who were all tied up in the same *guanxi* networks. The reporter said that he felt bold enough to defy the first official who had banned all reports on the explosion because the second official who helped him clearly wanted the story told. Ironically, in the end his newspaper, probably fearing retribution from propaganda officials for being too negative, ended up pressuring the reporter to put a more positive spin on the story, and the reporter decided to kill it himself rather than cave in to that approach.

Steering Clear of Well-Connected Organizations

Another reporter recalled a case where his own editors ultimately decided to kill a story due to concerns that publication could raise the wrath of well-connected individuals who might then take out their displeasure on the newspaper. That case occurred in the 1980s when the reporter's newspaper learned about a plane that crashed while flying from the southern city of Guangzhou to the mountainous city of Guilin about an hour away. Xinhua first put out a short story confirming the crash but providing few additional details. The reporter's paper decided to send him to the scene, where he discovered that the case was far more complex than the Xinhua report had indicated. He learned the crashed aircraft was actually a military plane that had been chartered by China's lone commercial airline, creating a potentially embarrassing situation not only for the airline but, more importantly, for the influential People's Liberation Army. In the end, the reporter said, the prospect of tangling with the army and the airline proved too big a risk, as both organizations were quite powerful and well connected, and the newspaper ultimately decided not to publish the story.

The police have also become increasing users of *guanxi* networks in a modern age where tales of miscarriages of justice abound and the Communist Party repeatedly tries to assure a jaded public that it is providing a safe living environment. Miscarriages of justice were most likely common in the first three decades of Communist rule through the 1970s, in an era where roughhousing, forced confessions, and even torture were routine, and where police were expected to solve every crime that happened by turning over a culprit, regardless of the strength of the evidence in the case. In such an era, any later findings of miscarriage of justice would have been quietly hushed up, with police using their extensive connections to keep embarrassing reports out of the public eye. But in the modern day, when the media have become bolder, in part empowered by a central government seeking to show its openness on public safety issues, media reports on cover-ups have proven much harder to squelch.

One notable case in that regard involved a police informant in central China's Hubei province whose wife had mysteriously disappeared in 1994. A woman's body was later found, leading police to accuse the man, Yu Xianglin, of her murder. He was originally sentenced to death for the crime, though that sentence was later reduced to 15 years in prison. Then 11 years later, in early 2005, his wife suddenly reappeared, making it clear that either the earlier case had been botched or the man was framed, and a bogus body had been produced. When it became obvious that Yu had been imprisoned for 11 years for a crime that he had not committed, he was immediately released and the media wrote about the case.

A few months later, one of the policemen involved in the earlier investigation killed himself. He had reportedly used his own blood to write a message saying he had been falsely accused, implying that he had been made a scapegoat for the earlier mishandling of the crime. One reporter I interviewed went to the officer's funeral, raising the ire of both local police and propaganda officials who were already unhappy about the huge volume of negative reports about the case. One propaganda official came up to the reporter and asked if he would leave the funeral out of concern that his presence might incite the local police, but the reporter refused. The propaganda officials finally diffused the situation by turning to their contacts at the central Propaganda Ministry in Beijing, who called the reporter's editor, who called the reporter and told him to back down.

In less-sensitive cases the result can be a warning delivered through the *guanxi* web. One editor recalled a case in 2003 where his magazine had sent reporters to cover a conflict between a factory in eastern China's Zhejiang province and local citizens who suspected it of dumping illegal toxins into a nearby river. The people had tried to force the factory's closure but met with resistance from the local government, which relied on the plant for tax and other revenue. A riot broke out, resulting in the death of a woman and numerous injuries before the police finally came and restored order. The magazine ran its story on the conflict, but that wasn't the end of the story. Later the town's Propaganda Ministry contacted someone from the magazine's business department, who was instructed to deliver a simple but threatening message to the editor: The magazine's reporters were no longer welcome in that town.

As far as media attacks on officials or specific government organizations or major state-owned enterprises are concerned, the *guanxi* web generally stopped any such reports from showing up in the media, where they could cause embarrassment and undermine public trust, not to mention airing the Party's dirty laundry. As a result, the headlines of China's newspapers were generally devoid of negative news on individuals and organizations for much of the nation's first 40 years, even as power struggles occurred constantly behind the scenes that often ended in purges of former rising stars within the Party. Looking at the papers of the past, one feels an eerie silence in the headlines during some of the most politically turbulent times, as once-promising politicians were deposed, often after they fell out of favor with Mao Zedong. Such was the case with Liu Shaoqi and Lin Biao, both once seen as potential successors to Mao Zedong, but who fell out of favor and were ultimately purged in the 1960s and early 1970s. In both cases, the papers contained little or no mention of either leader's downfall as each was removed from power and eventually placed under house arrest, as was the case with Liu, or died, as was the case with Lin, whose life ended in a plane crash when he tried to flee the country.

Starting around the late 1980s, the Party began to tolerate some negative reporting in the media on individual officials in its drive to tackle rampant corruption and other misdeeds, effectively lifting its umbrella of *guanxi* protection for those unlucky people whose highly publicized cases were meant to serve as a warning to others. But even today such attacks are still generally allowed only when they fall within the Party's broader agenda, be it a campaign to root out corruption or to improve working conditions at factories and mines.

One exemplary case of an attack that was meant to serve as a warning to others occurred during my tenure as a reporter on China's high-tech sector, involving the downfall of Zhang Chunjiang, a former top executive at China Mobile, a state-run behemoth that is the world's biggest mobile carrier, based on its huge subscriber base. After his detention under the Party's internal system for rooting out corruption, the media suddenly exploded with reports of a hidden world of corruption and decadence, where Zhang not only accepted huge bribes, but also entertained others with lavish meals and expensive gifts and had numerous mistresses. He was ultimately found guilty in 2011 of accepting $1 million in bribes, and was given a suspended death sentence and stripped of his Party membership, all in a very public series of reports from Xinhua that were picked up widely by other media. The reality is that many high officials like Zhang exist in the upper ranks of the Communist Party and major state-owned enterprises, many using their positions for personal gain. But, for whatever reason, the Party chose to make a case out of Zhang, not only punishing him for his misdeeds but doing so in a very public way.

Use of the media to publicize this kind of corruption and other social problems on the Party's agenda is increasingly common today, but these cases are still mostly the exception. For the most part, higher officials are generally still considered untouchable in terms of attacks in the media, although some are still quietly removed from office and later fined, imprisoned, or both when found guilty of corruption or other misdeeds.

While government officials and Party members are generally protected from negative media reports by the Party's own sprawling *guanxi* networks, the exact opposite is true for individuals who fall outside those networks, most notably in the country's fast-growing private sector. Many reporters at more aggressive publications, frustrated by the general prohibition on attacks against well-connected officials, often channel their energies instead into uncovering misdeeds by some of the country's new generation of private-sector tycoons and celebrities. The Party probably quietly encourages such reporting, as it diverts attention from its own internal problems while satisfying a jaded public's desire for scandals involving big names. By letting investigative reporters do such work, the Party also provides an outlet for their energies and takes pressure off itself and the government in general.

It has become a running joke that having one's name appear on any of a growing number of "Richest People" lists in China is a virtual death sentence, drawing unwanted attention that often results in digging by officials and reporters who uncover misdeeds surrounding that person's rise to riches. A steady stream of scandals has erupted in recent years around some of the nation's wealthiest entrepreneurs after their names have appeared on such lists. One typical case that dragged on for years involved the downfall of self-made tycoon Huang Guangyu, founder of Gome, one of China's biggest electronics chains. Huang made headlines in 2004 when, at the age of 35, he was named by *Euromoney China* as China's richest man, with a net worth of more than $1 billion. But his fortunes quickly changed starting in 2010, when he was suddenly accused of insider trading and bribery. Since then, his name has become regular fodder for the nation's media, which happily report not only his misdeeds but also on a heated battle for control of his company.

Like these homegrown tycoons, foreign companies also lack strong *guanxi* networks and thus have become another popular target for attacks by Chinese media, which, forbidden from reporting on many problems at major domestic companies, often turn their attention to foreign ones, where such reporting is fair game. A string of strikes at factories connected to Honda and Toyota was a steady source of media reports for several weeks in early 2010, until local officials finally called their networks into action and killed the story due to concerns about the potential for social unrest. Likewise, the slightest deviations from China's strict labor code, which is commonly ignored by domestic companies, become big news when they happen at factories with ties to big multinationals. US toy giant Mattel's name frequently comes up in negative reports when any of its scores of Chinese suppliers are found to be abusing employees with long hours or substandard working conditions. The same is true for Apple and other big names like Wal-Mart that rely heavily on China as a manufacturing base. When subjected to such attacks the big foreign names usually become contrite and sometimes even issue apologies, fully aware that anything else would merely result in more negative news from domestic media frustrated by their inability to channel their investigative energies elsewhere.

Among the wide array of multinationals active in China, foreign media are also attractive targets for their occasional missteps or perceived biases. Such attacks provide not only a distraction from domestic issues, but also give the government an opportunity to show domestic readers the fallibility of foreign media, which are usually far more trusted by most Chinese than their own domestic media.

During my time at Reuters in 2005 and 2006, we were subjected to two such attacks, both involving incidents that probably would not have created much of a stir if they had happened elsewhere in the world but nonetheless resulted in a steady stream of negative reports in the Chinese media. In one case, a reporter received a tip that the government had shut down the blog of a prominent noisemaker. After determining the blog was indeed no longer accessible, we issued a quick story on a matter that is relatively routine in China. Later, it turned out that not only had the site not been blocked, or at least not permanently, but the blogger himself also came out and publicly criticized Reuters for the inaccurate reporting, adding fodder for a stream of reports that criticized Reuters, and the Western media by extension, for bias in a hidden agenda to portray the Chinese government as a relentless censor of everything that fell outside the Party line.

The second instance had nothing to do with news, but involved a Chinese Reuters employee who ultimately left the company over a routine dispute that was poorly handled by the human resources department. In that instance, the worker ultimately sued Reuters in China for money she believed she was owed. She gave the story to the Chinese media, which gave it prominent coverage for several days, painting the woman as a victim of a major foreign company trying to take advantage of one of its Chinese employees. In the end, the case faded from the headlines, as usually happens, but not before slightly tarnishing the Reuters name in the eyes of Chinese readers, and also reminding Reuters and other foreign media that their status as outsiders in the country's *guanxi* web made them fair game for similar future attacks.

Chapter 4

Reporters

The Party's Eyes and Ears

T o fully understand the media in China, it's important to look at the thousands of people who chose to go into the profession, as well as the broader role and image of reporters in Chinese society since 1949. Central organizations like Xinhua have always occupied the top spot in China's media pyramid, but more broadly speaking the thousands of smaller newspapers and broadcasters across the country have performed a dual role, not only as tellers of the Party's story for the masses, but also as the Party's eyes and ears to help central leaders better understand the pulse of the nation. This two-way role was established early on by the Party, which since the founding of modern China has referred to the media as its "ears, eyes, throat, and tongue."

Due to this critical role, reporters at all levels were generally held in great esteem by Chinese society, especially in the early decades after the Communists came to power, and that image lasted up through the 1980s and even into the 1990s. As the anatomical analogy implies, reporters were the central leaders' primary eyes and ears for getting the information they needed to understand what was happening in the country and to govern effectively. At the same time, as the Party's throat and tongue, the media, through their reporters and articles, were also the primary voice for those leaders to deliver their message to the masses, making them a powerful tool in shaping public opinion.

One reporter who worked for Xinhua in the 1970s recalled that he was attracted to the job partly by the prestige of being a reporter. Working for Xinhua in those days brought reporters not only a high level of respect, but also a certain level of awe and even some fear stemming from the agency's sheer scope and power. That level of respect led to all kinds of perks, with Xinhua reporters often feted with big banquets, gifts, and chauffeur-driven cars when they traveled around the country on reporting trips. They received similarly lavish treatment at home from those hoping to make a good impression on people through this pervasive organization that reported directly to central leaders in Beijing.

Another reporter who worked for a regional newspaper said that working for Xinhua was almost like being a government spokesman, that Xinhua reporters would often receive the same treatment usually reserved for mid- to high-ranking government officials, and that more senior reporters were even regarded as leaders in their own right. But he added that being a journalist at any level was still considered very prestigious all the way through the 1990s.

This prestige has faded somewhat in the past 20 years as a wide array of other choices emerged for ambitious people in China, leaving journalism as just one of many career options alongside other white-collar jobs like teaching and medicine. Within the reporting realm, major regional newspapers remain attractive employers for most reporters, while Xinhua is still the gold standard for anyone aspiring to the top echelons of journalism in China, much as the *New York Times* or *Washington Post* is in the United States.

In addition to offering job security and a wide range of opportunities for career advancement, one reason Xinhua manages to maintain its attraction for journalists and prestige in the public eye is its role as intelligence provider for the central government. This role sees the agency performing certain tasks that would usually be handled by a spying organization like the Central Intelligence Agency in the United States, and means that Xinhua reporters need to be reliable, trustworthy, and capable of strong news judgment.

This less-visible role of reporters as gatherers of street-level information throughout China is best summed up with a single word: *neican*, the general name for all the internal reports written by Xinhua and other reporters. *Neican* actually means "for internal consideration," which would roughly translate to the "internal use only" stamp that often comes on internal publications in the West. *Neican* can cover a wide range of topics, from innocuous matters like crop harvests and public opinions, to much more sensitive ones like situations on the ground after the outbreak of riots in restless areas like Tibet. The *neican* system is largely based in Xinhua, but reporters at all publications are also expected to write up their own *neican* reports when they come across information that might be useful to government leaders.

The actual *neican* system was set up in 1951, shortly after the Communists came to power, when China was still closely allied with the Soviet Union, which already used its own version of *neican* for intelligence gathering. An interesting offshoot of *neican* and its base in a news agency like Xinhua is that China to this day still treats foreign reporters with a high degree of suspicion due to its own lingering image of journalists as partly writers and partly intelligence gatherers. Any foreign correspondent with China experience will have numerous tales about the many restrictions placed on his or her movements and activities. Before working in China, all foreign reporters must be accredited by Beijing, a process that takes weeks and often even months while the foreign ministry conducts extensive background checks. Once inside the country, foreign reporters were historically restricted over where they could live, and were technically supposed to work with local authorities whenever they traveled outside their home regions.

Most of my foreign peers believe that their offices and cell phones are tapped, although few believe that their lines are actively monitored, with the possible exception of the few people who are in regular contact with dissidents or have access to sensitive information. Most foreign reporters, especially those who lived in China in the 1980s and 1990s, can recount tales of being followed when going to meetings, or being detained and questioned by local police when traveling unannounced to sensitive areas. Many of the heavy restrictions are enforced with a much lighter hand since Beijing hosted the Olympics in 2008 and made an extra effort to showcase its growing tolerance of outside criticism. But most restrictions do remain technically in effect, and foreign journalists are still occasionally detained or followed when they pursue sensitive topics.

In the early days of *neican*, reporters sent abroad by China were often subjected to the same kind of scrutiny by their host countries, especially in the West, as most were assumed to be acting in dual roles as spies and reporters. One Hong Kong reporter who worked for Xinhua in the 1970s and 1980s said many of his friends and acquaintances automatically assumed he was a spy. This image of reporters as spies lingers somewhat to this day, and I can recount numerous times when my ordinary Chinese friends and acquaintances asked me outright or indirectly if I was a spy working for the CIA because of my journalistic background. The situation is somewhat mutual, as most foreign correspondents in China suspect the presence of local spies in their midst at their offices, and the question of who these "plants" might be is often a subject for mostly playful speculation. According to popular thinking, such spies are usually local Chinese reporters or news assistants who work alongside their foreign colleagues during the day, but also report to mysterious "handlers" from time to time to write *neican* about what is happening inside their offices.

The *neican* system was particularly important in the first three decades of Communist rule when China was still a closed society with few windows onto the outside world. The reporter who worked for Xinhua in Hong Kong recalled that in the 1960s and 1970s, the former British colony was one of the few windows that China had onto the outside world, making it a key place to gather intelligence. Accordingly, one of his major roles was to simply read through a wide range of regional newspapers that came in each day, mostly from other Asian countries, and write up *neican* summaries of regional hot topics. He was assigned to focus on Southeast Asia, an important spot in the battle of communism versus capitalism at that time. His daily routine involved getting newspapers each day from the Philippines, Indonesia, Thailand, Singapore, and Malaysia. He would then go through them, pick out stories that might be of interest to Beijing, and write up *neican* summaries.

In other instances, he would write up *neican* based on his own fieldwork, including during sensitive negotiations for the return of Hong Kong from British to Chinese rule in 1997. Other matters were more routine. In one case, he recalled, a US military ship, the *USS Enterprise*, stopped in Hong Kong in the 1980s, and locally based reporters, including some from Xinhua, were invited to come aboard for a tour. In that kind of situation, he would often write up two separate reports, one a news story for publication on the Xinhua wire, and the other a longer *neican* with a more detailed account of events and details like the layout of the warship.

The *neican* system in those days was a bit more mundane than its top-secret image implies, with most articles ultimately bound into volumes called *cankao xiaoxi*, roughly translating to "news for consideration," prepared for different levels and types of officials on a daily basis by a special team at Xinhua's Beijing headquarters. Within that system, most *neican* were grouped into three basic categories: *xiao cankao*, or small matters for consideration; *da cankao*, or big matters for consideration; and finally the top level, simply known as *neican*. "Small matters for consideration" volumes were available to a wide range of people, including officials as well as university students and graduates and people at similar levels, and were published in a newspaper format. Circulation for "big news for consideration," which was traditionally published in a book-like format, was limited mostly to government division heads and above. The highest-level news, *neican*, was divided into international and domestic editions, and was available only to top-level leaders. These high-level reports were compiled by a separate editing team, unlike the first two levels, which were handled by a central team of editors in Beijing.

Most of the reporters I interviewed said all Xinhua journalists are expected to write *neican*, as are reporters at other publications who see and hear things in their daily routines that might be of interest to the government. One former Xinhua reporter said everyone in the organization feels a certain duty to write up anything unusual he sees, be it a traffic accident or a gathering of gay people at a bar. He added that as Chinese society liberalizes and the media are given freer rein to report on a wide range of issues, many items that formerly would have been material for *neican* are now simply reported openly in the mainstream media.

While most rank-and-file reporters write *neican* from time to time, Xinhua also has its own elite team of "reporters" whose sole job is to go out on assignment to write *neican* reports. One reporter working in the 1970s in a small town in central China said that any visit by a Xinhua reporter during that time was treated with the utmost respect and assistance, since most people assumed the purpose of the visit was to compile material for a *neican* report. In one particular case during the Cultural Revolution of 1966–1976, he said, the area had been thrown into disarray after the central leadership ordered everyone to adopt a double-planting season to boost their harvests, even though that particular region's growing season was too short for such an approach. As a result, many people ended up hungry and even starved. However, local officials, in the kind of reaction typical of that time, were reluctant to make truthful reports to Beijing for fear of being demoted or called antirevolutionary. So Beijing leaders who suspected that all was not so rosy turned to the *neican* system, sending a Xinhua reporter to the rural area to find out the true situation. Worried local officials sent a couple of people to tail the reporter during his visit and tried to guess what he might write. However, there was little they could do to stop him or influence his report, which in fact may have helped the central leaders realize what a mistake the double-planting policy had been.

Another reporter outside of Xinhua said that during unsettled times like the Cultural Revolution, *neican* were sometimes used as weapons to attack officials who had fallen out of political favor. He recalled one such instance where a brazen reporter in Shanghai filed a *neican* on Ba Jin, one of China's most influential authors of the 20th century, who was subsequently persecuted for his counterrevolutionary views. In that instance, the reporter wrote the *neican* after Ba Jin made some negative remarks to him privately about the Cultural Revolution, which later became fodder for future attacks and forced Ba Jin to formally renounce his words.

Investigating Trouble in the Provinces

More recently, the *neican* system has returned to its roots as an investigative unit for determining the situation in trouble spots. One reporter who recently worked for the Xinhua *neican* team said that he and his peers would often get sent on assignment when central leaders wanted to know what was happening on the ground because they suspected that local officials weren't telling the full story in their reports. In such cases, the Xinhua "reporter" would typically show up unannounced, and then spend three to five days in the locality before coming back and writing up his findings. Sometimes a local Xinhua reporter would accompany the *neican* reporter and sometimes the latter would work alone, but in nearly all cases the *neican* reporter would try to keep a low profile to avoid attracting too much attention.

He recounted a typical case in his work, which illustrates not only the importance of these jobs and the difficulty of performing them, but also a certain level of the ordinary and mundane involved in the work. For this job, officials in Beijing had heard about shenanigans taking place at a village in central China's Henan province, where a group of people had formed an organized crime ring that engaged in a wide range of illegal activities. No one wanted to openly report the group, possibly because many of its members were bribing local officials. Lacking the ability to obtain more reliable information, the government turned to the Xinhua *neican* team and sent the reporter to investigate. In these situations, he said, local officials would usually figure out what he was doing there and do their best to have him followed and influenced to write a positive report. But in the end such reporters had relatively free rein to do their work because of their strong connections in Beijing.

Due to their important role as both intelligence gatherers and tellers of the Communist Party's story, reporters were historically recruited through a fairly rigorous process that targeted the best and brightest to join its ranks, especially at Xinhua. Equally important in the past was recruiting reporters who believed in the Party's agenda, although that element of the process has diminished somewhat in the past 20 years.

In the 1950s, 1960s, and even 1970s, when skilled reporters and journalism schools were rare, referrals were often the main ticket into Xinhua and other media for a new generation of idealistic young people. Two former reporters I interviewed said they both joined Xinhua after being approached by respected teachers and other authority figures, who gauged their interest, and talked about the prestige and opportunities for advancement that jobs at the agency could offer. One recalled how the headmaster of his school called him into his office one day and suggested he consider joining Xinhua, saying that he could make the necessary recommendations. The reporter added he was probably selected because of his left-leaning activities at his school, which made him a strong candidate despite his lack of a college education.

In that earlier era, many reporters, both inside and outside Xinhua, came from non-journalistic backgrounds. One reporter I interviewed estimated that most of the country's reporters born before 1960 were people who simply liked to write but had little formal training and often came from the countryside. That contrasts strongly with modern China, where most reporters are college graduates.

One editor recalled how he got noticed by higher-ups after submitting unsolicited articles to a local publication, a typical practice of those times. His big break came when he was working in the countryside in the 1970s, a time when the state-owned work units that employed everyone were testing out different sidelines to earn some extra money. At that time many had started raising pigs, and each area would hold a contest each year to see who was doing the best. This reporter's work unit had gotten the top award each year by raising the biggest pigs, but he noticed that its pigs didn't usually yield good-tasting pork, as many were older and their meat had become fat and oily with age. So his article described the paradox, discussing the burden of raising big pigs. He mailed his story in to a local paper, setting his journalism career in motion.

While media are still first and foremost the tellers of the Party's story, a newer, more subtle role they have taken on in the past two decades is that of maintaining social harmony and stability. In the same 2010 lecture mentioned in Chapter 1, where a top Xinhua editor discussed a restaged reemergence by China's first astronaut from his space capsule to hide an unsightly injury suffered during his descent, that same official, Xia Lin, also talked about a different case involving civil unrest to further illustrate Xinhua's mission in that regard. In that case, he cited the example of rioting in western China's Xinjiang region in 2009 between Uighyrs, the indigenous people, and Han Chinese as an instance where Xinhua should clearly take two different approaches in its reports for mass readers and Beijing leaders. Those riots were some of China's worst in recent memory, leaving 200 dead and ultimately resulting in death sentences for 14 people found guilty of fomenting the unrest. The fact that the riots were race related made them even more sensitive, as such ethnic tensions remain a taboo subject for the Chinese media in general.

On the one hand, Xia said, Xinhua reporters who covered the riots were instructed to conceal the extent of the violence in their reports for general distribution over the Xinhua news service, for fear that revealing the truth could stir up indignation and cause the unrest to spread, especially since much of the early violence was directed against Han Chinese, who make up the vast majority of China's population. During the lecture, he recounted how ethnic Uighyrs had set buses on fire, burning passengers alive, and raped and beheaded children—all details he said would have stoked anger and hatred among Han Chinese toward the Uighyrs and minorities in general. On the other hand, he added, it was critical to include those graphic details in the *neican* for central leaders in Beijing so they could accurately understand what was happening and decide how to proceed. It was only after reading some of those internal reports that Chinese President Hu Jintao himself decided to cut short an overseas tour and return to China to deal with the situation.

While reporters are still highly regarded by society in general, one problem that has crept into Chinese media over the past three decades, and pervades many organizations in general, is that of corruption. The best reflector of this problem is "red envelopes," the cash-filled envelopes given out to reporters for simply attending many news events. As a reporter working in China, I would often see these envelopes, euphemistically referred to as "transport money," given out at press conferences, even though organizers at these events were always strictly told not to give them to foreign correspondents. In the one or two instances when I accidentally received one, I would politely give it back to the event organizer, who would instantly blush at his or her mistake.

On more than one occasion, PR people from both foreign and Chinese companies would quip and complain to me informally about the rising cost of this "transport" money when staging an event. In the early days one could get by with a relatively modest $15 to $30 per envelope, many said. But in more recent years the amount has shot up to as much as $100 or more per reporter. The hard reality is that event organizers who offer too little or who give out no red envelopes at all will gradually find their press conferences poorly attended, if at all, as the word gets out there is no reward for coming to such events. One reporter said the reality is that important news will always attract a large turnout, regardless of how much or little is in the envelope. But for smaller stories, such payouts can make a big difference in attendance.

In a similar vein, some reporters have recently found other ways to earn money through lucrative side businesses to their core jobs. Some write positive reports to bring in new advertisers for their newspapers, and then get commissions for their efforts. And in other cases, reporters sometimes even blackmail companies by threatening to write negative stories unless they get hush money. Most reporters don't see much conflict in taking the red envelopes or getting paid for positive stories, and rather think of such kickbacks as part of their pay, much the way a waitress in the United States regards tips. But these practices are also relatively common knowledge among many ordinary Chinese, adding an extra layer of skepticism to their view of journalists in modern society.

Two younger reporters I interviewed reflected the current state of thinking surrounding journalism with the very different paths each took in their careers. One said his father was very upset at his decision to go into journalism, saying the profession was very difficult, with long work hours and low pay. By comparison, the reporter said, his father was a small businessman who had the freedom to make his own work hours and other lifestyle choices—an option unavailable to most Chinese before the 1990s when everything was still largely state-owned. Another former reporter recalled how he was hand picked from his journalism school for a career at Xinhua, where he quickly saw that with the right attitude and work habits he could someday attain a top-tier position. He worked hard at the agency for about a decade, rising steadily from its lower ranks to more senior positions in the new media businesses. Then one day he decided he could find a better future outside of Xinhua, and ended up taking a high-level marketing job at a private high-tech startup with little revenue but lots of potential. He recalled his Xinhua boss's reaction when he informed him of his decision: "Have you lost your mind?" was all his boss could say.

While other options abound for ambitious young people in today's China, the media do still retain a certain attraction for many, especially those looking for influential careers in the Party and government. That said, it's worthwhile to take a brief look at Xinhua's internal organization and role within the broader media sector, which provides a glimpse at the lay of the land inside many traditional Chinese media and also reflects government priorities.

Simply put, Xinhua is Big Brother Number One among the many younger siblings that make up China's media landscape, providing the first and final word on any important matter, be it the latest national effort to rein in an overheated housing market or the death of a major political figure. Xinhua uses a wide range of languages to make its point, both literally and figuratively. Through years of practice, seasoned China hands have learned how to read between the lines of the hundreds of stories that Xinhua puts out each day, scouring them for the latest government buzzwords and campaigns, as well as where and how prominent Party members are mentioned as indicators of their future careers. On sensitive issues where the message is meant for outsiders, English has become Xinhua's language of choice, as was the case for Beijing's angry reaction when prominent Chinese dissident Liu Xiaobo won the Nobel Peace Prize in 2010. In other cases, such as anything involving the banned Falun Gong spiritual movement, Xinhua's total silence can be just as telling, signaling that public discussion of the subject is off limits for all Chinese media.

Xinhua: The Party's First Take on History

If the Chinese media broadly represent the Communist Party's view of history, reports from Xinhua are the first and most important versions of that history. Most of the world's major governments and media carefully monitor the Xinhua newswire 24 hours a day, looking for the latest shifts in government policies and other directives, as well as the latest slant on how the government wants people to see individual matters like civil unrest or industrial accidents. China watchers also closely follow whose names appear and in what order in Xinhua reports, which often contain long lists of government officials present at a particular event or those on hand to greet a foreign leader. In a country where the inner workings of the Communist Party are hazy at best and often outright opaque, such lists offer some of the only public clues about who is in charge and whose star is on the rise. Equally important are the names that Xinhua leaves off its reports, again providing the only clues of when someone has fallen out of favor.

In many ways Xinhua is like the pitch-pipe in an orchestra, setting the tone on all major topics for other Chinese media to follow. For that reason, the domestic media closely watch their Xinhua newsfeeds to make sure they are staying on key in terms of what is acceptable to report, how to report it, and what remains off limits.

Reports on industrial accidents at factories and the rampant disregard of their management for the environment were taboo subjects for domestic media as late as the early 2000s, amid government fears that such reports could expose its lax oversight of industry and even fan civil unrest. But then the government decided such issues needed to be exposed and rectified, resulting in a steady stream of Xinhua reports over the past decade that signaled to other media that they were permitted to write about such subjects.

A good example of such shifting winds is China's coal mining industry, which has one of the world's worst safety records and is plagued by major accidents at both private and state-run mines. Reports of such accidents were largely absent from Xinhua throughout the 1990s, but then suddenly began to appear in earnest in the early 2000s, with the result that barely a week now goes by without word of the latest disaster. During this time such reports became so common that Reuters, which, like other foreign media, relies heavily on Xinhua for its domestic Chinese coverage, had to adopt informal guidelines that saw us writing stories on only the worst disasters, typically involving the death or injury of a set number of people or more. Anything smaller would simply fall by the wayside.

An interesting footnote to that story shows that while Xinhua may call the shots on broader sensitive topics, other media must still watch their step to avoid raising the ire of central officials. In one case illustrating this point, China's flagship English TV station took Xinhua's green light on reporting coal mining disasters to heart in 2005, sending out its own reporters to compile a series of stories on the problem. Soon after those reports were broadcast, however, the station got a call from the Foreign Ministry, complaining that the stories, which were seen by the station's mostly foreign audience, were hurting China's international image. As a result, many of the station's top managers and journalists who reported the story were forced to write self-criticisms.

In the early days of Communist China, domestic media used Xinhua reports word-for-word on a wide range of topics, whether local, national, or international, to ensure that they were conveying a consistent message from the Party. But in the Internet age, where the number of news outlets has exploded and many have little or no direct connection with central leadership in Beijing, Xinhua has taken on the more subtle role of thought leader, with local media often left to examine previous reporting patterns to determine whether it is acceptable to cover individual incidents or disasters. Xinhua is also often the first and only voice for anything that happens outside of China, from diplomacy to wars and international incidents, and domestic media are expected to carry its stories directly if they want to report on such matters.

In the past, Xinhua exercised strong control over China's domestic media by supplying nearly all the outside news that such local outlets received. Whereas big Western media typically use a wide range of sources for their coverage, such as Reuters, the Associated Press, CNN, and the BBC, Chinese media in the past relied exclusively on Xinhua for all of their non-local reports. Xinhua itself was the only Chinese media organization allowed to monitor news from outside. It used its monopoly to pick and choose the global stories that it wanted to reprint to advance the Communist Party's latest agenda. Nowadays, of course, nearly every Chinese media outlet, large or small, has easy access to the Internet and often carries reports from other sources. This is technically illegal but widely tolerated, as long as no one strays too far from the official Xinhua line.

China's opening to the outside world and a newfound wealth at many of its newspapers, TV stations, and web sites have also radically changed the situation with regard to stationing reporters outside one's home base. In the older days, when China was still quite poor and closed to the outside world, Xinhua was the only media organization with reporters throughout China and outside the country, giving it a lock on all broader-based regional and international reporting. But as the country has prospered, and travel both at home and abroad has become more common, a growing number of media now station reporters abroad, resulting in a wider range of voices on major domestic and international affairs, which again are tolerated as long as they don't stray too far from Xinhua's official line.

In many ways, foreign correspondents living in China today see Xinhua as a press release machine, comparable to US services like PRNewswire and Businesswire, which put out steady streams of company press releases for others to receive and interpret. News from Xinhua is often the closest thing to an official statement on the latest government policies, leading most reporters to take such stories with a grain of salt, much the way they would when reading a press release on the White House's latest initiative to eliminate poverty or provide affordable housing. But while most international media take the Xinhua slant on stories with a large degree of skepticism, the agency's unique status also means that its reports are usually quite credible, with the result that Xinhua will often be first to "break" big stories coming out of China, such as the death of a major leader or announcements of new government programs. As far as the foreign media are concerned, if the information is related to government and Xinhua says it, it must be true.

From an organizational and historical perspective, Xinhua is set up much like any major company, with its headquarters in Beijing and dozens of satellite bureaus and offices scattered throughout the country and increasingly around the world. A look at Xinhua's own web site provides some interesting insights into how the organization sees itself. The page itself is difficult to find, with only a numbered web address, and I learned about it only after a knowledgeable person pointed it out to me. For anyone wanting to take a look, the page itself is at the cryptic but publicly accessible address http://203.192.6.89/xhs, reflecting the extremely low profile that Xinhua tries to assume in broader Chinese society. Divided into simple sections on its history, leadership, and mission, the site states that Xinhua was founded in 1931 as the Red China News Agency in Jiangxi province, and is the Communist Party's oldest news organization. The agency and all of its staff took part in the Long March of 1934, as Mao Zedong and other top Party leaders trekked thousands of miles through some of China's poorest regions to evade capture by the Nationalists, who ruled the country at that time. It officially changed its name to Xinhua, literally meaning "New China," in 1937.

Xinhua also takes pride in the fact that it was not only a mouth-piece for the Party, but has also counted most of the Party's top leaders as contributors over the years, including Mao himself, who penned more than 100 articles and commentaries. Other big names who have penned Xinhua articles over the years include Zhou Enlai and Deng Xiaopeng. In the mission section of its site, Xinhua proudly proclaims that the first of its four major functions is to act as the "ears, eyes, throat, and tongue" for the entire Chinese people.

Xinhua now has 33 bureaus throughout China, Hong Kong, and Macau, including one in each province. It made its English debut with a broadcast in 1944, and began a broader global push after the Communists defeated the Nationalists in 1949. But its real world-wide expansion began decades later with China's opening up in the 1980s. Xinhua now boasts 140 bureaus scattered throughout the world. Reflecting its own sense of accomplishment, Xinhua says that it considers itself one of the world's top four news agencies, alongside Reuters, the Associated Press, and Agence France Presse.

Organizationally speaking, Xinhua resembles any major news service in many ways. At its center is a general editorial desk in Beijing that receives and edits stories, acting as gatekeeper for all news that goes out with the Xinhua name. This desk is headed by top-level people, most of them Propaganda Department appointees with years of experience working in and with the media. As high-ranking Party members, these officials are in regular contact with high-level Party brass, who let them know all the latest policies, who is in, who is out, and any other important matters that should be included in or left out of Xinhua stories. Underneath that editing desk Xinhua is divided broadly into two major departments, one for domestic news and the other for international. Another department looks after Chinese news for overseas consumption, which is usually written in languages other than Chinese.

Beneath Xinhua's basic top layers is a sprawling network of more than a thousand reporters, with the biggest single concentration in Beijing and the rest spread out among the various provinces and international bureaus. Beijing is home to several larger teams focused on specific industries such as agriculture, whereas reporters in the regional offices tend to be generalists.

One former reporter in Xinhua's English service remarked that there was relatively little mixing between reporters writing in foreign languages and those working for the Chinese-language audience, mostly because the two groups focused on different kinds of stories. Whereas foreign-language reporters tended to focus on bigger issues and softer news, those writing in Chinese would often write about very local issues to highlight the government's latest accomplishments, or focus on domestic issues such as crime and corruption to show the average Chinese how the Party was working to root out the many problems that have come with the country's rapid development.

The reporter also noted that Chinese-language reporters were generally treated better than foreign-language ones writing for international readers, as the role of the former group was seen as more important. Whereas articles penned by domestic reporters would mostly go out soon after submission, he said, stories for an international audience, which were often less time sensitive, were more likely to get caught in a larger editing process that could often require days or even weeks before publication. In terms of prestige, the most coveted jobs were postings in Xinhua's international bureaus. Before China's opening to the outside world, Xinhua was one of the few options for anyone who wanted to live and work outside China, making a job there extremely sought after. But as the country has become more open and opportunities to travel, live, and work abroad have grown, Xinhua has lost that part of its attraction as an employer. It is not uncommon now to meet people who moved on after several years at Xinhua to pursue other career options.

While different stories get different editorial treatment based on their content and audience, most of the people I interviewed said the broader editing process at Xinhua wasn't too heavy-handed for anything except the most sensitive stories. Most noted that Chinese reporters in general, both within and outside of Xinhua, all practice a form of self-censorship, avoiding sensitive topics that could cause an article to get bogged down in the editing process and eventually killed. Such self-censorship certainly isn't unique to China. For example, most Western media don't report on suicides unless the circumstances are unusual, and many will also practice self-censorship on the personal affairs of elected officials. But in China, the number of taboo topics is much larger, including long lists of both people and subjects, past and present, that the Party doesn't want to see discussed in big public forums like the media.

From a political standpoint, Party membership isn't actually required to join Xinhua, but is strongly encouraged, especially for people with big advancement potential. Generally speaking, Party membership is mandatory for anyone beyond the level of ordinary reporter, and the ratio of members to nonmembers rises steadily as one goes up the ranks, with top editing and other management jobs reserved for members only.

One reporter remarked that only senior reporters who are Party members are entrusted to write stories involving sensitive social or political topics. He commented that anyone who works daily in Zhongnanhai, the complex where China's top leaders live and work, must be politically reliable and therefore is almost certain to be a Party member. Anyone who regularly meets top leaders, equivalent to being a White House correspondent in the United States, must also be a Party member, he said, estimating that around half of the people at Xinhua were Party members. He said that anyone with management responsibilities, from the lowest section chief and all the way up to department and bureau chief, is almost guaranteed to be a Party member.

Despite its Western image as a propaganda machine, many inside of Xinhua take their work as journalists very seriously and frequently engage in the same kinds of debates about their profession as other reporters around the world. One such case that remained famous in Xinhua newsrooms for many years occurred in the 1950s, involving the eternal debate on what constitutes a doctored photo and what is allowable to improve an image to tell a story better. In that case, Xinhua's photo department hosted a heated debate after a senior photographer arranged things in one of his pictures before taking the actual shot. Similar cases of this nature occurred during the US Civil War in the 19th century, when photographers would often arrive at battlefields after the fighting was finished and then rearrange bodies and other objects to give their pictures more drama. Such practice is usually frowned upon or prohibited outright in most journalistic circles today.

In the Xinhua case in the 1950s, the camp opposed to such practice eventually won the day, and the photographer who arranged the scene was punished and everyone instructed to only take photos of actual scenes. But the reporter who recounted this story also noted that during the Cultural Revolution, many journalistic principles were thrown to the wind completely, and practices like manipulating photo compositions returned.

Many journalistic practices have improved markedly in the past 20 years during the Reform era, with Chinese reporters adapting many Western standards. But that said, today's public is increasingly jaded over the steady stream of growing pains that have come with China's transformation from a planned to a market economy, leading many to suspect the media don't report the full story due to government fears of stoking civil unrest. One reporter said that many average Chinese feel the media are no longer there to serve the people, but rather just want to manipulate what they see and downplay all of the problems. Another reporter said that many people still see Xinhua reporters as organs of the state whose job is to spout the latest Party line, regardless of whether it reflects reality.

Chapter 5

Korea and Tibet

China Finds its Voice

US Marines engage in street fighting during the liberation of Seoul, September 1950. North Korea invaded the South in June that year in a bid to reunify the divided peninsula, but was pushed back when the United States entered a war that would also see China later join on the side of the North.

Photo Credit: Reuters/OTHK

Having examined China's media from a broader perspective in the first four chapters of this book, in the remaining chapters I will look at how the media have reported on several major events since 1949. In doing so, I hope to showcase many of the major themes already discussed, including how China's media are far from a stagnant force, and indeed have evolved quite a bit since their early roots as a simple government propaganda tool. The best place to start this journey is in the country's earliest days, after Mao Zedong famously stood atop the gates of the Forbidden City to announce the formation of the People's Republic of China on October 1, 1949.

This chapter and the ones that follow will focus mostly on media coverage in the initial days or weeks of a major event, as that is when reporting is typically at its most intense and revealing. This chapter will focus on the Korean War and the occupation of Tibet, two events that actually dragged on for months or even years, with media coverage dropping off sharply after the initial days or weeks, a pattern also seen with most major Western media.

The year 1950 was a pivotal one for China and its newly empowered media. The Communist Party was basking in the glow of its victory against the ruling Nationalists just a year earlier, a victory that had taken nearly everyone by surprise as a classic battle of David versus Goliath. But beneath that glow were large pieces of unfinished business as the Communists moved to consolidate their power. Perhaps most importantly, the Communists needed to retake control of the country from a wide range of local powers that had sprung up during more than a decade of war. At the same time, the new government still faced threats from outsiders, most notably the United States, which was determined to destabilize a regime that was clearly allied with the Soviets in a fast-evolving Cold War. As the government sought to consolidate its position, China's media were undergoing their own transformation, with the Communists slowly silencing the many voices that had existed under a more open Nationalist administration in favor of their preferred single-voice approach.

Two of the biggest challenges in these days for both the government and its state-run media, now empowered with the force of a formal government behind them, were in Tibet and Korea, though for very different reasons. In Korea, the situation was largely out of China's hands with the division of the Korean peninsula into North and South after the end of World War II. The conclusion of the war had also brought an end to the 35-year occupation of the peninsula by Japan, and both the Soviets and Western powers had installed their own governments in the newly formed nations of the North and South. The Korean War of 1950 formally began when the North, headed by Soviet-installed leader Kim Il Sung, invaded the South in June of that year. Both the United States and China would quickly join the war, the former supporting the South and the latter the North.

From China's perspective, the Korean War was hardly one in which it wanted to fight. The Chinese military, while still basking in their victory of less than a year before, were exhausted after years of civil war and a painful occupation of large parts of China by the Japanese during World War II. More recent records and analysis have shown that many in the new Communist government were less than thrilled with the idea of getting into a major clash with the United States so soon after their own civil war had ended.

At the same time, however, China was nervous about its borders, especially its border with Korea, where the United States had gained a foothold just 150 miles away with the creation of South Korea. Following the flight of the Nationalist government to Taiwan in 1949, many in Beijing worried that the United States could use South Korea as a base to restart the civil war in China, a move that would most likely first require gaining access to North Korea and its long border with northeast China's Liaoning province.

Communist China also had history and a new global political reality to consider when deciding how to react to the first major conflict on its borders. The country itself had just suffered through a period now known as the "One Hundred Years of Humiliation," which began with the Opium Wars of the 1840s when the Chinese, then ruled by the Qing dynasty, suffered a series of embarrassing defeats at the hands of the British—a humbling experience for a nation that once considered itself the most advanced on earth. That humiliation only grew in the following decades, when Britain and other foreign powers laid claims in a number of major Chinese port cities that they ruled as de facto colonies. It culminated with the occupation of much of China during World War II by Japan, a much smaller nation that had lived in China's shadow for most of its history.

As China was emerging from this humiliating period, it was also contending with the rise of the Soviet Union to its north, as well as with the United States as a global power. For Mao in particular, it was important to show both the Soviets and the United States that China was also a force to be reckoned with, as part of Mao's greater vision that China could someday become a leader of the global Communist movement in its own right, a role clearly held by the Soviets at that time.

During this turbulent period, the Chinese media most closely resembled the classic "mouthpiece" that most have come to equate with Communist nations and single-party states where everything is government owned. The messages were loud and clear, and seldom wavered from the central points that the new Communist government was trying to make, with regard not only to Korea but also to Tibet, which will be discussed later in this chapter. China used its media at this time to announce its formal presence in the Cold War, as a kind of presentation of credentials, and to call for other countries to give it the same respect as that reserved for other major powers. It wanted the Soviets to take notice, and also for its own people to see that it could stand up to the kinds of powers that had bullied it for the past hundred years.

China's Korean War coverage in particular saw the media develop many of the tricks that would later become staples in its tool kit for the decades to come. Those included the use of external conflicts to divert attention from issues at home, a sort of "blame the foreigner" approach, playing on sensitivities from the hundred years of humiliation. It also saw the media develop what I like to call a guerilla-style form of news coverage, which typically includes reports on a wide range of activities from many sources, all of which are carefully crafted around a theme to drive home a single message.

The Korean War formally began on June 25, 1950, when the North attacked the South. Northern leaders expected a quick victory that would reunify the briefly divided peninsula under the Communist leadership of Kim Il Sung. The North was clearly allied with the Soviets at that time, with the result that the Kim regime informed the Chinese of its plans merely as a sort of courtesy just a few days before the actual attack took place. China stood on the sidelines in the first week of the war, happy to focus on its own affairs and let the heavily armed North reunify the peninsula on its own.

All that changed, of course, when the United States entered the war less than two weeks after the conflict began, setting off alarm bells in Beijing for some of the previously mentioned reasons. Despite strongly backing the North in the nation's earliest days, the Soviets were reluctant to get involved in what could potentially become a major new conflict with the United States, and instead deferred to the Chinese to help out the North if necessary. Mao and other Communist leaders were initially opposed to providing such help, but soon changed their minds after the South Koreans, now with US backing, not only turned back the invaders but actually began pushing past the north–south border into North Korean territory. Before long, the South was fast approaching the Chinese border at the Yalu River.

China responded to the threat by secretly massing its troops on the Korean border, and then sending them across on October 19, nearly four months after the war began. Its troops began to fight with the South Koreans and Americans about a week later, marking a major escalation that saw the South's troops driven back to the former border. The war dragged on for three years before finally ending in 1953 at largely the same borders as at the start. The casualties were huge. China reported 150,000 of its troops killed in the war, although some estimate the number of Chinese dead may have reached as many as 400,000. The United States also suffered big losses, with nearly 37,000 killed, and another 92,000 wounded.

Four Media Approaches

One can find four distinctly Chinese media approaches over the course of the Korean War. The first two, which occurred as the war began, both reflect tactics commonly used in the early days of media under Communist rule, which is to distort the truth in order to reflect the message the Party wants to convey. The third is use of what I have referred to as "guerilla reporting," which prevailed once the United States entered the war; and the fourth is non-reporting of real news, a tactic used to cover up unsavory facts that would subvert the Party's message.

Coverage during the first phase, the North's surprise attack on the South on June 25, was relatively muted and distorted to hide the fact that the North was the aggressor. At the same time, the Chinese media were quick to point out the conflict could ultimately result in the reunification of the peninsula under a Communist-allied government, a clear victory in the new global Cold War. The day after the invasion the war was featured in a front-page story of the *People's Daily*, the Communist Party's official newspaper, with a map showing where, according to the paper, the South had transgressed beyond the 38th parallel dividing the two nations, a trumped-up excuse for the North's invasion. The headline was upbeat, reflecting the "good-news-only" theme that would dominate the Chinese media for years to come, saying that the North had already begun to turn back Southern troops. Such bold distortions of the facts are rare or nonexistent today, as easy access to outside information for most Chinese would make such untruths easy to detect and expose. But reporting of half-truths or sometimes even outright lies was common practice in the Chinese media as late as the 1960s, when the country was still quite closed to the outside world and the central government's tight control meant that there were few if any outside channels to confirm or refute the official version of events.

In addition to the main story announcing the outbreak of war, the first-day coverage in the *People's Daily* also included a related report of a meeting in the North where hopes for peaceful reunification of the peninsula were discussed, and an editorial stating the North had the right to defend itself in the face of aggression from the South. This relatively low-key reporting looks designed not only to hide the fact of the North's aggression, but also to prime the Chinese people for the much bolder headlines that the Party eventually was hoping for, announcing the North's success in reuniting the peninsula—trumpeting a major victory in the battle of communism versus capitalism.

Of course, those headlines were never written, as the United States entered the war around July 5, less than two weeks after the start of the conflict, and quickly turned the tide. At this point the low-key approach quickly vanished and the conflict was suddenly blown up into a massive story in the *People's Daily*. This marked the beginning of the guerilla-style coverage mentioned at the beginning of the chapter. On July 6, the day after American troops entered the war, much of the front page of the *People's Daily* was devoted to stories condemning the US move. The words "enemy," "imperialist," "invader," and "aggressor" were used copiously in a series of articles and editorials blanketing page one. In its guerilla coverage, the paper also used as many story formats as possible to create the impression of "many voices," all with the same theme of condemning America's aggression. It featured a wide range of people blasting the US entry, including officials from the Chinese Foreign Ministry, a domestic group promoting international peace, and an economic development group. Lest readers think the condemnation was coming only from official channels, the front page also featured a report from a small city called Pingrang, where numerous local groups were also expressing words of protest. All of those event-based articles, called "spot stories" by journalists, were supplemented by a long editorial from the newspaper itself commenting on "The Victorious Road Ahead in the War for Liberation by the Korean People." This kind of over-the-top chatter was commonly used by the Chinese media throughout the first few decades of Communist rule, sometimes consuming entire editions of newspapers, as if trying to convince the reader that the sheer volume of coverage from so many different "sources" means that the event as reported must be true.

The guerilla coverage continued almost daily for much of the first few weeks after the United States entered the war, as the tide quickly turned against the North and as South Korean troops advanced toward the Chinese border. I particularly liked the front page of the July 19 edition, which featured a colorful caricature of General MacArthur trudging through a swamp, a pistol in one hand while blood drips from the other and people hang from his hairy arms. The newspaper also took advantage of the situation to complain about America's "invasion" of Taiwan, as the United States embarked on a long-term policy of protecting the Nationalists holed up on the island from a mainland invasion. Given the way that Taiwan began appearing in a growing number of headlines around this time, it is feasible to infer the Communists were worried that the United States might use the Korean War as an excuse to invade China and rekindle the civil war that drove the Nationalists out of power in the first place.

Collectively the media seem to convey a sense of constant handwringing and worrying by the Chinese during this period, as the US "imperialists" began to overwhelm the North. As time went on, two refrains came up repeatedly in the news coverage. One of those involved stories of Foreign Minister Zhou Enlai sending regular protests to the United Nations, usually by telegram, each time the US–backed South made any move that posed even the smallest threat to China, such as military flights that crossed over Chinese territory. The other was a nonstop barrage of protests by a wide range of domestic organizations, from citizens groups to business and government bodies, which held endless rallies and organized petitions all calling for an immediate US withdrawal. Looking at this guerilla coverage in hindsight, it seems to have been aimed not only at selling the story to the Chinese people, but increasingly also at preparing them for China's eventual entry into the war.

That entry began on October 19, 1950, nearly four months after the war began, when China secretly started sending troops across the Yalu River. Chinese soldiers began to engage US and South Korean troops about a week later. Yet throughout this time, no mention was made in the media of Chinese participation in the war, and the news blackout stayed in effect for a full three weeks after Chinese troops first crossed into Korea. This kind of blackout tactic, which sees the Chinese media simply ignoring certain sensitive matters as if they had never happened, was common all the way through the 1960s and even into the 1970s, when even big events like a major earthquake in the city of Tangshan, which left more than 200,000 dead in 1976, received minimal coverage.

The *People's Daily* finally broke its silence on China's entry into the war in its November 8 edition, more than two weeks after the actual event, with a lead front-page story opening with the headline, "With

Participation of the People's Volunteer Army Behind Them, North Korea Wins an Important Victory." At a glance, it is apparent why the government chose that day to disclose to the public China's participation in the war, with the paper reporting that Chinese troops had already begun to turn back the South Koreans and their US allies.

Throughout the coverage of the war, the fact that the North's aggression started the conflict was never revealed. Also not mentioned was the fact that China's so-called "volunteer" army was anything but voluntary. Later history would show that many of the troops sent by the Chinese to fight the Americans were actually captured soldiers from the Nationalist army, who were then forced to fight in the Korean War. The presence of these unwilling conscripts would ultimately complicate prisoner exchanges after the end of the war, as the United States insisted on giving captured soldiers the right to decide whether they wanted to go back to China, despite Beijing's insistence that all POWs be sent back. Not surprisingly, many of the captured troops with Nationalist backgrounds opted not to go back, and ended up emigrating elsewhere.

The Korea conflict provides a good springboard for the other main subject of this chapter, Tibet. Media reports of China sending troops into the Himalayan region first appear at about the same time that Chinese troops are secretly entering Korea. Historically speaking, the relationship between China and Tibet has always been complex, hence the wide range of views on the subject. Tibet was part of the Chinese empire from the late Qing, China's final dynasty, which began in 1644 and formally ended in 1911 with the founding of the Republic of China under the Nationalists. It was never a formally independent country during that time, and Britain and neighboring India both had influence in Tibet and their own designs on it as internal strife increasingly consumed China in the waning days of the Qing dynasty. Against that backdrop, one could reasonably argue that China's initial sending of troops to Tibet in October 1950 wasn't even a formal invasion, but rather just a reassertion of control over what it perceived as its own territory, as it sought to head off competing claims from India or Britain or even a formal declaration of independence. Other parts of what is China today might try to make their own cases for independence, but few historically had such well-defined governments and identity of place as Tibet, which even had its own emissary in Beijing.

Prior to the Chinese troop movement, the Dalai Lama, often called the spiritual leader of Tibet, had been allowed to travel to other countries for meetings and to return. Even after 1950, he continued to be cautiously optimistic about the potential for a high degree of autonomy under the Communists. For his part, Mao also considered the Dalai Lama a relatively moderate force within Tibet who could be used to help marginalize more radical Tibetans.

In terms of events, what happened in 1950 is rather straightforward: Chinese troops marched into Tibet in the middle of October to assert control under the year-old Communist government, meeting with relatively little resistance in what China would later call a "peaceful liberation" from both outside forces and also a Tibetan government that it would later portray as highly exploitative of many Tibetans. Tibetans accepted the occupation by Chinese troops, though the situation remained uneasy over the next nine years, with each side looking for advantage. Even some central leaders reportedly felt the approach in Beijing to governing Tibet was heavy handed, including widespread discrimination against ethnic Tibetans. Then in March 1959, relations began to grow tense as rumors circulated in the region of a plan by Beijing to kidnap the Dalai Lama. Locally based uprisings began soon afterward, with tens or even hundreds of thousands of protesters coming out in support of the Dalai Lama and growing calls for independence. The Dalai Lama fled about a week after those protests began, ultimately taking refuge in India after a 15-day journey. A BBC report at the time put the number of dead during the three days of fighting at 2,000, although Tibetan leaders who fled the country would later put the figure much higher, at more than 80,000.

Tibet: A Lost Family Member Returns to the Fold

Chinese media coverage of the developments in Tibet was similar in tone to reporting on Korea, with headlines mostly spouting the Party line that Tibet had always been a part of China and was simply returning to the fold, as China moved to show both domestic and global audiences that it was a force to be reckoned with under its young Communist government on issues within and around its borders.

The media also used other, smaller tactics in their then-nascent portfolio, again blaming foreigners for helping to incite the unrest and repeatedly using key catchwords, most notably calling the 1950 campaign a "liberation" of the Tibetan people—a buzzword still used to this day and a view widely accepted among the Chinese.

Within the Chinese media, the *People's Daily*'s first major mention of Chinese troops in Tibet came in early November 1950, three weeks after the troops had actually begun entering the region to reassert control. The newspaper's November 2 edition contained the first big report on the subject, placed at the bottom of the front page, simply proclaiming "The People's Liberation Army Has Begun Advancing into Tibet." The single headline was actually an umbrella for a series of smaller Xinhua stories, most composed of fewer than 10 sentences, with the main one a largely factual account of the advance, which at that point was several weeks old. The term "liberate" appeared frequently throughout the stories to describe the advance of the People's Liberation Army.

The main story was followed by another brief one recounting how Chinese troops received an "enthusiastic welcome" on their arrival from local Tibetans, Muslims, and ethnic Chinese, including four living Buddhas who would have been highly esteemed in the devoutly Buddhist Tibetan community. The other major story that day cited a Tibetan army officer calling Mao Zedong to say that Tibetans wanted to return to the big family of the People's Republic of China, and that local Tibetan officials and troops would work quickly with the Chinese to liberate all Tibetans. This again drew on a recurrent media theme that Tibetans were members of a feudal society in which the powerful elite, many of them high-ranking Buddhists, had enslaved the majority of the average population before China's arrival in 1950.

The coverage on the following day, November 3, was equally succinct, again featuring three short stories at the bottom of the front page, one an editorial and two Xinhua reports. The editorial sang the praises of the Chinese army and the many difficulties it had to overcome to reach such a rugged and remote area as Tibet. This reflects the high place that the military holds in Chinese society, so much so that to this day it is exempt from many established government controls in terms of media coverage, and military brass can largely determine for themselves what can and can't be written about them. The second story simply summarized an article that had appeared in a British labor newspaper, comparing Tibet's relationship with China to that of Wales to the United Kingdom, and explaining how that made Tibet a part of China. This kind of article is typical of a pattern that occurs repeatedly in the years ahead, whereby the Chinese media print words of encouragement, approval, and understanding from overseas voices to try to create an aura of broader consensus around controversial moves, thereby somehow validating the government's actions. The third article simply reported on the warm welcome given by native Tibetans to Chinese soldiers advancing into an area called Xikang, again drawing on the liberation theme.

From a broader perspective, the generally low-key nature of the *People's Daily* coverage during this initial advance is quite telling. Whereas this kind of news would qualify as a top story in most Western countries, this muted approach, which sees all coverage relegated to the bottom of the front pages, and the relative brevity of stories in general reflect the broader sensitivity that remains in effect in China's media to this day when reporting on anything involving racial tensions. Such tensions are among the several dozen major taboo categories that seldom make it into the news.

While the situation was generally understated in the media in 1950, coverage was much more prominent in the case of the 1959 uprising, which came as a surprise to the Chinese. The uprising began around March 10 that year and ended with the Dalai Lama's flight from Lhasa with a small entourage one week later. Throughout that time, reports of the riots and deaths in Tibet were completely absent from the pages of the *People's Daily*, in an encore of the kind of blackout seen during the early days of China's entry into the Korean War. As with the Korean War, the blackout seems to have been aimed at waiting until there was "good" news to report to the Chinese audience—in this case the end of the protests with a triumph for the Chinese, and the flight of the troublemaking Dalai Lama, who would be labeled in media reports for decades to come as a "splittist" and a "traitor."

The first mention of the uprising in the *People's Daily* didn't come until March 29—nearly three weeks after it had begun and two weeks after the Dalai Lama's flight—when the story suddenly appeared from nowhere to take up the entire front page, in another typical case of gue-rilla coverage. Not surprisingly, the coverage reads more like a *fait accompli* than a developing story, with the lengthy first article declaring that China had calmed the uprising, which was blamed on a small group of people who had "betrayed their motherland in the name of imperialism" against the larger will of the Tibetan people. The reports clearly pointed out that Tibetans, including the extremists and some government offi-cials, had instigated the violence by attacking Chinese troops first, and added that many local governments were now being disbanded.

This approach of blaming social unrest on small groups of radicals is yet another recurrent theme in the media in such times of upheaval, including the Tiananmen Square student movement of 1989, in which a small group of "black hands" were continually blamed for inciting otherwise-innocent Chinese to rise up against the government. In fact, the usual preference would be to simply black out, or minimize as much as possible, any news related to social unrest, which, like racial tensions, the government considers off-limits for reporting in the media. However, in the cases of the Tibetan uprising and Tiananmen, the news was too prominent to sweep under the carpet, leading the government to turn to its next-best option of minimizing the real significance of the story by placing blame on a handful of "radicals" in its media reports.

The guerilla coverage of March 29 continued into the next day, March 30, when the front page was again filled with Tibet-related stories that seemed to reflect a growing angst about the potential for more tensions between ethnic Chinese and the many other minorities in and around that part of western China. Such minorities are numer-ous throughout that region, though China generally allows them a high degree of autonomy and thus relations between the two sides are usu-ally relatively harmonious. One typical story on this second day of Tibet coverage proclaimed how people in the provinces of Qinghai, Inner Mongolia, and Xinjiang, all with large non-ethnic Chinese populations, had come together to discuss the "traitorous" Tibetan groups. The head-line was a virtual collage of buzzwords and phrases that would become part of the lexicon for later discussions of Tibet in the Chinese media, including "a very small group," "reactionaries," "traitors," and "the moth-erland." Another article that day reported on similar mass meetings and other activities in Beijing, Shanghai, and Tianjin, where people were congratulating Tibet on its "beginning of a new democratic and socialist era," a reference to the official line that average Tibetans were heavily persecuted in the past by a ruling class that would now be marginalized. A final exemplary headline that day, again playing on the unity theme, cited a Buddhist organization in China calling the Tibetan rabble-rousers nothing more than "wolves in Buddhists' clothing." The addition of Buddhists themselves to the groups condemning the uprising was an important way to dismiss the religious persecution claims made by many of the uprising's instigators, relegating them to the realm of simply opportunistic troublemakers.

Coverage of the uprising continued in a similar vein for the next few days, but the flight of the Dalai Lama wasn't mentioned until April 3, again more than two weeks after his initial departure. Here, the reason behind the timing of events was a bit clearer, as the Dalai Lama's whereabouts were unknown to most people for the greater part of the two weeks of his flight, which ended with his crossing into India around March 31. That first report on April 3 actually consisted of just a two-sentence news brief at the bottom of the front page of the *People's Daily* that looks almost like an afterthought, stating the Dalai Lama had fled to India. Such briefs, which often look more like official statements than real news stories, are again relatively common in the Chinese media even to this day. They typically appear during sensitive times and are the government's way of saying "we want you to know about something that happened, but no further discussion is allowed."

The initial brief on the Dalai Lama's flight to India was followed by several days of silence, even as the *People's Daily* contained a steady stream of reports about the return of order to Lhasa. The next mention of the spiritual figure didn't come until another five days had passed, when the newspaper broke its silence with a brief article stating that the Dalai Lama had sent an apologetic letter to Beijing explaining that the insurgents had taken their action to protect him and wanting to see if he could mend fences. The article was essentially a translation of the letter, written in Tibetan, and was accompanied by a photo of the original letter—a relative rarity for Chinese newspapers of that era, whose pictures were mostly limited to government officials, mass rallies, and other positive portrayals of life. Despite extending that olive branch, and the Chinese media's use of the letter to justify the government's actions, the two sides never reconciled and the Dalai Lama never returned to Tibet, remaining in exile to this day.

Thus, this ended two of the earliest chapters of conflict reporting for the young media in the People's Republic of China. In Korea and Tibet, we see early reporting patterns that will become staples of the Chinese media for decades to come. Perhaps first and foremost, the "good-news-only" theme became a regular feature, as the media blacked out China's entry into the Korean War and the uprising in Tibet, and lifted the veil only after a positive story had emerged to be told. Reporting of those events also gives rise to many of the other media tools that will later come into common use, including the coinage and repetition of key buzzwords and phrases, guerilla coverage, and the minimizing, avoidance, or outright prohibition of certain taboo topics like racial tensions.

Last, but not least, this period also exemplifies the rise of Xinhua as the primary source of reports for all media on sensitive stories, a legacy that continues to this day. In discussing general coverage patterns, one old-time reporter commented to me that few if any domestic media from the 1950s all the way through to the 1990s would dare to use any report other than the official Xinhua version of events in situations comparable to Tibet or Korea.

In the final analysis, coverage of these two important events in early Communist China shows how the government used the media as a kind of blunt tool to ensure that everyone got the same, consistent message. The media during this era were the government's megaphone, which it used to tell the public which issues were important and why readers should adopt those views as their own.

Chapter 6

Cultural Revolution

The Ultimate Media Movement

A man walks past a poster depicting the Chinese Cultural Revolution at a film studio on the outskirts of the city of Yinchuan in April 2007. Mao launched the Cultural Revolution in 1966 in a bid to sideline his political opponents and rekindle the revolutionary spirit in the general populace. The movement lasted a decade and formally ended with Mao's death in 1976.

Photo Credit: Reuters/OTHK

The first half of the 1960s was not a good time for Mao Zedong, generally considered the primary founder of the People's Republic of China and the country's dominant political figure from the nation's establishment in 1949 until his death in 1976. His vision of creating a truly Communist country where everything was owned by the state and people all worked for the common good had received a massive setback with the Great Leap Forward of 1958–1961, one of the biggest tragedies in modern Chinese history. That movement saw the Communists try to collectivize the nation's privately owned farms, only to create a massive manmade disaster instead that left millions dead of starvation and Mao's credibility as leader of the country seriously damaged.

Like most of Mao's movements, the Great Leap Forward started with good intentions, even if its means were extreme. Less than a decade after the founding of the People's Republic of China, Mao wanted to show the world that agricultural communes could be far more productive than the individual plots and farming methods practiced by millions of Chinese for centuries. To do this, he embarked on an aggressive campaign of collectivization, moving legions of poverty-stricken farmers from their homes to a new generation of massive agricultural communes.

Eager to show Mao the correctness of his policy, the leaders of these new communes quietly started inflating crop outputs in their reports to the government to show that the new system was more productive than the old farming methods. Encouraged by the inflated numbers, Mao and other central leaders set even more aggressive targets for the communes, whose officials happily played along by further inflating their latest harvest reports. The spiral of inflated figures continued, and soon the new agricultural communes were giving nearly all of their actual output to government collectors, while keeping the remainder—which looked good on paper based on the inflated figures but was actually little or nothing—for themselves.

The national hoax finally culminated in massive famines that saw tens of millions of people die of starvation. When the central government finally woke up to the reality of what was happening, it quickly took steps to ease the suffering and the famines quickly disappeared— dealing a big blow to the image of Mao Zedong, who was the movement's top backer. His credibility badly damaged, Mao subsequently took a backseat and let other, more practical leaders run the show. But by 1965 he was again getting restless and felt the Great Leap Forward was far enough in the past that he could begin to resume his revolutionary agenda.

Thus the Cultural Revolution was born—arguably the most turbulent period in China's history since 1949. The media suddenly became a massive bullhorn for Mao and his allies to popularize their latest slogans and topics of the day. Most of these slogans revolved around a revolution that would see the control of culture wrested from the urban elite and returned to the rural masses. Meantime, those same urban elite were often sent down to the countryside for years as part of their "reeducation." From a media perspective, Mao and his allies literally took the "news" out of newspapers and other media during this period, replacing it with slogans and opinion pieces on their new revolution. Ironically, this period was one of the freest in the Communist era for the media in terms of direct government oversight, as most central and local officials were suddenly too caught up in the widespread power struggles of that period to pay attention to what the media were writing. Barely a week would go by during this turbulent decade without the purge of one major leader or another, as Mao's favorites one day would end up his adversaries the next and branded as capitalist roaders, counterrevolutionaries, or running dogs. With no one directly watching over their shoulder, most media no longer were forced to simply reprint the stories coming out of Xinhua or the *People's Daily* each day, and could instead write their own articles, editorials, or other story formats. Still, they were highly constrained in terms of what they could write about, having to stick to topics of the day, usually toeing the latest line coming from Mao in Beijing.

One reporter who lived through the period said that the mantra for the media and society in general boiled down to one word: *struggle*. He said that Mao proclaimed in 1962 that class struggle must be discussed all year on every day of every month, and the media took this message to heart. It was a signal for them to turn away from traditional news reporting and instead focus on more editorial-style writing, with a special eye to criticism. From that time, he said, the newspapers became full of editorials and a wide range of other opinion-piece formats criticizing just about anything, from intellectuals to movies to Confucius, setting in motion a media pattern that would remain in place until the Cultural Revolution formally ended in 1976. In effect, the media's job during these tumultuous 10 years became that of cheerleader, reminding the masses with a steady blare of slogans, editorials, and other new and creative story formats of the importance of maintaining the daily struggle. Despite the "anything goes" freedom for most media to write their own articles and commentaries, many smaller magazines and newspapers were still shut down by Mao loyalists when they failed to toe the Party line or were simply allied with people on Mao's bad side.

The tumultuous atmosphere that evolved at this time became even more so as traditional mass media, mostly newspapers and radio, were quickly joined by a noisy chorus of micro-media that suddenly appeared everywhere in such forms as slogan-shouting mobs, propaganda posters, and another form of individually penned piece called the "big-character poster"—long and often ranting proclamations written by average people using traditional brush and ink.

Another Cultural Revolution hallmark that could also be characterized as a form of micro-media is the "struggle session," an all-too-familiar term to most Chinese but an alien concept to Westerners. Such sessions were usually led by groups of overzealous youth, often members of Mao's Red Guard of civilian soldiers charged with rekindling the nation's revolutionary spirit. They would travel from neighborhood to neighborhood and hold their struggle sessions in buildings and on the streets, sometimes verbally attacking long-dead figures like Confucius but just as often going after local residents who had been branded as "anti-revolutionaries" for such innocuous acts as owning a private business or having a parent who worked in a foreign company in pre-Communist China. Last, but most definitely not least in the micro-media parade was the circulation of millions of "Little Red Books" with quotations from Mao, which would become one of the period's most lasting symbols. While apparently similar on the outside, even these seemingly homogeneous books had a certain variety, as editors picked out which of Mao's thoughts they considered the most significant from his larger body of works, resulting in a wide range of volumes.

The noise that came from this incredible plurality of voices is what I like to call the "sound of ten thousand bullhorns," with just about any individual empowered to speak his or her views from the top of personal soapboxes by writing big-character posters and attending struggle sessions where anyone could call out or interpret the latest slogan and condemn the latest antirevolutionary individual. The enthusiasm many ordinary Chinese felt toward Mao and his various movements during this period was genuine, the product of years of virtual deification and frequent repetition of his many real achievements in areas such as land reform and redistributions of wealth to create a more equal society. As a result of his near-godlike status, even opportunists who didn't necessarily believe in Mao's greatness could advance their own agendas by singing his praises. On the other hand, anyone who criticized Mao immediately opened himself to attack as an antirevolutionary.

From the historical perspective, many see the Cultural Revolution as a last-ditch effort by Mao to remain relevant and seal his place in the history of the modern country he had helped to found. While Mao had proven himself to be a brilliant commander and a shrewd strategist in leading the Communists to an unlikely victory over the Nationalists, his record was far less impressive at the more mundane but equally important tasks of running the country on a day-to-day basis and trying to lift its hundreds of millions of destitute citizens out of poverty. His first big attempt to leave his mark with the Great Leap Forward not only set the country back several years economically but also left tens of millions of dead, and is now recognized as one of history's worst manmade disasters. Some say that Mao's Cultural Revolution was in some ways simply a form of payback for those who had to clean up his mess after the failure of the Great Leap Forward, making him look bad.

Against the backdrop of that major fiasco and a desire to leave a more positive mark, Mao was also looking closely to the north at what was happening in the Soviet Union, which had been China's close ally and role model in its earliest days. Mao was specifically concerned about what had happened after the death of longtime Soviet leader Joseph Stalin in 1953. Stalin had led the Soviets through World War II and run a regime during which he had brutally repressed his adversaries. But then his legacy had been rapidly dismantled posthumously by the country's next leader, Nikita Krushchev, in a process that would later become known as de-Stalinization. It is thought that Mao feared that a similar de-Maoification process might take place after his own death at the hands of another top leader, Liu Shaoqi, his heir-apparent, who would ultimately become one of the Cultural Revolution's biggest victims. Mao's dethronement of Liu Shaoqi was followed by the rapid rise of another heir apparent, Lin Biao, the man who created the cult of the Little Red Books. But like Liu Shaoqi, Lin Biao would meet with a similar fate several years later when Mao began to distrust him as well.

Mao knew he could control people while he was alive, but was also acutely aware that he needed a stronger legacy in the form of a lasting revolution that would continue after his death to truly seal his place as a great man in the history of modern China. The Cultural Revolution was his final effort at greatness, as he aimed not only to avoid Stalin's fate but also to overtake the Soviets as leader of the global Communist movement.

I've already mentioned some of the media themes that appeared during the Cultural Revolution, including the rise of the micro-media as part of the sound of ten thousand bullhorns. As my metaphor implies, the media of this time may have had ten thousand voices, but it's also important to note that all of those played on the same handful of themes, namely the latest directives from Mao and his top-level supporters who delivered his daily messages.

Guerilla Coverage at Fever Pitch

The Cultural Revolution marked a crescendo in many trademark practices of the Chinese media. At the top of the list, guerilla coverage reached new highs during this time as newspapers went for weeks and months on end with entire editions composed of little more than symphonies of slogans, opinion pieces, and praise of the latest thoughts of

Mao Zedong, along with condemnations of anyone opposing the movement. There was an almost frenzied use of buzzwords, though many of the key catchphrases that were thrown up during those times ultimately lacked the kind of staying power seen in the Korean and Tibetan conflicts, which gave rise to words like "splittist" to describe the Dalai Lama. By comparison, most buzzwords from the Cultural Revolution have fallen out of use since the movement formally ended with Mao's death in 1976.

Also rising to prominence in this period is the use of the editorial, and the use of other media devices such as slogans and banners that appeared daily at the top of each page, to drive home the latest Party line. Finally, the period also saw regular use of the blackout tactic, where the rapid and often spectacular fall of former rising Communist Party stars went completely uncovered by the media, whose complete silence on such major matters takes on a surreal, almost conspiratorial quality for readers like me leafing through old newspapers decades after the events.

It's hard to pinpoint an exact beginning to the Cultural Revolution since, as previously mentioned, newspapers were under direct or implicit orders to write about class struggle as early as 1962. Historians generally put the formal start at August 1, 1966, the anniversary of the founding of the People's Liberation Army. But other views also exist. One old-time reporter working for a major Shanghai daily during that time said that the movement actually began with a series of reports in his newspaper in 1965. He pinpointed the beginning to an editorial published on November 10, 1965, where the writer, a man named Yao Wenyuan, criticized a contemporary Beijing opera about a historical official named Hai Rui who wasn't afraid to speak his mind and voice criticism, even if that meant criticizing the emperor. The reporter said that everyone at his newspaper, himself included, was completely baffled when the commentary appeared on page two of that day's paper under the cryptic headline "Hai Rui Was a Ming Dynasty Official." Some reporters even went to Fudan, the local big-name university, to ask experts there what it meant, and others put the question to local Shanghai politicians. It was impossible to ask the author himself, as he was only an occasional freelancer and not well known to most of the staff.

Later on, according to this reporter, people would learn that the article had been written at the request of Mao himself, and was meant as a veiled attack on Liu Shaoqi, the former rising star and heir-apparent who was already falling out with his former ally. In this case, Mao, who had adopted a low profile at that time after the failure of the Great Leap Forward, may have seen himself as akin to Hai Rui, using the editorial to attack Liu Shaoqi, who by then had moved to center stage and was seen as the country's next leader. Mao, it turned out, had read some of the editorial writer's works before and liked them, leading him to handpick the man to pen one of his earliest attack articles in the prelude to the more formal launching of the Cultural Revolution.

From around that time, this reporter said, all newspapers and other media gradually began to change their reporting style and content, with the result that conflict and criticism became common themes on their pages. He said that this new era of struggle erupted into open conflict at his own newspaper in January 1967, several months after the Cultural Revolution formally began, when a power grab saw most of the former top editors thrown out and replaced with people more supportive of Mao and his latest revolutionary themes.

In terms of actual events, one can look at both the political events taking place behind the scenes, as well as actual happenings on the street that were throwing people's lives into turmoil, to trace the development of the Cultural Revolution. From a political perspective, I will focus on two key figures, the previously mentioned Liu Shaoqi and Lin Biao, who were both once considered top contenders to take over as leaders of the Communist Party, only to rapidly fall from grace after Mao turned against them. In Liu's case, the beginning of the end came in the fall of 1967, about a year after the Cultural Revolution formally began, when Mao called a series of meetings to discuss his former protégé's problematic "case," which included numerous "transgressions" pulled up from his long history in the Party. By the middle of 1968, a group of Mao supporters had compiled three volumes of condemning materials on Liu, many dating back to his early days as a member. He was soon stripped of his Party post and his name completely disappeared from the public realm around that time. He died a year later in 1969 after harsh treatment, his death completely unnoticed by the average Chinese—a sharp contrast to his earlier days in power when he was regularly featured on the front pages of major newspapers.

After Liu, Mao's next heir apparent, Lin Biao, experienced a similar fate, although in much shorter order. Lin rose rapidly to high positions during the Cultural Revolution in lockstep with Liu's decline, only to tumble just as quickly as he fell out of favor with Mao. In the end, Lin is believed to have tried to flee to the Soviet Union after a failed coup attempt in 1971, and he died when his plane crashed in Mongolia.

For the average Chinese and by most historical accounting, the Cultural Revolution began on the first day of August in 1966, when Mao used the anniversary of the founding of the People's Liberation Army as the occasion to start his movement. His launch would ulti- mately last for most of the month, culminating with a mass rally on August 18 at Tiananmen Square, when Mao personally greeted the newly formed Red Guards, the legions of vigilante-style youth charged with rekindling the nation's revolutionary spirit by bully- ing ordinary citizens with endless streams of rallies, struggle sessions, and other impromptu events. The chaos that began that month would continue for much of the next decade, when schools and universities were closed and other features of ordinary life as many people knew it suddenly ceased. During that time, countless people whose histories that were deemed "bad" for reasons such as their past status as property owners or working for foreign companies were persecuted and jailed, and millions of ordinary Chinese were sent to the countryside to redis- cover the revolutionary spirit.

In terms of mainstream media reports, my review of the Cultural Revolution focuses on the month of August 1966, when coverage was most intense as Mao formally began a movement that he hoped would seal his place in history. The August 1 edition of the *People's Daily* set the tone for things to come, with pages virtually devoid of real news, save for the occasional mention of visits by a foreign leader or two. Instead, the paper was filled with stories and editorials singing the praises of Mao Zedong thought and generally extolling his virtues. One theme in those first few days of August was the repeated appearance of a catchphrase in various forms calling on the world to become a school of Mao Zedong thought—one of many such slogans that came to characterize this period. Indeed, one headline on August 1 that would be repeated for days to come proclaimed: "The Entire Nation Should Become a Big School for Mao Zedong Thought."

More revolutionary slogans started to appear on the following day, August 2, including more talk of turning the world into a school of Mao Zedong thought, and one of the first uses of the word "revolution," with one headline calling on factory workers, farmers, academics, and soldiers to engage in revolution. Again, the onslaught of articles lacked any real news. The first use of the term "Cultural Revolution" in the *People's Daily* came just two days later, on August 4, in a long-winded editorial condemning a deputy at the Culture Ministry named Zhou Yang of "damaging and attacking the Cultural Revolution." The first mention of big-character posters was also made that day. These posters quickly became a hallmark of the movement and a popular starting point for many of the campaigns directed against various individuals, from major figures all the way down to the local schoolteacher who said something "antirevolutionary" in class. By this time, articles about Mao Zedong thought had quickly multiplied to take over the *People's Daily*, appearing throughout the newspaper.

On August 6, the condemnatory editorial rose to new heights, with pages three and four of the paper taken up by a single article accusing the same deputy culture minister, Zhou Yang, of trying to subvert Mao's revolution through the manipulation of culture. Looking at the coverage in retrospect, it is hard not to feel sorry for Zhou, who was the subject of yet another attack in a lengthy editorial the next day, headlined "What Poison Has Zhou Yang Planted in the Northeast?" One of the first signs of another theme to come, the widespread persecution of anyone with higher education, a group loosely termed as "intellectuals," came around the same time, with a *People's Daily* editorial headlined "Intellectuals Can Never Escape the World of the Laborer." All this seems aimed not only at the intellectuals, whom Mao disdains in general, but also at the many leaders in government who Mao feels have been co-opted by the educated class and have lost their revolutionary spirit.

One of the strangest themes during this time—at least from a Westerner's perspective—was a new genre of "Odes to Chairman Mao" that began appearing regularly in the papers that August. These pieces were quite unlike anything else in today's media. The two most common formats for these odes were story-less headlines simply singing

Mao's praises, and simple musical scores with melodies and lyrics for revolutionary songs. One story-less headline appeared in the August 7 edition of the *People's Daily,* simply reading: "Ah, Chairman Mao, You Are the Sun in the Hearts of All Peoples of the World!" A good example of the song format appeared in the September 8 edition of the *People's Daily*, with the printing of the words and melody of a ditty entitled "Closely Follow Chairman Mao to Victory." The lyrics proclaim:

> The working class is the leading class,
> There is no battle the People's Liberation Army can't win.
> Serious pursuit of struggle and self-correction,
> This is what intellectuals, workers, farmers, and soldiers all welcome.

Such proclamations and songs in the newspaper when viewed in retrospect have a surreal quality that would almost be laughable except for the fact that the words represented a very real and dangerous movement that would ultimately destroy the lives of millions and create what many in China now call the "Lost Generation." Such songs were probably designed to educate the masses about the meaning of the Cultural Revolution in as simple a form as possible, in a country where illiteracy rates were still high and many still lacked access to basic education.

Educator of the Masses

Another format that appeared early in the Cultural Revolution was the simple instructive article, the aim of which was to inform people of what exactly Mao was trying to do through his massive new movement. One of the earliest articles in this format appeared on August 7, when the inside pages of the *People's Daily* contained a small box with a simple letter from the editor explaining what was meant by the new Cultural Revolution. Another article that day in a similar format came from a deputy engineer at a factory in the relatively poor interior province of Shaanxi, with the headline "Let Culture Return to the Hands of the Laborers." These instructive stories reached a crescendo on August 9, when the entire front page of the *People's Daily* officially proclaimed the launching of the Cultural Revolution and gave a detailed explanation of what the movement was all about. This was followed three days later by another front page devoted entirely to coverage of Mao's greeting of the masses to discuss the new movement.

By now, one probably gets a good sense of the kind of guerilla coverage that went on in the media in August 1966. That said, one final development worthy of note was the first mention of the infamous Little Red Books, which were formally unveiled in the August 8 edition of the *People's Daily*. There, Mao and his followers announced the biggest book launch in history with the headline "The Central Committee of the Communist Party Decides to Publish Large Volumes of Chairman Mao's Works," accompanied by a story that mentioned an initial run of 35 million copies. As an interesting aside in all this, one of the few real international news stories in the *People's Daily* at this time was a series of articles on the struggle of black people in America during the Civil Rights Movement then taking place. The inclusion of this solitary major outside story seemed to be Mao's way of telling the average Chinese that similar struggles were also taking place elsewhere in the world, especially in other major powers like the United States.

Clearly the media were instrumental in helping to launch the Cultural Revolution in August 1966 and the following months, but the same can't be said of their coverage when first Liu Shaoqi and later Lin Biao were deposed in 1968 and 1971, becoming the movement's two biggest victims. The media reports during both of those major news moments are easily summarized, since both cases are the same: In each, the *People's Daily* contained no reports about the downfall of either man. Liu Shaoqi's finale came in September 1968, when Mao's supporters formally presented evidence of his crimes. Yet, during that time, the headlines in the *People's Daily* still mostly focused on Mao and his latest directives as the Cultural Revolution entered its third year, with no mention at all of Liu Shaoqi, who had already fallen out of the headlines for some time at that point. Likewise, the *People's Daily* contained no references to Lin Biao's downfall, which ended with his death in a plane crash in September 1971. Such news blackouts continue to this day in the official media, though they are far less effective since news inevitably gets out via backdoor channels, most of them over the Internet.

For a former reporter like myself, the Cultural Revolution is especially interesting since many of the reporters who staffed the nation's newspapers and other media at that time are still alive to recount what things were like. One journalist, who worked first at a rural radio station and later at a provincial newspaper, recalled how he and his colleagues spent most of their time on non-news activities, such as criticizing the latest person under attack by Mao. In those days, he said, struggle sessions at local communes were usually top stories. More broadly, he added, reporters could write stories on only a limited number of themes, such as how to learn from the People's Liberation Army and the embrace of class struggle.

Another journalist, who covered the sanitation industry in Shanghai during those years, recalled how he and his peers were at first uncertain over what to make of Mao's official launch of the movement. So most continued writing about their usual beats as if the chaos breaking out around them didn't exist, resulting in the all-too-common blackout of a major news story that was otherwise obvious to anyone walking the streets. He said his paper continued in that manner, with reports on the chaos expressly prohibited, until its editors were ousted and replaced. From that point on, starting in early 1967, the newspaper became a "spreader of the revolution," falling into line as part of a wave that would eventually overtake all major media. In Shanghai, the month of January 1967 would later be called the "January revolution" as one newspaper after another took the new Party line to heart and began the guerilla, sloganeering form of reporting that would quickly become the central hallmark of the Cultural Revolution.

The reporter said that one big change after the coup at his paper was the rise of the social editorial, a free-form sort of commentary on the state of society unrelated to any specific event, which quickly became a daily staple. Many such commentaries were personally reviewed and edited by Mao himself. As the transformation progressed, many reporters were taken off their previous beats and placed onto new teams that exclusively wrote such social editorials, which would eventually come to consume about a tenth of the newspaper's total writing staff. Being named to the team was a high honor, even though members had little or no freedom to pick their own topics and instead were instructed on what to write based on the latest Beijing directives. In most cases, the assignments involved writing about Mao's latest doctrines, resulting in a huge diversity of actual reports even though the messages were the same.

One other reporter working in Hong Kong said all Chinese media in the territory, then still under British control, were instructed to label the period with the catchphrase of "anti-British resistance," as widespread riots broke out. He added that the British ended up arresting two Hong Kong–based Xinhua reporters who wrote about the unrest as tensions soared between Britain and China. In response, the Chinese placed a Reuters reporter in Beijing, one of the few Western correspondents in China at that time, under house arrest.

So went the Cultural Revolution, which would go down somewhat ironically as at once a period with little direct government oversight but also one of the least free in terms of topics that individual media could write about. During this time the media quickly splintered from the single voice that simply reprinted the words of central news sources like Xinhua and the *People's Daily* into thousands of different voices, though each was still allowed to comment on only a narrow range of topics, mostly related to Mao's latest directives. This noisy chorus would continue for a decade and only formally end in 1976 with Mao's death. Above all else, this period epitomizes the Chinese media's unique form of guerilla coverage, with a wide range of editorials, commentaries, sloganeering headlines, cartoons, and even the odd item like a musical score on the latest revolutionary theme filling the papers day after day under bold banners instructing people to join the movement. Actual news evaporated during the period, with the exception of reports on a march, rally, or struggle session that complemented broader themes of the day. Along parallel lines, the Chinese form of news blackout reaches its own new highs during this period, with the downfall and death of two former political superstars and heirs apparent to Mao locked out of most or all media coverage during that time.

The period also saw the rise of thousands of new catchphrases, many taken from Little Red Books and the latest words from Mao. Many of those dominated newspaper headlines for weeks or even months at a time as reporters repeated them in their daily social editorials and other commentaries, only to fade just as rapidly when everyone moved on to the next message. A few of these words and phrases, such as "Mao Zedong thought," "counterrevolutionary," and "class struggle," would later become synonymous with the movement itself, long after the end of the Cultural Revolution, etched into the minds of a generation whose lives were thrown into turmoil during the period.

At the end of the day, I think of the Cultural Revolution as China's "ultimate media movement" for which I have titled this chapter. The movement marked the culmination of a steady series of smaller ones that preceded it, most notably the Great Leap Forward, and gave Mao one last chance to use the nation's vast media as his personal soapbox. In many ways the media during the Cultural Revolution functioned exactly as Mao and the Communists intended them to from the get-go, as a platform to promote the Party's latest goals, accomplishments, and other agenda items. In this case, Mao exploited the media with a surprising degree of success, using them to create the sound of ten thousand voices all promoting his latest ideas and goals, and turning them into the true propaganda machine most closely associated with totalitarian, single-party governments.

Chapter 7

A Nixon Visit, the Death of Mao, and the Road to Reform

A Softer Approach

Former US secretary of state Henry Kissinger delivers a speech in front of pictures of late US president Richard Nixon meeting with his Chinese counterpart, Mao Zedong (top), and Nixon meeting with late premier Zhou Enlai (bottom), during a ceremony in Shanghai to commemorate the 30th anniversary of the joint US–China communiqué, also known as the "Shanghai Communiqué," April 15, 2002. Nixon issued the communiqué on February 28, 1972, to begin the process of normalizing US–China ties after years of hostility.

Photo Credit: Reuters/OTHK

The 1970s marked a major turning point for China's media, as Mao's influence—and his noisy tactics—faded with his dying Cultural Revolution and ultimately the death of the man himself in 1976. The end of the Maoist era would also mark a major shift for China's state-run media, which would quickly retire many of their rowdy, blunter tactics for a more subtle approach that continues to this day.

Put differently, this period saw the media evolve from the more classic propaganda tool usually associated with Big Brother–style regimes to more of a soft-power tool. Such a transformation around this time is by no means limited to China, and was also occurring in Western countries where the rise of public relations and marketing as new disciplines was giving governments new tools to influence public opinion by shaping how the media wrote about them. But none of these democratically elected governments had the media so clearly at their direct command as China to use as a tool to implement this new approach.

The changing of the guard in China would see the government agenda shift to more pragmatic matters like opening up to the outside world and economic development, supplanting the old revolutionary agenda under the first two decades of Communist rule. During this period, the media also revert to one of their previous roles as an important tool for the government to maintain social stability, as massive changes in the transition from a socialist to a market economy lead to major upheavals with the retirement of the "Iron Rice Bowl," the previous welfare state where everything from jobs to education and healthcare was provided by the government, and the implementation of a system where people must fend for themselves. As this occurs, revolutionary messages and guerrilla tactics are gradually retired from the pages of China's newspapers and its airwaves, to be replaced with a new, softer approach that includes trumpeting of economic and diplomatic accomplishments and downplaying or outright censorship of social unrest in the form of widespread protests over issues like corruption, poor working conditions, and other government shortcomings. Such problems also existed in the Iron Rice Bowl days, but they became more apparent in the Reform era as the leadership in Beijing tried to create a more open society.

This groundbreaking shift is perhaps best exemplified by the landmark visit of US president Richard Nixon to China in 1972, which was followed four years later by the death of Mao, drawing a solid line under his nearly three decades of turbulent leadership and opening the way for the rise of a group of more pragmatic leaders.

At the geopolitical level, 1970 was a vexing time for Mao. His four-year-old Cultural Revolution, meant to seal his place in history, was already showing signs of fading as China was getting tired of yet another major movement and the upheaval and chaos that came with it. The movement itself would last another six years until the death of Mao himself in 1976, when pragmatists would quickly step in and officially bring down the curtain with the arrest of the "Gang of Four," four of Mao's closest allies, including his wife, who would be officially blamed for all the chaos. But Mao, who was in his seventies and in failing health, could already see the writing on the wall in the early 1970s, and was willing to try something new by reengaging with the outside world, specifically with the United States, which still officially recognized Taiwan as Free China while the mainland remained Red China.

Such engagement was driven as much by political and economic necessities as by any change of heart by Mao. Outside of China, US–Soviet relations were starting to thaw under the Détente policy of Nixon and Leonid Brezhnev after two decades of frost during the height of the Cold War. Significant tensions still remained nonetheless, as Nixon tried to extricate the United States from the unpopular war in Vietnam, where the Soviet-backed North was nearing its final victory over the US–backed South.

In the meantime, China's own relations with the Soviets—which had already soured under the leadership of Krushschev following Stalin's death in 1953—had grown progressively worse, culminating with a series of brief border/territorial disputes in the 1960s. From the economic standpoint China was also stuck in a rut due to years of neglect and mismanagement under Mao's revolutionary agenda, and he probably realized that more investment and trade with the West could help to improve the situation.

Against this backdrop of movement fatigue at home, souring relations with the Soviets, economic stagnation, and his own failing health, Mao realized it could be in his and China's own best interest to reengage with the United States. The main problem was that he had spent so many years vilifying America, first during the Korean War, and then for years to come for its official backing of Taiwan as the representative of China at the United Nations, that he would be putting himself at incredible risk of attack by his political rivals by softening his stance. Any softening of that stance would also deprive Mao of a convenient whipping boy to plaster across the front pages of the nation's newspapers whenever he wanted to divert attention from problems at home. He finally managed to achieve his goal by prepping the public for the breakthrough visits with a carefully crafted media strategy that made the United States appear to take all the initiative, which will be detailed below, and by making the primary mover on the Chinese side appear to be Zhou Enlai, China's premier and a highly popular figure who had managed to survive all the purges of the Cultural Revolution by maintaining relatively cordial ties with Mao.

At the end of the day, China's final rapprochement with the United States and the West in general would ultimately result in retirement of carte blanche vilification of outside countries in the media. But individual perceived misdeeds by foreign countries—most notably Japan—are still used to this day as nationalistic rallying points to unite the Chinese and divert attention from problems at home.

The foreigner-as-villain theme would largely bow out with the move to a softer media approach, even as a number of more subtle tactics that continue to the present would see their widespread debut before and during the Nixon trip. The new softer approach will see widespread use of the public announcement, or *gong gao*, form of article as Mao and propaganda officials use the media as a tool to prepare the public for a major policy shift as China takes the first steps to embracing a former enemy and opening up to the outside world after years of isolation. Another interesting theme that looms large during this time is the widespread use of articles that are little more than laundry lists of names. This style of article is common throughout the era of Communist Party rule, and revolves around a story format that often opens with one or two sentences of news, followed by long lists of dozens of names of people who attended the event. This format is probably meant to tell average readers who is in charge as China prepares to open up and move away from its past of revolutionary movements and a rigidly planned economy.

One other minor major shift that will occur during this time is the move to more real-time news for the average Chinese consumer via television and later the Internet. Newspapers, radio, and other means such as rallies and conferences had served as the major channels for informing the public in the first two decades of Communist rule. Reports from such forms of media would often reach the average consumer days or even weeks after the fact, with timing often determined by propaganda officials who would release information to the public when they determined it would be most beneficial to their agenda. But as the country's economy started to gain steam in the Reform era dating from 1978, TV ownership would quickly take off as China became the world's largest manufacturer of televisions. That would be followed by the rise of the Internet in the 21st century, forcing the government to hone many of its media tactics to deal with an increasingly real-time news environment.

But back in 1970, China was still a closed society and the vast majority of Chinese could access news from both inside and outside their country only through the tightly controlled state media, which were still largely engaged in the news-less guerilla form of coverage that had become the norm during the Cultural Revolution. Most of the earliest developments that would ultimately pave the way for Nixon's historic trip were top secret and remained out of both the Western and Chinese media.

The real activity that would pave the way for Nixon's trip began in October 1970, when US diplomats, using Pakistan and Eastern Europe as intermediaries, quietly reached out to the Chinese to gauge China's potential interest in a meeting. The Chinese were indeed interested, and around the same time both Nixon and Mao started sending out signals through their own home media to ready the public for the historic shift. In Nixon's case, the first public hint that something was happening came in October 1970, when he told a *Time* magazine reporter that he wanted to visit China before he died, and if that wasn't possible he wanted his children to go. During a toast at a banquet in Romania where he first broached the subject, Nixon also reportedly dropped his use of the term "Red China" for the first time and instead called the country by its proper name, the People's Republic of China.

From the Chinese side, Mao did much of his public communicating through an old friend, Edgar Snow, an American journalist who had been a strong supporter of the Communists during the Chinese civil war. Mao told Snow that he would welcome a Nixon visit if a meeting could be set up. Concurrent with those remarks, a large picture of the meeting between Mao and Snow also appeared on the front page of the *People's Daily*, which, as a senior Chinese diplomat recalled many years later, was meant to signal Mao's interest in a meeting.

Kissinger's Secret Trip

Following that initial flurry of activity and consensus that both sides wanted to proceed, Nixon's secretary of state, Henry Kissinger, made a secret trip to Beijing in July 1971, or about nine months after the initial exchanges, to make preparations for an official visit. One key development during that meeting was an agreement that there could be only one China, and that there would be no independent Taiwan. At the end of that meeting, both sides issued simultaneous statements announcing Kissinger's visit and Nixon's desire to come to China. Kissinger would make a second visit to Beijing three months later in October to finalize plans for Nixon's trip.

Concurrent with all this were important developments taking place at the United Nations, where China, which wielded veto power as one of five permanent members of the UN Security Council, had been represented since 1949 by the Nationalist government in exile in Taiwan. In October 1971, just before Kissinger's second visit, the UN—clearly with support from the United States—voted to give the seat held by the Nationalists over to the Communist government in Beijing, another clear indication that a rapprochement between the two countries was moving forward.

With all the necessary preparations concluded, Nixon made his trip to China, arriving on February 21, 1972. His trip would last for a week, during which he would spend most of his time in Beijing, followed by short trips to Shanghai and Hangzhou. The two sides issued a joint declaration known as the Shanghai Communiqué on February 28, including the US acceptance of a one-China principle, and Nixon would leave the same day. While the fact was never widely publicized, reports much later from China would say that Mao's already-failing health had taken a serious turn for the worse not long before Nixon's arrival. Mao's interpreter at the time would later recall that Mao, who was then 78, seldom met with foreign leaders at that point, and that he had actually been unconscious just nine days before the historic meeting. He managed to remain alert for the entire dialogue, which ended up lasting more than an hour despite being scheduled for just 15 minutes. But the event was so draining that Mao immediately had to start breathing oxygen through a mask as soon as Nixon left the room, the interpreter said.

While the reality of the situation was quite dramatic and groundbreaking, China's media coverage of the event was just the opposite, especially in the very beginning when both sides were in a testing-the-waters mode aimed at preparing their respective publics for the dramatic shift. In China, part of the preparations saw the media carrying numerous negative reports about the Soviets. One reporter working in central China at the time recalled that in the run-up to the first reports of improving US relations, Chinese newspapers were regularly filled with a range of articles critical of Sino–Soviet relations. His own outlet, a broadcasting station, ran reports on a daily basis blasting the Soviets with a range of labels like "imperialists" and "revisionists" to drive home the point that China was exploring its options as relations with its former Communist ally soured under the uneasy relationship between Mao and the Soviets.

The first actual report in the *People's Daily* that something was happening came in the July 16, 1971, edition, shortly after Kissinger's first secret visit to Beijing. While the news may have been seminal and groundbreaking in nature, one would hardly get that impression from the way it was presented in the Chinese media. Top headlines that day were devoted to the importance of physical exercise and several stories about a visit by a North Korean delegation to China. Meantime, coverage of the Kissinger meeting, which had been formally announced the day before by both the United States and China, was limited to a tiny box consisting of four sentences at the bottom right side of page one of the *People's Daily*. The story, taken from a Xinhua report, contained no headline at all but was simply labeled "public announcement" and set off from the rest of the day's news by a line of dots and dashes. Adding to the intrigue and ambiguity, the Xinhua story didn't cite any formal sources for its information, a relatively common phenomenon for a news agency whose word was generally assumed to be the truth, making the naming of sources unnecessary. Instead of specifying a source, the Xinhua report simply used the Chinese construction of *juxi*, roughly translating to "it is understood that," as its primary sourcing. Actual information in the brief announcement is mostly factual, stating simply that Zhou Enlai and Kissinger met in Beijing to discuss Nixon's wish to visit China. It further stated that Zhou formally extended an invitation for a visit before May of the following year, 1972, which was happily accepted by Nixon. The stated purpose of the visit was a desire by both sides to normalize relations and trade ideas, the carefully worded article said. Nowhere in the brief announcement is Mao's name ever mentioned, and the wording leaves the reader with the clear impression that the initiative is all coming from Nixon and the United States, and that Zhou Enlai is handling matters from the Chinese side.

This use of the public announcement, containing no headlines, with basic details and just a few sentences of carefully chosen background information, will become a staple of Chinese media reports on the two Kissinger trips, and is one of the most commonly seen news formats during this time. From my own Westerner's perspective, these announcements, carefully set off from other "real" news stories with broken lines of dots and dashes, almost read like a "coming attractions" teaser, designed to create buzz and excitement by being both cryptic and slightly tantalizing at the same time, leaving the reader wanting to know more. But for the average Chinese, who had lived for decades in isolation from the outside world, the effect was probably far less pronounced, simply prompting readers to take note of yet another foreign government initiative. The low-key approach of the announcements and inclusion of Zhou Enlai as the only Chinese name also allowed Mao to keep a safe distance from the story, as he continued to officially pursue his Cultural Revolution even as growing questions were emerging about his health and ability to lead.

One veteran reporter told me the government commonly uses the public announcement format when it wants to directly communicate something with the public. He said such announcements are still sent out through Xinhua, but at the same time the format makes it clear that these are the direct words of the government. Use of the format is also a subtle warning to local media that the article is meant to be used as is, and that any changes, additional background, or inclusion of opinions from local editors are strictly prohibited. It's the government's way of saying: This is happening, and no further discussion is allowed. In many ways, such public announcements are the equivalent of putting a press release verbatim in the newspaper. The reporter said such low-key announcements are often used to prepare the public for bigger news, and are used only sparingly for major developments.

The July 16 *People's Daily* and its handling of the Kissinger trip set the tone for coverage throughout the run-up to Nixon's actual visit less than a year later. The story completely disappeared from the paper the day after the first public announcement, with coverage in the July 17 edition again focused on stories extolling Mao and his thought. The next stories didn't appear until Kissinger's second trip, October 20–26, 1971. The first story from this cycle comes at the bottom of page one of the *People's Daily* on October 21, shortly after Kissinger's arrival. In a slight deviation from the public announcement format, this story contains an actual headline with Kissinger's name, saying "Doctor Kissinger Arrives in Beijing," though it is still limited to a curt four sentences in a brief Xinhua item. The article contains limited information, including the fact that Kissinger has come to work out details for a Nixon visit and the names of eight leaders who were on hand to meet him, again with Mao's name notably absent as he sought to maintain his distance from the ongoing rapprochement.

Alongside the article is another brief Xinhua item saying Zhou Enlai and two other leaders, Ye Jianying and Ji Pengfei, will meet with Kissinger. This item marks the first of many name lists that will also characterize coverage of the Nixon trip, including 14 people who will represent China and eight representing America at the talks, in the first appearance of the laundry-list format to tell readers who in their government is calling the shots. Both of the Kissinger items are neatly set off at the bottom-left corner of the front page with a series of dots and dashes.

The day after Kissinger leaves, another brief item appears in the October 27 edition of the *People's Daily*, again at a familiar spot at the bottom-right corner of the front page, saying simply that he has left, and including another laundry list of people who saw him off at the airport. The edition also contains another story of rapprochement, with a short front-page story announcing China's reestablishment of formal ties with Belgium. And yet, in the same edition, the *People's Daily* also abandons its low-key approach with a much louder headline as its lead story on Beijing's taking over of China's seat at United Nations from the Nationalist government in Taiwan. Despite warming ties with the West behind the scenes, the *People's Daily* continues to take a tough public anti-American stance in this UN story, with coverage conveying a strong sense of vindication after years of being wronged. The main sub-headline to the article nicely sums things up, calling the giving of the UN seat to China "a victory for all peoples of the world" and "a disgrace for the American imperialists."

This bit of schizophrenia recurs the next day, October 28, when the *People's Daily* returns to its preferred public announcement format with a simple Xinhua item stating that everything "went well" during Kissinger's trip, and that a definitive announcement about a Nixon visit will be released before long. But as if to remind everyone that America is still officially the villain, a lengthier story also appears on page five denouncing the "imperialist" United States for its conspiracy to invade Cambodia, as the US war in Vietnam was spilling over into that country. I attribute this schizophrenia to the different sources for the Nixon trip compared with all other news. On the one hand, Propaganda Ministry officials were continuing to write in their usual style with the US-bashing headlines; on the other hand, the Nixon stories were probably coming directly from top leadership and were therefore exempt from changes and other spin from lower-level officials.

From the Kissinger preparatory trips, we'll skip ahead to Nixon's actual visit, which began with his arrival in Beijing on February 21, 1972.

For this examination, we'll look at coverage in the *Liberation Daily*, the official Party newspaper of Shanghai, to give some variety of sources, even though most of its reports on the Nixon trip would come from Xinhua and its coverage would typically be similar or identical to the *People's Daily*.

Starting with a Handshake

The newspaper contains no notice or any other indication that anything major will happen in its February 21 edition, the day of Nixon's actual arrival, which passes much like any other day with the usual mix of revolutionary stories. All of that changes in the next day's edition, as the Nixon trip takes up the paper's entire front page, including a large photo of Nixon and Mao shaking hands and a smaller one of a larger, seated group with Nixon and Mao in the center, surrounded by their various aides. Given the meeting's landmark nature and the huge place it suddenly assumed in the Chinese media, it is somewhat ironic that the top story on the front page of this edition is itself only three sentences long. The first of those says simply that the men met for serious discussions in Zhongnanhai, the complex next to Tiananmen Square where all the country's top leaders live. That is followed by one sentence containing the names of who attended from the US delegation and, finally, one saying who represented China.

This article and the two accompanying photos will ultimately be the only mentions of Mao during Nixon's visit, which perhaps isn't surprising in light of Mao's deteriorating health and the fact that he wanted to keep a certain distance from the country he had vilified for so long. In Mao's absence, Zhou Enlai quickly steps in to become the center of attention in the coverage. The second and only other article in this first day of Nixon trip coverage on February 22 makes Zhou its lead character as the top-ranking person to meet Nixon at the airport and later as host for a banquet in Nixon's honor. This article, which is actually two Xinhua reports patched together, gives a rather boring blow-by-blow of Nixon's movements in Beijing, from his arrival at the airport to his trip to the guest house where he stayed and finally from the banquet he attended in his honor at the Great Hall of the People adjacent to Tiananmen Square. Those basic facts are heavily padded out with long lists of names of who attended what event from both sides, with an accompanying smaller picture of Zhou shaking Nixon's hand as he gets off the plane at the airport. Despite Mao's personal and media absence for the rest of the trip, this front-page arrangement clearly shows that Mao is still in charge, and that Zhou is taking the number-two position at the historic meeting. Coverage of the trip continues on page two of the paper, and includes more photos and the text of Nixon's and Zhou's speeches at their banquet.

This first day of coverage from the trip will set the tone for the next few days, with most reports in the *Liberation Daily* little more than simple descriptions of what Nixon did that day, followed by long lists of who attended what event. Zhou Enlai's name heads nearly all of those lists, indicating this is his show, and Mao's name completely disappears. I attribute this disappearance largely to Mao's ill health, which made it impossible for him to attend most of the events, as well as his continued attempt to maintain some distance from this rapid turnabout in relations with a former foe. Once Mao leaves the picture the story immediately loses its lead-story position in the *Liberation Daily*, but still remains on the front page in secondary positions. Coverage becomes decidedly low key as the talks continue, with two stories on February 24, now three days into the trip, focused on softer, more personality-type coverage, such as Nixon going to see a revolutionary opera and the comings-and-goings of his wife, Pat, the previous day. The story regains some of its former high position as the talks wrap up, with more prominent coverage given in the February 26 edition on a banquet, this time hosted by Nixon to thank Zhou Enlai and China for their hospitality. Not surprisingly, coverage of the banquet includes texts of the toasts made by the two men and long lists of who attended, with Mao's name again absent.

Nixon would leave Beijing for side trips to the scenic city of Hangzhou and then to Shanghai before his return to the United States. The only major substantive coverage during that time comes on February 28, when the lead story is the joint declaration issued by Nixon at the end of his trip, also known as the Shanghai Communiqué, laying the groundwork for normalization of relations between the two sides, which would ultimately result in reestablishment of formal diplomatic ties in 1978. Despite the historic nature of the announcement, the article is again simply headlined with the words of the "joint public statement" that was finally agreed upon by the two sides.

One Shanghai-based reporter at that time recalled that, ironically, no one from his newspaper—one of the city's largest—was sent to cover Nixon's brief stop in the city, adding that most or all local media were simply not told about the visit. Despite the clear opportunity for some strong local reporting, all newspapers at that time would have had to use the Xinhua stories even for something of that magnitude happening in their own backyard, he said, adding that anything involving foreigners was off-limits at that time for local reporters due to sensitivity in Beijing about how outsiders were viewing China. As an interesting aside, this reporter also said he was actually aware that a major figure was coming to town, though he didn't know who, after being tipped off by one of his contacts who helped to put up some of the decorations at the hotel where Nixon stayed. Another reporter in central China said the news wasn't really all that interesting to the average Chinese, many of whom were still living in the countryside and were more focused on daily matters.

One reporter who worked for Xinhua at that time recalled how the visit marked a turning point for the news agency in its global reach, as China's return to the world stage and establishment of diplomatic relations with one country after another allowed the news agency to set up its own new network of overseas bureaus in many of those countries. Before the trip, Xinhua and its reporters were largely a closed organization, keeping to themselves in their limited number of bureaus outside China and even at home. But from that point onward, the agency and its journalists and other staff would become much more active in reaching out to others, including not only correspondents but also diplomats and other political and business figures. The agency would also make a concerted drive to bring more English speakers and writers into its network as it reengaged with the rest of the world and tried to tell China's story to a more global audience. In some instances, a Xinhua bureau could even serve as the de facto embassy or consulate in a place where China had no official diplomatic representation. Such was the case in Hong Kong under British rule in the run-up to its 1997 return to China, when the Xinhua office became a popular site for protests by Hong Kongers worried about losing freedoms.

Xinhua's global expansion is part of China's larger "soft-power" drive, which has the government trying to positively influence global opinion of the country through more low-key initiatives like these English-language reports and previously mentioned Confucius Institutes where foreigners can learn Chinese in their own countries.

I want to end this chapter with a brief look at the media's coverage of the death of Mao in 1976, an event that, along with Nixon's trip, is a fitting ending to the first two turbulent decades of modern China's history under Communist Party rule. With Mao's death, China's new leaders would quietly put aside many of the items from his revolutionary agenda in favor of more practical matters like economic development, resulting in a sharp reduction in the cloak-and-dagger and guerilla-style tactics that had become media staples by then.

If the Cultural Revolution was the sound of 10,000 bullhorns, then China's media were holding one final blast of those trumpets in reserve for the death of Mao, the movement's main architect, on September 9, 1976, at the age of 82. From the historical perspective, Mao's death scared many Chinese for the simple reason that few could imagine what might happen to the country in the absence of the man who had played such an integral part in its first quarter century. Mao may have been responsible for many of China's problems, but no one had any idea what might happen next since there was no new game plan or heir apparent waiting to take over.

Despite the graveness of his situation, there was no indication of anything amiss in the *People's Daily* on September 9, the day that Mao actually died. That day's edition is filled with the usual revolutionary chatter, including a lead story from Xinhua on how to properly guide youth and another story about North Korea's future road to victory. All of that changes, of course, on September 10, when the media embark on a final round of guerrilla coverage, an appropriate send-off for the man who helped to perfect the format.

With no warning from the previous day, the *People's Daily* suddenly becomes all about Mao, with most of the issue devoted to his death.

Coverage kicks off with a front page that is totally taken up by a photo of Mao with the headline "The Great Leader and Advisor Chairman Mao Lives on Forever," a common phrase used to remember someone who has died. Complementing the photo and headline is the slogan at the top right of the front page, "Long Live Marxism, Leninism, and Mao Zedong Thought"—a sort of last-gasp effort at grouping Mao together with these other Communist greats to try to preserve his legacy. Nowhere in the front-page coverage is there any mention of the fact that Mao has actually died, again in what looks like an attempt to focus on the man's legacy rather than his actual death. Pages two and three that day are filled with eulogies to Mao, while the rest of the issue contains stories about the importance of continuing the revolution, again in what looks like an attempt to preserve Mao's legacy. In all this first-day gue-rilla coverage, one can almost taste the previously discussed fear that Mao must have felt at the prospect that his legacy might be rapidly dismantled by the next generation of leaders after his death, similar to what had hap-pened to Stalin in the Soviet Union.

After the first reports of his death, pages of the *People's Daily* would all contain the banner "The Great Leader and Advisor Chairman Mao Lives on Forever" for weeks to come. In the spirit of the guerilla cover-age he helped to pioneer, the *People's Daily* on September 11, the day after the first reports of his death, is chock full of photos of Mao at various times in his life, starting from his youth all the way until 1933, when he was still quite a handsome young man. Further back in the issue, pages six and seven are filled with a pouring in of condolences from leaders around the world. The next day, September 12, the front page contains a photo of Mao's body lying in state, with other leaders bowing their heads in respect, while the inside pages contain a parade of articles reminiscing about his younger days, accompanied by more com-plimentary photos. This montage of laments, condolences, and youth-ful images continues for the next week until September 19, nine days after the first report of his death, when the *People's Daily*'s lead story described the masses gathering in Beijing to bid their final farewell.

One reporter recalled how the public remained completely unaware of Mao's fading health and death until the official announce-ment. He said he and his peers at the radio station where they worked were notified by central broadcasting authorities on the afternoon of September 9 that there would be a big announcement at 4 o'clock that afternoon, and to urge everyone to gather around the radios in their communal halls to listen. His own station directly relayed the Beijing broadcast, and continued to rebroadcast bulletins from Beijing and the provincial broadcasting authority for the next half month before finally resuming its own programming. Another Shanghai-based journalist recalled how he was out reporting in the countryside when he heard about the death on a loudspeaker from a local broadcaster, at which point many ordinary people broke down crying. He said regional reporters like himself were later allowed to write their own locally oriented stories on Mao's death and the nation's mourning.

Thus occurred two seminal events in the space of four years that would at once mark the beginning of China's reengagement with the outside world and the start of its road to reform, while also bringing down the curtain on a largely failed revolutionary agenda under Mao that had left millions dead and the lives of millions more badly disrupted or destroyed. From the media perspective, the period would see a broader retirement of the guerilla-style coverage that characterized the Maoist era in favor of a more subtle approach, in this case the use of understated public announcements to set the stage for major news. This softer approach would continue to the present, as China transformed its media to a force of persuasion rather than the old style of coercion. Even as that occurred, China would continue to play on nationalistic and anti-foreign themes in the media, tactics that continue to this day on a more selective basis.

The Nixon visit would also see widespread use of the old-style name list as a form of pseudo-news, providing one of the few public clues about who was in and who was on the way out during this time of major transition. While the guerilla coverage has largely faded in today's media, name lists and the placement of names in general are still important, and remain primary tools used by China watchers trying to determine what is happening behind the scenes in the opaque world of Chinese politics.

Chapter 8

The Tiananmen Square Divide

The Media Gains, Then Loses, its Voice

Student protesters arrive at Tiananmen Square to join other pro-democracy demonstrators during the Beijing Spring movement of 1989, passing the portrait of the late chairman Mao Zedong. The demonstrations were crushed by the People's Liberation Army on June 4, 1989.

Photo Credit: Reuters/OTHK

I f Mao's death in 1976 marked the end of a period of dogma and guerilla coverage in China's media, then the period that followed was one of reform and openness that reached a crescendo with the Tiananmen Student Movement of 1989, only to come to a screeching halt with the movement's brutal suppression. The crackdown marks a clear shift for China's media story, with an unprecedented degree of plurality and freedom of expression on the side leading up to the movement, followed by a return to many of the strong-arm themes and tactics afterward. This kind of swinging of the media pendulum occurs not just in China but throughout the world under other authoritarian regimes, where periods of experimentation and openness are often followed by conservative backlash at the rapid pace of change. In the case of the Tiananmen movement, that reversal came quickly and decisively, setting the media back on a conservative course that they follow to this day, where they once again must toe the Party line dictated by Xinhua and other central news sources.

At the most basic level, four major elements converged to give rise to the Tiananmen movement that would catapult China into global headlines for months starting in April 1989. The first and most important was directly related to China's economic reform that saw major changes taking place for the average Chinese. The same people advocating that reform were also advocating a more open society, which would be a second important factor. A third critical element was an internal power struggle taking place within the Communist Party between reformers and conservatives, while the final factor was related to global conditions that saw other socialist countries, led by the Soviet Union, also start to experiment with their own reform.

The most critical factor that gave rise to the movement was simple economics, an element not widely discussed or understood by foreigners, but without which the movement never would have gained the widespread support it did outside the university realm. Following the death of Mao and launch of the Reform era in 1978, a new generation of Chinese leaders led by Deng Xiaoping were slowly steering the country to a more market-oriented economy from the old socialist model where everything was owned by the state. The new system, then referred to as "socialism with Chinese characteristics," brought huge changes to Chinese society in its first decade, both in terms of the way goods were produced and also in the levels of corruption that suddenly blossomed as many people took advantage of gaps in the system to advance their own fortunes.

From the consumer standpoint, the situations before and after reform were polar opposites. Under the old state-run socialist system, supply was often limited for even the most basic goods like rice and oil, and selection was almost nonexistent in terms of different brands for different products. The old Soviet image of consumer choice was true in China as well, with store shelves often bare and any goods that were in stock all coming from a single producer. To ensure that people could lead at least a basic existence, everyone received monthly rationing coupons for essential items. It was the classic socialist state, featuring limited supplies of goods at low state-set prices that allowed everyone to lead a simple, stable life with little room for anything else.

The advent of reform saw the gradual abolition of rationing coupons and state-set prices for many basic items, as free markets sprang up throughout the country where farmers and a new group of entrepreneurs could sell their goods at prices that were largely set by market forces. That change resulted in inflation—an unheard-of phenomenon for most Chinese, who were used to paying the same low prices for goods all their lives out of modest incomes of around 10 to 20 dollars per month. Wages also started to rise in the Reform era, but inflation was growing even faster by 1989, due in part to the central government's lack of experience with handling a phenomenon that had been absent in the centrally planned economy. That inflation was a major grievance of the average citizen during that time, and led many to sympathize with the antigovernment elements of the student movement of 1989.

The other major grievance of the common citizen was corruption. In moving from a centrally planned to a market economy, many people in high positions under the old socialist system suddenly found themselves in a golden position to make some extra money—often a lot of extra money. The equation was simple: They could buy goods through their old state-run channels at the government-set prices, and then turn around and sell those same goods on the open market at market prices, earning huge profits in the process. This general corruption as a result of the switchover from planned to market economy was accompanied by a parallel jump in more traditional corruption that saw just about anyone and everyone using his or her connections to earn a quick buck, be it by assisting someone in getting a new apartment or helping their child find a job after graduation. I experienced the phenomenon second hand during my years in China at that time, with friends constantly complaining to me about the high cost of doing just about everything. Cartons of cigarettes and expensive liquor became the currencies of choice for bribing officials, and the expression "cigarettes and liquor" became a popular catchphrase for corruption in general, playing on a homonym for the "research" fees for which such gifts acted as a form of payment.

The widespread discontent over inflation and corruption would ultimately provide the fuel to send millions of ordinary people onto the streets in support of the movement in 1989, but several other factors were also at play. Chief among those was the unprecedented openness that was suddenly being tolerated at all levels, from broader platforms like the mass media all the way down to the individual. People who once kept silent on even the most innocuous issues for fear of being attacked as anti revolutionaries could suddenly say whatever they wanted with little or no worry of consequences. Major limits remained on this freedom, most notably in a continued strict ban on public expression in any kind of organized forum. But on an individual basis, people were largely allowed to speak their minds as long as they limited their words to simple complaints between friends and acquaintances—a new right that they exercised wholeheartedly, as I can personally attest to from my time in Beijing. That freedom continues largely to this day, though, again, complaints in any sort of organized forum are still strictly forbidden.

A similar new degree of openness was also being tolerated in the media, which were being allowed to do more of their own original reporting and editorial writing outside the usual Xinhua stories and central Party line. Traditional Party-backed publications were also being supplemented by a new breed of semi-independent newspapers and magazines that began to spring up, providing even more voices to the national dialogue as China emerged from decades of isolation. At the center of this broader reform was Zhao Ziyang, the biggest advocate of the new openness and ultimately the most prominent leader who would fall from power during the Tiananmen crackdown. In the period during the 1980s leading up to the movement, Zhao became widely known for calling on the media to use the "language of humans," versus a former approach that saw them relegated to the far less flexible "language of officials."

A third important element that enabled the movement occurred largely behind the scenes, where a growing divide was emerging between reformers and conservatives within the Party. The reformers were a group of free-market, open-society advocates headed by Zhao Ziyang, who had been hand-picked to lead the country by Deng Xiaoping, who favored economic, if not political, reform. They were countered by the more conservative faction behind Li Peng, then China's premier, who were concerned that things were changing too quickly and that the country's new openness could ultimately undermine the Communist Party itself. While Zhao Ziyang was still in control and setting policy, the student movement and subsequent popular support that would see mass demonstrations take place throughout China was allowed to go on, due at first to Zhao's policy of openness, followed by the inability of the conservatives to bring the movement to an end through martial law when they finally got the upper hand. In the end, Deng Xiaoping, who held real power, sided with the conservatives on the issue of the student demonstrations, resulting in the ouster of most top reformers and paving the way for the Chinese army to march into Beijing and retake Tiananmen Square, killing hundreds of protesters who tried to block the advance of troops into the city.

Outside of China, some global factors also helped to set the stage for the popular movement. Most significant among those was the new policy of openness, called *glasnost*, being rolled out at the time by Mikhail Gorbachev, the reform-minded leader of the Soviet Union. Aware that his own socialist state was rapidly failing, Gorbachev was trying to overhaul a Soviet system that, like China's, had suffered from years of repression and mismanagement under a centrally planned economy controlled by a single party. History would later show that Gorbachev's efforts would ultimately prove too little too late. The fall of the Berlin Wall in 1989 marked the end of the Communist era in Eastern Europe, and Gorbachev himself was deposed soon afterward, with the sudden and dramatic collapse of the Soviet Union in 1991. Somewhat ironically, Gorbachev was set to make a historic visit to China in May 1989, right in the middle of the movement, not only throwing a spotlight on a new rapprochement between China and the Soviets, but also highlighting the road to reform that both were undertaking in different ways. Gorbachev would ultimately go ahead with his visit, but much of the media coverage during what otherwise would have been a groundbreaking moment ended up going to the student movement, which was already more than three weeks old at that time. Adding to the embarrassment, most of the pageantry that had been planned for the Gorbachev visit, including a reception at Tiananmen, had to be canceled or moved as government handlers did their best to keep students and other demonstrators from ruining the Party's Kodak moment of rapprochement.

In terms of media themes, the biggest one to come from the Tiananmen Student Movement is easily the one of openness, which saw hundreds of voices emerge in the traditional media and also in many makeshift publications that were produced during that time. One reporter said that in that period it was easy to write and publish stories that were critical of just about anything, even the Party. Things were so open that in one instance he was allowed to write and publish a 50,000-character article, which would have taken up several pages in an average newspaper, on the harm being done to wild animals due to lax environmental protection. Reporters could basically propose anything during this time, and their editors would let them write it. He recalled that his own *piece de resistance* was a story criticizing some of the practices at a liquor factory that was one of his area's main employers, which ultimately led to the resignation of the top county official.

Another theme to emerge during this time was the rise of more real-time news. The early reform period had led to an explosion in the production of television sets and shortwave radios, with the result that many Chinese households in major cities owned one or both by the late 1980s. Many of my friends in Beijing relied almost exclusively on shortwave broadcasts in Chinese from the BBC and Voice of America for their news during those years, and I can still vividly recall being told about the latest developments at Tiananmen based on these offshore broadcasts. Despite personally living in Beijing at the time of the movement, where I was working as an English teacher at one of the city's many universities, I also often relied on these broadcasts for reliable big-picture information, especially after martial law was declared and later after the military crackdown. The beginning of the real-time news era would later accelerate with the popularization of the Internet, effectively killing the old system of news blackouts and strategically timed releases of information through the mainstream media often days or even weeks after major events.

A third theme was what some would later refer to as a blind admiration for anything Western that also came to characterize this period. In terms of the media, that admiration led to a belief that anything carried by major Western media outlets like the BBC and Voice of America must be true, ignoring the reality that even reports that appear to be objective will contain certain inherent biases because of the writer's mission or the agenda of his or her publication. This blind admiration of the West was also often credited for feeding the free-for-all style of journalism that emerged, as many Chinese reporters believed that what they were doing was similar to what the Western media did, even though the reality was often much different. This type of freewheeling, experimental journalism during this period led to a number of new and innovative reporting formats and styles, most of which are seldom if ever seen in the West, which will be discussed below.

Several major new themes also emerged just after the crackdown, as the media rapidly swung from their newfound openness to the older dogma characterized by central control and stories conforming to the Party's latest agenda. One major theme to emerge after the crackdown was the role of the media as a tool to maintain social stability, an important function in a society where issues created by the move from a planned to a market economy were resulting in a considerable amount of discontent and unrest. The media hadn't really played such a role in

the past, as social unrest was less problematic in the earlier era characterized by economic stagnation and a broader intolerance for dissent that
made most people afraid to speak their mind. Along similar lines, one
of the media's major new missions after the crackdown was to create a
moderate form of consensus that downplayed or outright avoided issues
like corruption or unfair confiscation of land that could lead to social
instability. From an ideological standpoint, the media's primary mission
would be to protect the interests of the Party above all else, with the
interests of the people taking a backseat after the Tiananmen crackdown.

The post-Tiananmen period would also see a revival of the anti-
foreign card in the media, as central leaders, feeling their own insecurities
after the mass movement, tried to quash the blind admiration of the West
that had sprung up in the 1980s. As previously mentioned, this new form
of anti-foreign tactic would be refined and used more selectively in the
decades after the crackdown. In place of blanket vilifications that once
saw nations like the United States and most of its Western allies tarred as
"imperialists" and portrayed as global bullies, this new use of xenopho-
bia would instead focus on specific incidents, with the aim of fanning
Chinese nationalism and shining a spotlight on Western shortcomings.

This new anti-foreign streak reached a height not long after the
crackdown with the global fall of communism in the early 1990s. During
this period, Chinese media reports took on an almost conspiratorial over-
tone, as the term "peaceful evolution" became a staple buzzword in the
early 1990s for an invisible Western plot to topple one Communist government after another. The anti-foreign theme would gradually subside in
the years after the crackdown, as it became clear that the Communists in
China would remain in power despite the collapse of the Soviet Union.
Nevertheless, the anti-foreign card remains an occasional staple in China's
media toolkit, as will be discussed in a later chapter.

Key Moments: Death of a Former Reformer

The chain of events that led to and sustained the Tiananmen Student
Movement were numerous and complex, but a few key moments are
worth mentioning before taking a closer look at the detailed picture of
a movement that, for the first time in Communist Chinese history, was

intricately chronicled in the media. The spark that set things in motion occurred on April 15, 1989, with the sudden death of Hu Yaobang, a reformer who had fallen out of grace a few years earlier for his progressiveness. The first mass gatherings began days after Hu's death outside the gates of Zhongnanhai, the complex next to Tiananmen Square where all of China's top leaders live and where a wide cross-section of Beijingers now came to pay their final respects. No foul play was ever suspected in Hu Yaobang's death, though some would later say the early demonstrations were an indirect criticism of Deng Xiaoping, who had picked Hu to lead economic reform but then deposed him for his liberal policies.

Zhao Ziyang responded to these initial protests with a lenient policy toward the students, so while he was still officially in charge, central leaders allowed the gatherings to continue. But when Zhao Ziyang left Beijing in late April 1989 on a previously planned visit to North Korea, Deng Xiaoping deemed the student demonstrations "turmoil" and backed a condemnation of the demonstrations by the conservatives in an editorial on April 26. That move only inflamed the demonstrators, resulting in a mass demonstration on April 27, after which a top Party official effectively lifted a blackout on coverage of the demonstrations and told the media to report what was really happening. The resulting flood of coverage gave the movement even more momentum, with more than a million people packing into the square at the height of the movement's popularity in late April and early May. In addition to calls for democracy, demands to curb inflation and stamp out corruption became popular themes discussed by the large numbers of both students and other people who attended the demonstrations. I went down to the square during some of the marches at the height of the movement and remember an almost-festive feeling there, as a wide range of groups, from factory workers to elementary and middle schoolteachers with their young students in tow, marched through the streets with colorful banners stating who they were.

After reaching a peak in early May, the movement started to lose some of its steam when the government, while entering into some dialogue with student leaders, remained largely silent about the marchers' demands and people began to tire of coming out day after day. The students launched a hunger strike on May 13 in a bid to make the leaders respond to their demands and also to breathe some new life into the faltering movement. By now many of the students had set up a tent city in Tiananmen Square, and I remember how the combination of hot early summer weather, poor sanitation, and lack of food caused a large number of hunger strikers to fall ill, with the result that the air was soon filled with the sound of sirens as ambulances rushed away student after student who had passed out from hunger and exhaustion.

The hunger strike ultimately had its intended effect, breathing new life into the movement and prompting very high-profile visits by the likes of Zhao Ziyang himself to talk with hunger-weakened students in the square. In the middle of all this, Gorbachev made his historic visit to Beijing, arriving on May 15. Because the square was occupied at this point with a tent city of hunger strikers and other students, a previously planned elaborate welcoming ceremony at Tiananmen had to be held at the airport instead, and the visit would remain largely upstaged, but not unnoticed, by the ongoing student movement.

As negotiations between student leaders and government officials continued with little or no results, behind the scenes Deng Xiaoping was not only growing impatient but may have also been getting military forces ready to clear out the square. At a meeting on May 19, Deng Xiaoping decided to declare martial law, implemented on May 20, and Zhao Ziyang stepped down in protest. The movement continued despite that, but began to take on a different tone as a stream of more radical students and others began pouring into the capital to take up residence at the square, replacing the Beijingers and local students who had been the main participants up until then. I visited the square a few times during this period and vividly remember the tense mood that set in, contrasting sharply with the more upbeat feel and drama of the earlier days. My other vivid memory of that period was of the squalor that had overtaken Tiananmen, which lacked basic necessities like the running water, toilets, and cooking facilities needed for long-term living. One of the other things I recall from this later period was a certain lawlessness that had taken over, with students, many wearing red armbands and headbands, often commandeering taxis, buses, and other vehicles to shuttle them around, and setting up roadblocks to stop anyone they considered unfriendly.

The end itself finally came with the infamous movement of tanks into Tiananmen on the evening of June 3 and into the early morning hours of June 4. The number killed has never been precisely determined, but Western media generally quote a figure of hundreds and possibly even more than a thousand. Contrary to the initial belief after the crackdown, most of the people who died were not students but ordinary citizens who had poured into the streets on the evening of June 3 when rumors began to circulate that troops would soon be moving into the city. Most were killed when they tried to halt the advance of troops, with some being shot after troops opened fire while others were crushed by the advancing tanks. The famous photo of a man standing in front of tanks was taken on one of the main avenues leading into the square, as he and others tried unsuccessfully to block their progress. After the troops finally reached the square, leaders representing the government negotiated with the remaining protesters, led by Liu Xiaobo, who would later win the 2010 Nobel Peace Prize for his efforts to bring political change to China. The army ultimately gave the remaining people camped in the square several hours to leave, with the result that there were few casualties at Tiananmen itself.

The days after June 4 were filled with tension, as Beijing remained under martial law and the conservatives reasserted control, even as groups of angry residents continued to show defiance by burning vehicles and sheltering former student leaders who were already being hunted. One of my last memories of this period is the complete impassability of the streets of Beijing, which were filled with burned-out buses and other vehicles, and littered with shattered glass and twisted road dividers put there by protesters in their last-ditch effort to stop troops from entering the city. The government would ultimately publish a list of the most wanted people from the movement, most of those student leaders. All but a few would end up being smuggled out of the country, most often through Hong Kong, to take up residence in other countries.

Media reports of the movement can be clearly divided into three stages. The first started with Hu Yaobang's death on April 15, and ran for the next two weeks, when most of the coverage was limited to official matters like funeral arrangements and condolences from abroad, with little or no mention of the earliest demonstrations or other non-official activities. The second stage began with the end of the media blackout around April 28, when stories on the movement suddenly exploded onto the front pages. The third and final stage began with the declaration of martial law on May 20, when many of the colorful, more enterprising reports began to drop out of the papers and more ominous calls for order started to appear, along with new buzzwords like "uprising" and "stability" that indicated a crackdown was looming.

For this event, I again looked at Shanghai's *Liberation Daily* for my most detailed analysis, but also compared its coverage with accounts in the *Southern Daily*, one of the main papers in south China's Guangdong province. In the earliest days, the reports in both papers were nearly identical and based on Xinhua stories, an approach that was standard for most major Chinese media at that time. But as events progressed, the volume of local reporting grew to include a large number of locally written stories, based both on related demonstrations in the newspapers' home cities, as well as material being submitted by reporters who were sent on assignment to Beijing to cover the main event.

The *Liberation Daily*'s coverage during the first phase of the movement was mostly muted, reflecting the diminished place of Hu Yaobang in the Communist Party following his fall from grace several years earlier. The first story appeared on April 16, with the lead story focusing on Hu's death the previous day, and including a short public announcement on the pending funeral arrangements. While it took the lead position, the story was just one of five on the front page that day, and there were no further references to Hu inside the paper. Coverage continued in a similar vein over the next few days. After no reports the next day, the story reappeared on April 18, with a small captioned photo of central leaders led by Zhao Ziyang holding a moment of silence in Hu's honor. Despite the first mass gatherings that began to occur around this time as people came to pay their last respects, newspapers were strictly forbidden from reporting on that element of the story.

The *Liberation Daily* continued its low-key coverage focused on Hu, with an announcement of a wake for Hu and a locally written report about a moment of silence that was held in Shanghai. As in the past, the use of the public announcement seemed to be the Party's way of saying that Hu Yaobang had died and was receiving an appropriate send-off, but that no further discussion was allowed. The faceless editorial also came into play with an April 21 piece headlined "How Should We

Mourn for Comrade Hu Yaobang?" foreshadowing a much wider use of
the format that would come both during the movement, when almost
any kind of report became fair game, and after the crackdown, when
the tone would turn defensive in explaining why the crackdown was
necessary.

Despite a broader ban on reporting about the unrest at this early
stage, the *Liberation Daily* did manage to include a hint of what was happening in Beijing as early as April 21, or just six days after Hu Yaobang's
death, with the headline that some students were conducting "noisy
affairs" outside the offices of the Xinhua headquarters in Beijing. But
even that report, and other similar ones in the following days, seemed to
have been aimed at sending a strict message to anyone who might have
wanted to take advantage of the situation, with the sub-headline that
the "Beijing City Government Issues a Public Announcement Warning
to a Small Number of Well-Intentioned People." Here we see the use
of another popular Chinese media device, namely the use of the phrase
"small number" and similar constructions to downplay volatile situations and pin the blame on a very small number of people whose views
do not reflect broader popular sentiment. The use of this tactic would
become especially prevalent in the third stage of the coverage, both during and after the crackdown, when the unrest and resulting widespread
disorder would be repeatedly blamed on a handful of conspirators,
dubbed "black hands," who are portrayed as working behind the scenes
to manipulate a generally guiltless and well-intentioned public.

A small stream of similarly low-key and slightly menacing reports,
many warning against acts that could lead to upheaval and unrest,
would pop in and out of the paper throughout the first phase of coverage, although all were carefully placed out of immediate view on the
inside pages. One of those, on April 23, significantly contained the first
use of the word "unlawful" when describing the behavior of a group
in the western city of Xi'an that burned 10 vehicles and more than 20
homes after a local memorial ceremony for Hu. Apart from this slightly
menacing thread, more Hu-related coverage continued to be featured on the front pages for most of the first two weeks after his death,
including the text of a eulogy offered by Zhao Ziyang, which appeared
in the April 23 edition of the paper, along with the familiar long list of
leaders who attended the event. This stage of strict limits on what can

be reported nears an end on April 26, when newspapers carry another ominous editorial, this time by Deng Xiaoping himself, declaring the demonstrations "anti-Party."

The second stage of reporting began in the *Liberation Daily* on April 28, nearly two weeks after Hu's death, when the newspaper took its first tentative stab at reporting the real news after the senior government official, Hu Qili, had given his okay. From this point, many of the loaded words like "unrest" and "unlawful" noticeably dropped out of the coverage, and the papers tried to take a more objective approach by publishing more straightforward reports on what was happening. Significantly, Xinhua itself led the charge in this new "just-the-facts" campaign, publishing a relatively neutral story with the bland headline "A Group of Students from Beijing Universities Takes to Marching in the Streets" appearing in the *Liberation Daily*'s April 28 edition. But the editors of the newspapers were clearly still listening to more conservative local Party leaders, as seen by the inclusion of a headline that day warning that unrest and disorder only hurt the masses.

Two days later, on April 30, the *Southern Daily*, now considered one of China's more progressive newspapers, published a story on government leaders meeting and holding a dialogue with students in Beijing, although the story was buried on page nine. This stage in the movement marked the beginning of an interesting divergence between the more conservative coverage in the *Liberation Daily* versus progressive-minded stories in the *Southern Daily*, reflecting the wide range of initiatives that were starting to occur at the local level in terms of what stories to report and how they should be reported. The *Liberation Daily* would ultimately be rewarded for its conservative coverage when the city's mayor, Jiang Zemin, was named the country's next Communist Party chairman just months after the fall of Zhao Ziyang.

Some of the populist issues that underlay the movement appeared in the headlines on May 1 in the *Liberation Daily*, which published a Xinhua report on a meeting between student leaders and government officials to discuss corruption, among other issues. An interesting development occurred two days later, on May 3, as the *Liberation Daily*, which had mostly followed the Xinhua line up until now, made one of its first attempts at local reporting on the Beijing movement, showing that it had already sent some of its reporters to the capital.

In this case the paper supplemented the usual Xinhua stories with its own report saying that 4,000 students had taken part in demonstrations. This story looks modest by Western standards, but its publication probably involved a great deal of deliberation behind the scenes. The students would go on to give a list of their demands to government officials, which also received straightforward coverage in the following days.

Students Go on Strike

Another big development came in the May 5 edition of *Liberation Daily*, with reports that students in Beijing had gone on strike by refusing to attend class—an event I remember well, as the last two months of class abruptly ended on that day at the university where I was then teaching. One reporter who worked for Xinhua at that time described for me an atmosphere of openness and boldness that swept over the news agency in those weeks. This was reflected in a May 10 *Liberation Daily* story about a group of 1,103 media professionals who were also demanding to hold their own dialogue with government officials to discuss reform. During those heady few weeks, Zhao Ziyang himself was also quoted several times talking on the importance of democracy and political reform, in what looked like his own attempt to engage the students through the media and address one of their main grievances.

May 15 saw a significant development, with a report that Premier Li Peng, head of the conservative camp, had held his own dialogue with a group of workers at Beijing's largest steel factory, one of the first reports showing that the movement had spread beyond the students who were the main subject of most articles so far. The story also noted that workers were most unhappy with corruption and inflation, drawing attention to those major populist themes, which had been largely overlooked in most of the coverage so far amid loftier calls for more democracy and political reform. The May 15 edition also contained the first reference to the new hunger strike that the students had launched two days earlier to bring some new momentum to their movement.

Amid all of these developments, Gorbachev arrived for his historic visit. His arrival was the lead story in the *Liberation Daily* the next day, and indeed his trip was the subject of the entire top half of the front page, although no mention was made of the fact that his welcoming ceremony had to be moved to the airport. Starting from this date, now around four weeks into the movement, the first signs of what would become a new theme in the lead-up to the crackdown also began to appear in the form of articles with an almost-pleading quality to them, calling on everyone to remain calm and orderly. I interpret these articles as possibly the first sign that Zhao Ziyang and the reformers were concerned about an eventual crackdown that was favored by Deng Xiaoping. In this case, the May 16 headline with this new pleading tone appeared at the bottom of the front page below the Gorbachev coverage, and was a call from one government official who "Once Again Reaffirms the Patriotism and Sincerity of the Many Students, and Hopes That Everyone Will Address the Issues with the Highest Degree of Rationality."

Gorbachev continued to dominate coverage the next day in meetings with Deng Xiaoping and Zhao Ziyang, with his historic visit taking up the top half of the front page in a nod to the fact that Party matters were still foremost above all else. But the bottom half of the front page was largely devoted to the student movement, including one of the first photos of the demonstrations. This showed that even traditional Party papers were getting bolder in their willingness to push the envelope, printing not only articles describing the scene but also photos that often evoked a stronger reaction. Also reflecting this growing boldness, the *Liberation Daily*, itself a Shanghai-based daily, reported on some local protests on that day, showing that the movement had spread beyond Beijing. In one other noteworthy sign of boldness, the paper also openly discussed for the first time that an activity involving Gorbachev had to be canceled due to the protests. The quiet pleas continued on that day as well, with a call by Zhao Ziyang for the students to remain rational, and another Xinhua report citing 10 universities that had sent an open letter to their students asking them to return to class.

These trends gain momentum from this point onward, with the *Liberation Daily*'s increasing boldness reflected in a string of its own reports, both on activities in Shanghai and also in Beijing, accompanied by a growing number of photos. Gorbachev rapidly disappeared from the news starting on just the third day of his visit, as attention quickly returned almost exclusively to the movement.

The following days also saw a growing number of articles from a wide range of voices, from government and school officials to worried parents, to women's and even artists' associations, calling on the students to remain rational, end their hunger strike, and return to classes. This media tactic was an interesting throwback to an earlier one that we saw in the Korean War coverage, when similar calls of protest came from a broad range of groups over the US entrance to the war. The use of such a tried-and-true tactic showed that even though the movement was in its most progressive second phase at this point in terms of media coverage, propaganda officials were still somewhat in control and resorting to some of their old methods to get out their message and give it more credibility by creating a broader feel of consensus from different groups in society.

In a similar vein, another recurring type of coverage that appeared during this time in the most liberal stage of the media coverage was the growing acceptability of top leaders being seen meeting with the students and discussing their demands. Reports starting in this third week of May were filled with various such meetings by top leaders, led by Zhao Ziyang himself, who paid a visit to recovering hunger strikers that was reported in the *Liberation Daily*'s May 19 edition. The paper went a step further by also carrying its own report, together with original photos, on top officials in Shanghai, including Mayor Jiang Zemin, meeting with some local students who had also gone on hunger strike.

After this brief period of open and creative coverage, in the third and final stage of reporting after Zhao Ziyang had been pushed aside the conservatives began implementing Deng Xiaoping's order for martial law in the last 10 days of May. During this stage, articles that formerly sounded like pleading requests began to take on a more menacing tone, reading more like warnings. One of the first of these menacing stories appeared in the May 20 edition of the *Liberation Daily*, the day that martial law was formally declared. The story, in a report about a big meeting by the central government military commission, contained some of the earliest references to ending the "unrest" and restoring order. An actual article on the declaration of martial law was, not surprisingly, front and center in the next day's edition.

During this final stage of the movement, the "public announcement" format reappeared, beginning with one such local item from

Shanghai leaders on May 21 stating that many activities had ended by now, but that some students were still "posing a threat to order." Such items, which would once again become a staple during this final period, looked like the government's way of calling on the students and others to end their activities, while reassuring worried local citizens that everything was under control and life would soon return to normal. Propaganda officials also turned to two other common tactics in this phase, trying to forge a consensus by saying things like "everyone wants order" and also trying to downplay the magnitude of the situation by repeatedly stating that the unrest was limited to a small group of people. Buzzwords like "unrest" started to pop up more regularly as the conservatives reasserted control.

Some of the more open-style articles from the previous phase continued for a few days into this final period, but the uncertainty that newspaper editors must have been feeling was clear from the placement of these stories in secondary positions and a relative drop-off in their numbers. One interesting locally written series that continued to be published in the *Liberation Daily* during this period was a string of "Beijing Diary"-type stories on what was happening in the capital during martial law, giving readers a very on-the-ground feel of what things were like at Tiananmen Square. But as the conservatives gained the upper hand, the volume of these locally written reports also quickly dropped off to the point where most items were once again coming from either Beijing or the Shanghai city government.

In place of the locally based reports, more articles on the military started to appear, informing people on what was happening during martial law and possibly preparing them for the final crackdown. Most of these stories tried to make the soldiers and martial law in general appear as benign and sympathetic as possible. Stories exemplifying this approach appeared in the May 24 issue of the *Liberation Daily*, one on a skirmish that saw a soldier injured and another Q&A–style article on what exactly martial law entailed. During this time, large numbers of editorials and other story formats calling on people to support the Communist Party and its policies also began to appear. Typifying this genre was the lead story on May 31, which simply called on people to "Seriously Study the Spirit of the Central Government."

Few references were made to foreigners during this period, or during the entire movement in general, even though large numbers of non-Chinese such as me were living in Beijing and witnessing the movement. During the final stage of the movement, one of the first foreign voices in the media to be heard was that of United Nations Secretary Javier Perez de Cuellar, who was quoted saying he hoped there would be no violence. Another martial law story from Xinhua detailed a notice sent out by the Foreign Ministry to foreign correspondents living in Beijing on what they could and could not do during this time.

A small burst of coverage on the movement occurred immediately after the final crackdown on June 3 and June 4, but the depth of the reporting was clearly limited and the news was clearly coming from central sources by this time, despite the widespread and graphic reports that were flooding out of China from the foreign media. A relatively detailed account of the crackdown appeared in the *Liberation Daily* on June 5, though no mention was made of anyone getting killed. The lead story on the subject came under a simple public announcement headline, and contained a rough timeline of the events, including the fact that the army had put an end to the movement and cleared the students from Tiananmen Square. The story introduced a number of catchphrases that would pervade the media for weeks and even years to come. For the first time, the movement was called an "antirevolutionary rebellion" and the participants were described as a small number of "hooligans."

From this point the media, now clearly toeing the Party line, went into justification mode, trying to explain to everyone why the government had to take the action that it did to restore order and prevent the country from plunging into chaos. Reports would appear about mobs of angry citizens who killed soldiers and burned their vehicles, and on the generally illegal and violent nature of many activities that occurred during the movement. While many citizens were indeed angry and engaged in some of the post-movement activities that were reported, the media did little or nothing to report on the reason for their rage, namely the killing of hundreds of unarmed citizens by the military during the crackdown. During this period, the media would also call on citizens to support the martial law troops who were acting to restore order. In a bid to quell a growing fear among the local populace that the crackdown could grow, a new stream of articles also appeared, calling on everyone not to believe rumors about food shortages and other potentially disruptive news that could create panic. My analysis ends with the June 8 edition of the *Liberation Daily*, which carried coverage of the first official government press conference to answer questions in what would ultimately become a damage control campaign that lasted for years.

The four reporters I spoke with who lived through and reported on events surrounding the Tiananmen movement all remembered the period for its openness and the big hopes it created for journalists accustomed to heavy restrictions on their reporting. The reporter with the most direct experience worked for Xinhua in Beijing, considered ground zero for the movement from a journalistic perspective. He recalled that, in one of the biggest ironies, but also perhaps befitting the situation, Xinhua journalists were never instructed on how to report on the events happening around them for much of the duration of the movement, but were instead left largely to their own devices.

This reporter said that a major turning point for him and his peers came less than two weeks into the movement, when many were infuriated by an April 26 editorial in the *People's Daily* penned by Deng Xiaoping himself, calling the movement antigovernment and labeling it as unrest for the first time. He recalled how he and his colleagues were briefed on the previous day to closely read the editorial and follow its lead, angering many who believed that the movement was neither organized nor threatening as the article implied, but instead was peaceful and spontaneous. From that point on, most of the younger staff at Xinhua, along with other major domestic media like CCTV and even the *People's Daily*, went out on the streets and joined the demonstrations.

He said that he personally went to Tiananmen almost daily after that, taking numerous pictures, even though he never wrote anything that was actually published. He remained at the square until the very end, spending much of his time at an informal press corner that had sprung up at the Martyr's Memorial. He said that he had actually photographed the forcible evacuation on the night of June 3 and morning of June 4, though his film was ultimately confiscated and never returned.

After June 4, all the young Xinhua journalists who had attended the demonstrations were forced to confess what they had done and to write self-criticisms, a Maoist-era practice, which was still common at that time, requiring people to write at length on the error of their ways in response to accusations of anything deemed morally wrong or as having antigovernment overtones. The reporter said he was forced to write such a self-criticism after someone wrote an anonymous letter accusing him of leaking military secrets, resulting in a three-hour interrogation and repeated harassment after that. He was able to keep his job after the police ultimately found nothing to substantiate the accusations, but said that morale at Xinhua sank to such a low level that he ended up quitting in 1991.

Another reporter, whose work at that time often took him to the countryside of central China, recalled how there were many students protesting in his home city, the provincial capital. But what was more remarkable, he said, was the fact that everyone—down to the poorest peasants in the countryside—was following the movement on their radios and TVs, ownership of which was starting to become relatively common at that time. He said that most such country folk, while mesmerized by the movement, weren't interested in actually joining or even supporting it, as many thought their lives were already improving under the decade-old reform policies that were slowly starting to lift many out of poverty.

A Shanghai-based reporter recalled how his newspaper sent many of its correspondents to Beijing during that time, although he was not among them. He remembered the initial confusion of his Shanghai editors at the time of Hu Yaobang's death, as many were unsure how to characterize a man who had been one of China's most powerful leaders just years before, only to largely fall from grace even though he was not subjected to the complete whitewash treatment often meted out during the Mao era. After it became clear that Beijing leaders weren't going to take a major stance on the issue, the media, including his newspaper, quickly took matters into their own hands, launching the period of great openness that came to characterize the early stages of the movement. He recalled how things changed rapidly and dramatically with the declaration of martial law, when all of the city's senior editors were called downtown to a meeting and instructed to follow the Party line from then on. Many reporters reacted to this by going out to demonstrate afterward, but all such activities quickly came to an end after the final crackdown, which also saw some of the most active reporters having to write lengthy self-criticisms.

Thus ended the Tiananmen Student Movement of 1989, a time bracketed by periods of traditional Party-line media tactics and behavior at either end, with a period of incredible openness in the middle. The anything-goes atmosphere that arose during that time was unparalleled in the history of Chinese Communist Party rule, and resulted in a wide range of reports that were basically accurate but lacked many of the journalistic standards seen in the more mature Western media, which many were trying to emulate. There's not much to say about media trends in general during this period apart from the broader openness that characterized it, as there were quite literally no rules and editors did largely whatever they wanted.

One of the few traditional tactics that still showed up during this time was the use of the media blackout in terms of reporting political news. Despite the huge openness of the time, little or no coverage was given to the major behind-the-scenes political fighting between the reformers and conservatives that would ultimately see the latter gain the upper hand for years to come and lead to the fall of lead reformer Zhao Ziyang and his followers. Such blackouts of internal Party politics remain common to this day, leaving most Chinese and China watchers to read the tea leaves through second hand channels such as scrutinizing name lists and political appointments. In rare instances, politicians themselves even write their own memoirs, which was the case with Zhao Ziyang, who secretly recorded his own experiences during the movement on cassette tapes that were later smuggled out of China and turned into a book, *Prisoner of the State*.

That said, the period just before the crackdown saw a return to many of the media tactics of old, a number of which remain in use to this day. Following the tone set by Xinhua once again became the order of the day in the final stage of the movement, with little or no deviation from the Party line tolerated for several years afterward. Smaller tactics would also come back into common use, most notably the introduction of both tried-and-true and newer buzzwords like "antirevolutionary," "rebellion," "black hands," and the "very small number" phrase used to characterize the movement and the numbers of people who participated. The public announcement also quickly came back into play as the government's way of laying down the law with no room for further discussion. Finally, the aftermath of the movement would see one of the first major uses of mass persuasion to try to explain to the average person why the crackdown was necessary, marking a sharp break with a past where coercion or outright black-outs on such sensitive topics were more common. That said, the subject of the movement remains essentially banned in public forums today, both in the traditional media and on the Internet, and a good many more years may have to pass before that prohibition is lifted.

Chapter 9

Falun Gong

Guerilla Coverage Returns

CCTV broadcasts the trial of four Falun Gong leaders at the Intermediate People's Court in Haikou, capital of the southern island province of Hainan, November 12, 1999. China jailed the leaders of the banned Falun Gong spiritual movement for up to 12 years in the first known trial of members of what the Communist government decreed "an evil cult."

Photo Credit: Reuters/OTHK

The Communist Party has gained confidence these past two decades after steering China through the difficult transition from a command to a more market-oriented economy, but two things that seem to evoke particular alarm are the prospects of social unrest and competition from rival organizations. These two phobias converged in the late 1990s with the Falun Gong spiritual movement, a quasi-religious meditation-based group founded by a charismatic leader, in what would result in one of the government's final guerilla-style media campaigns that would ultimately end with the outlawing of the group and its being branded as an "evil cult."

To understand what happened with Falun Gong and why it evoked such a harsh response in the government and media, one needs to understand that religious groups in China, and rival groups in general, have a long history of stirring up fear among Chinese rulers. Religious groups in particular were especially problematic, as they often had the potent combination of strong central organizations that could call on broad bases of devout followers to do their will, often in direct opposition to the government. For much of Chinese history indigenous Taoism and later Buddhism would dominate the political landscape, although Christianity would make its own strong entrance and challenge to the central leadership with the arrival of Catholic missionaries in the 16th century.

One of the biggest threats to central power in the modern era came from such a group during the Taiping rebellion of 1850 to 1864, which nearly toppled the Qing dynasty before the central government finally put it down. That case saw a highly organized group loosely linking itself to Jesus literally build a nation within the borders of a China ruled by a rapidly weakening Qing dynasty that was already facing

157

strong pressure from the major Western powers. The Taiping ultimately extended its reach to a big chunk of eastern China along the Yangtze River basin, exercising its power through a highly organized government complete with its own army. The group would only be crushed in the end by the Qing army with strong support from the foreign powers, who preferred the Qing emperors to the uncertainty of what might happen to their interests under a new Taiping leadership. Later conflicts in the late 19th and early 20th centuries would see other quasi-religious homegrown groups spring up, often as secret societies over which Beijing wielded little or no control.

After the establishment of the People's Republic of China in 1949, the Communists mandated that all religious groups must be registered with the state and receive a strong degree of government oversight. As a result, most Chinese-registered religions were little more than puppet organizations of the state for the first three decades of Communist rule. Oversight has loosened a bit since China started to open up in the 1980s and people have shown a greater interest in joining religions, but all groups must still officially operate within government control.

One of the most contentious relationships as a result of the insistence on strong government oversight has been the one between Beijing and the Roman Catholic Church. The Catholic Church has seen its China numbers swell in the past two decades amid a broader growing interest in religion, with practicing Catholics now thought to number more than 10 million, a sizable figure though still only a tiny fraction of China's 1.3 billion population. And yet, despite that, the Chinese Catholic Church still takes its orders from Beijing rather than the Vatican, with the central government making most high appointments and approving all major leadership changes. Of course, this flies in the face of the Vatican's own centrally organized system for the rest of the world, where church leaders in Rome appoint all top officials and have a strong say in other major matters as well. Beijing's refusal to allow similar Vatican oversight of the Chinese Catholic Church has resulted in frequent run-ins with the nation, which to date remains the only major Western country without formal diplomatic ties with China.

Given that stormy relationship with religions in the past, Beijing's current insistence on strong direct control of all such groups today should come as no surprise. In fact, the government's fear of religious groups is really part of a broader phobia of any major group with the power to challenge the Communist Party government. Organizations of any kind, religious or secular, must all register with the government, and often have their applications refused without any reasons given. Those that the government did not approve, including largely apolitical industry and business groups, now operate in a gray area that leaves them exposed to the risk of closure at any time at the smallest sign of trouble or disagreement.

Many attribute the rapid rise of Falun Gong to a number of factors that all came together in the late 1980s and lasted into the 1990s. The group itself was founded by a charismatic man named Li Hongzhi, who now lives in the United States and whose name is banned in all China-based media and Internet forums. The central tenets of the faith Li created combined Buddhist ideas with the practice of *Qi Gong*, the ancient Chinese art of using breathing exercises to regulate internal energy and generally improve one's health.

One of the chief factors that helped give rise to Falun Gong was a spiritual vacuum that developed in China during the 1980s, as the Communist Party rapidly abandoned many of its old ideologies in favor of more practical market-oriented policies. While many of those policies lifted people's living standards, the Party had little or nothing to offer in terms of new ideas to satisfy a broad-based desire for a richer spiritual life to complement the new material prosperity. This spiritual vacuum was a major factor that led to an explosion of interest in *Qi Gong* during that time, with "masters" popping up overnight throughout the country, each with his or her own techniques and small groups of followers. I can personally recall the rise of the fad during that time, as many of my friends, most of them college educated, wanted to talk with me about their latest lessons and demonstrate their skills. I would usually roll my eyes and play along, even though most of it seemed to lack much substance.

In that kind of climate, it's not difficult to see how many quasi-religious groups using *Qi Gong* as their basis might start to spring up, catering to a younger generation of Chinese who at once had many new opportunities in front of them but very little spiritual guidance on how to proceed. The government probably saw the rise of these groups as minor and insignificant, and paid them little or no heed, as most were far too small and lacked the organization to challenge its decades-long rule. Of course, all of that changed with Falun Gong, a very well-organized group whose ranks quickly grew to include thousands of followers, even though that rapid rise went mostly unheeded by a central leadership that was tackling much bigger issues as it steered China from a centrally planned to a more market-oriented economy. Falun Gong members covered a broad spectrum of everyday Chinese, from younger people interested in *Qi Gong* and the movement's more spiritual side to older people who saw its regimen of meditative-style exercises as good for one's health. In the earlier days before the group was banned, it wasn't at all uncommon to meet people whose friends or relatives were members or who were members themselves. From a Westerner's perspective, the group was probably the equivalent of some of the new-age groups that spring up from time to time in the United States or Europe, many of which are shunned by the majority as slightly nutty but which still manage to attract a following. What differed in the case of Falun Gong was that the group managed to grow quite big due to its strong organization, and initially counted mostly mainstream people as its followers, including many Party members. To this day it is one of the few groups that, despite its officially banned status, can mount successful challenges to the Communist Party in China, launching occasional acts of sabotage by hijacking TV signals and helping people to get around Beijing's various Internet firewalls to access sites on sensitive subjects like Falun Gong itself. The group also runs its own extensive media empire outside of China, including a network of web sites, publishers, and even a TV station, in its bid to counter Beijing's own attempts at global influence through similar channels. The group is a master at staging public demonstrations, and it's not at all uncommon to see its members parked outside major Chinese embassies and consulates worldwide protesting its suppression inside China. Falun Gong members are also adept at organizing protests whenever a major Chinese leader travels abroad, and have a reputation for getting out numbers and making their voices heard on such occasions. While some might say the group has become more political than its meditative roots, many of its followers would argue they are just advocating for the freedom to practice their own religion without the heavy oversight of Beijing.

Starting with a Stealth Demonstration

In terms of media coverage, this analysis will focus on the months of April through October 1999, which correspond to a massive stealth demonstration staged by the group at Tiananmen Square, followed by a weeks-long central government media campaign that ended with a formal ban on the group and its being labeled an "evil cult." The most striking thing about this period in terms of media coverage is its resurrection of the old-style guerilla campaign, which by 1999 had become a relative rarity. The guerilla coverage that characterized this campaign saw the pages of the *People's Daily* almost completely filled for days with Falun Gong–related articles in all shapes and sizes, giving the impression of widespread opposition and social disapproval of the group from everyone and justifying the government's final ban. True to the guerilla style, the coverage included a wide range of formats, from editorials, testimonials, and general commentaries to other news events all harping on the same theme, namely the harmful and destructive power of Falun Gong and the dangers of associating with the group or its practices. Together with the broad-based coverage, this period also saw the use of another familiar tactic with the introduction of repeatedly used buzzwords to denounce and vilify the group, along with daily banners designed to highlight its broader badness.

Equally striking during this period was the virtual blackout of the topic that occurred in the national media after the few months of intense guerilla vilification, with the effect that the name Falun Gong essentially disappears from public discussion from that point. This kind of on-again-off-again pattern is relatively common in the Chinese media, with the government turning on the media spigot when it wants to make its point and then turning it off when it has accomplished its objective. To date the group remains one of the most widely censored topics in the Chinese media, with any searches of its name or any of its leaders on the Internet coming back empty, and any references in chat rooms quickly deleted. Seldom does one see such blanket and ongoing censorship on a single topic in the Chinese media, underscoring the uneasiness the Communist Party continues to feel about Falun Gong to this day.

From a broader perspective, the government's vilification of the group also reflects its increasing reliance on the media as a tool for maintaining social stability in the current change-filled era. In the minds of top Party officials, Falun Gong represents a group with the power to upset social order through its large base and competing agenda of lobbying for freedom of religion, even though the organization has made few if any serious moves to challenge Communist authority in the political arena.

While the Falun Gong issue finally came to a head in the spring and summer of 1999, the Party was aware of its growing influence for several years starting in the mid-1990s and would print opinion pieces from time to time denouncing it. One of the earliest attacks came in the influential *Guangming Daily*, a Party-run newspaper for intellectuals, back in 1996, giving the unofficial green light for other media to follow with similar editorials. A stream of critical editorials would appear in papers throughout China for the next few years, but even so Falun Gong would remain largely a peripheral factor in the Communist Party's field of view as it contended with its more pressing agenda of economic transformation.

All that changed on April 22, 1999, when Falun Gong members held a large surprise demonstration in the city of Tianjin, just a short distance from Beijing. That was followed three days later by the main event—a massive sit-in of around 10,000 members lobbying for freedom of religion outside Zhongnanhai, the compound next to Tiananmen Square where all the country's top leaders live. Historians would later comment that the sit-in was less remarkable for its size, and more so for the fact that it came as a complete and total surprise to the Communist Party government, whose extensive domestic intelligence networks failed to detect the event so that it could stop it from happening or deal with it in another manner.

After a full two months of deciding what to do, the government launched its frontal assault on the group on July 22 with a massive media campaign, including a formal declaration that Falun Gong was illegal and condemnation of its leader, Li Hongzhi, and its legions of followers. The next two months saw the government wage its guerilla media campaign to formally vilify the group, ending with the formal branding of Falun Gong in October as a *xie jiao*, which literally means "evil religion" and is generally translated by the Chinese and Western media as "evil cult."

After the government's assault ended, Falun Gong members continued to engage in periodic acts of sabotage like hijacking TV signals, mostly defiant in nature rather than actual attacks on people or property, to remind the Communist Party of its existence. Such acts are occasionally mentioned in the Western publications, which have taken an interest in the topic from a human rights perspective. But any reports are strictly forbidden in the Chinese media. Several of the reporters I interviewed said the subject is strictly forbidden from reporting at the local level in China, and most media try to avoid the matter completely but will always use stories from Xinhua if they ever need to report. One notable exception to the broader coverage ban in China involves a January 2001 event, when five Falun Gong members reportedly tried to set themselves on fire at Tiananmen Square. The group would later deny its people were involved, even though Xinhua reported that they were. Later, the government would frequently roll out footage of the attempted self-immolations on domestic television to remind everyone why Falun Gong was dangerous and needed to be banned in China. The broader campaign has been largely successful, helping to mobilize broader Chinese public opinion against the group.

The story of Falun Gong in the Chinese media is quite colorful from a coverage perspective, though entirely one-sided as the group itself completely lacks a voice throughout the process. As mentioned above, one of the earliest salvos in the media offensive against the group came in the June 17, 1996, *Guangming Daily*, in the form of an editorial on page four calling on people to "Raise the Alarm and Cry Out to Oppose False Science." The story goes on to mention Falun Gong by name, and blasts it as a false science that attracts unsuspecting followers with its claims of curing illness and taking people to a higher spiritual level. The editorial raises the curtain for similar condemnations that appear throughout China for the next three years, and introduces the term "false science" as one of the first catchphrases that will become part of a rich media lexicon used to blast the group.

Skipping ahead to 1999, the *People's Daily* contains no mention of the April 22 rally by Falun Gong members in Tianjin on any of the days immediately after the event. The hometown *Tianjin Daily* also contains no mentions of this relatively major local story, indicating the demonstration received the usual blackout treatment in most or all major Chinese media. Even the more liberal English-language *China Daily*, which caters more to foreigners and often carries stories that other domestic media won't touch, fails to cover this first major sign of defiance by

Falun Gong members in China. Likewise, the bigger April 25 sit-in at Tiananmen Square is also completely blacked out in the Chinese media as central leaders figured out how to respond to this sudden and unexpected challenge without openly acknowledging it domestically or to the world at large.

A full two months pass after these groundbreaking events with literally no mention of Falun Gong or anything related to the group in the *People's Daily*, in an eerie calm before the storm for anyone who knows what's coming. All of that abruptly changes in the July 23 edition, when the newspaper suddenly comes out with guns blazing against the group. July 23 sees the *People's Daily*'s entire front page devoted to anti–Falun Gong stories, with a number of related stories on the inside pages as well. In an interesting twist on the usual routine, the newspaper uses stories reported by its own staff—rather than the usual Xinhua stories—for its two lead articles, one announcing a ban on any Communist Party members from joining, and the other a consensus-style story saying how everyone agrees on this ban. The decision to forgo the usual Xinhua stories underscores how seriously the Communist Party is taking the situation, since the *People's Daily* is the Party's official newspaper and anything written by its staff reporters is the equivalent of the Party's direct voice. From the opening day of this assault, all references to the name Falun Gong will be in quotation marks, again employing a common Chinese media tactic that uses the placement of a word in quotes to help de-legitimize and subject it to a certain disdain and ridicule.

Other front-page stories on this opening day of the assault include a Xinhua report pointing out that the group never legally registered with the proper government bodies, and that it has held a wide range of illegal activities promoting superstition. For these reasons, the organization itself has been declared illegal, the article states, in the first use of a refrain on the group's legality that will appear repeatedly in the weeks ahead. The guerilla coverage continues on page four of the *People's Daily* with a Xinhua spread on the group's charismatic founder, Li Hongzhi, whose teachings are proclaimed to be based on "crooked reasoning and evil preachings." Interestingly, this anti–Li Hongzhi section sees the Party finally acknowledge the April protests, referencing the events in both Tianjin and Beijing, the latter of which it says was attended by more than 10,000 people. The raising of the issue at this point, now two months after the fact, and its placement within the spread on Li Hongzhi, seem to be the Party's way of saying "Watch out for this guy. He's both crooked and manipulative." This first day of guerilla coverage also contains one of the first of many banners that will appear in the weeks ahead, this time an umbrella heading on page five saying "Worship Science, Oppose Superstition."

The *People's Daily* spreads its attack throughout the paper by including related stories in a weekly East China supplement that day dedicated to news from Shanghai and surrounding areas. In addition to an article generally condemning Li Hongzhi, the East China pages contain another format that will become common in the weeks ahead, namely the testimonial from ordinary people whose lives have been shattered by Falun Gong. In this case, the testimonial comes under the headline "Falun Gong Killed My Wife," and features a family photo of a man, his wife, and two children, presumably from a happier time before the wife was seduced by Falun Gong. The article contains a rare "pull-out" quote in a separate box, a common journalistic tool in the West but one used far less in China, which cites the grief-stricken husband, a bespectacled man named Lu Xingchong, saying: "If my wife was alive today, she would be 51. It was 'Falun Gong' that hurt her to the point where my home was broken and someone died! After becoming mesmerized with 'Falun Gong' she didn't think about eating or drinking, but it didn't cure her illness and finally she wanted to die, blinded by a religion that made her kill herself." The story goes on to detail the woman's obsession with Falun Gong, describing 18 audio cassettes; nine videos; and a big pile of books, magazines, and statues of Li Hongzhi that were found among the woman's possessions.

The guerilla coverage gets even louder the following day, July 24, when most of the inside pages of the *People's Daily* are devoted to trumpeting the dangers and evils of the group. In a switch from the first day, the subject drops off the front page completely on day two, with a couple of page-one articles on the importance of upholding the law as the only indirect reference to the campaign. This move to the inside pages also looks like the Party's way of taking the issue off the top of its agenda, saying it has bigger fish to fry, while preserving the battle at the grassroots level with a continued barrage of editorials, testimonials, and reports of excess and harm from the provincial level.

Explaining the Evil

Many of the articles on this second day seem focused on explaining to the reader why the government outlawed the group, and the use of a new catchphrase, "The Falun Gong Problem," comes into use in many reports. Another story on page three talks about how everyone basically agrees with the central leadership's decision to outlaw the group, and a number of groups are shown opposing it as well on page four, all implying that such a decision must be right if so many people agree, as the Party attempts to build consensus around the issue.

The assault continues for the next week with more of the same. The campaign clearly had its desired effect, as one of my friends recently recalled to me how many people were suddenly "outed" during this time as Falun Gong followers, to the surprise and shock of those around them. He remembered the scandal that erupted at his own school when the principal himself was formally outed as a follower, leading to a period of shock followed by criticism and ostracism of the man himself. Similar scenes were undoubtedly repeated all over the country, proving just how effective the government's campaign was.

I won't go into a day-by-day account of the coverage from this point onward, as most of it starts to look the same, with themes that include pointing out why the group was declared illegal, the harm it causes to society, and the importance of upholding the law. The papers also include a steady stream of attacks on Li Hongzhi, including one on July 28 ridiculing him for having once taken medicine to cure an illness, implying that if Falun Gong really worked it should have cured the illness itself. One of my favorite anti-Li headlines comes in the August 11 *People's Daily*, in an understated editorial with the simple headline "Li Hongzhi Is a Demon."

The social stability theme also comes into play during the attack, with the group portrayed as a threat to public order. For the most part stories are confined to the grassroots level, with different associations and other local organizations holding discussion forums, signing petitions, and taking other actions to show their disapproval. More catchphrases also enter the media lexicon during this time, with "resolutely supporting Communist Party policy" and variations on that theme becoming yet another mantra. Other buzzwords also come into use, with a special focus on the theme that Falun Gong's pretenses of having a scientific basis are a scam, and that the group's teachings are based simply on superstition. A new stream of stories also begins to appear in these days about the confiscation of massive amounts of Falun Gong materials, which are collected by authorities and put on display for the public before being destroyed, reminiscent of book burnings of years past in the West.

From my perspective, I find the large number of testimonials the most interesting prong of the campaign for the personal touch they bring to the Party's vilification campaign, which attempts to portray Falun Gong as not only a deviant teaching, but also a massive commercial enterprise that sucks the money out of its gullible victims by selling them large volumes of books, magazines, videocassettes, and other materials. Page four of the July 25 edition of the *People's Daily* is completely devoted to such testimonials, including one on scores of Falun Gong followers who suddenly quit the group after realizing the error of their ways; another on how the group ruined the life of one man's wife; an article on a group of former followers who filed a lawsuit alleging they were harmed by the group; and one editorial simply headlined "It Should Have Been Banned Sooner!" Two more moving testimonials appear the following day, one involving a 74-year-old man who turned himself in to local police, handing over eight books and two Falun Gong discs in the process, and another about a father who leaped to his death into a rushing river while clutching his son after becoming bewitched by Falun Gong.

And so the barrage of reports continued, with most inside pages of the *People's Daily* now headed by the "Worship Science, Oppose Superstition" banner on a daily basis at the height of the attack. The assault finally starts to fade in the early days of August, even as the by-now-rich vocabulary of buzzwords and catchphrases shows up regularly in the slowing stream of stories. In terms of my analysis, the assault unofficially ended on October 28, when the *People's Daily* carried a large article at the bottom of its front page stating that Falun Gong has officially been declared an "evil cult." Presumably by this time the Party has determined that its campaign has had its desired effect, and it's time to retire a subject that is still banned in the Chinese media. To this day, Falun Gong is largely shunned and even feared by the big majority of Chinese, showing how effective the campaign of 1999 was. Large numbers are still believed to secretly practice Falun Gong inside China, though few will ever admit so openly to an outsider.

From a reporting perspective, the half-dozen journalists I asked about how they or their papers reported on Falun Gong answered in nearly identical fashion: All said they and their papers would never attempt to report on the subject at the local level, and most would be likely to avoid it altogether. On the rare occasion when they had to print something, all would use official Xinhua stories verbatim without any local contributions. One reporter observed that Falun Gong essentially gets the blackout treatment to this day in China, with Xinhua and other central news sources acting as if the group doesn't exist despite its occasional acts of defiance.

Another reporter observed that Falun Gong is just one of a number of matters that his newspaper would never report on, alongside other taboo topics like foreign affairs, religion, minorities, and ethnic conflicts. These subjects are strictly off limits to all except for Xinhua and other centrally controlled media, which more often than not simply give them the blackout treatment and pretend they don't exist. Another reporter at one of China's more liberal publications said his magazine is always trying to push the envelope on sensitive subjects like religion, especially underground religions that exist outside the official realm of state control. But he also echoed the others in saying that Falun Gong is such a forbidden topic that even his publication wouldn't dare to do any stories on it, as doing so would almost certainly result in severe punishment and possibly even a government-ordered shutdown. So sensitive is the subject that one other reporter said rank-and-file journalists aren't even allowed to write about the group in *neican*, the internal-use reports that are meant only for leaders.

Thus ends my brief look at Falun Gong, a unique topic for its media coverage that represented a sort of bridge between many of the cruder, traditional media tactics of the first three decades of Communist rule and the softer, more subtle approach that has evolved in the past decade. Many of the media tactics used to report on the group fall more clearly into the traditional school, most notably the guerilla style of coverage that harks back to previous treatment given to events like the Cultural Revolution and the Korean War.

That kind of frontal assault includes many of the usual reporting tactics, such as a wide range of editorials, government proclamations, social group activities, and testimonials all driving home the same message, which is reinforced with a stable of buzzwords and catchphrases that are rapidly introduced at the outset of the coverage. In this case words like "superstition" and "evil cult" become common themes throughout the attack, along with the use of quotation marks around the term Falun Gong itself to de-legitimize and ridicule the group.

Finally, the media employ a healthy dose of the blackout tactic as part of their coverage strategy, most notably waiting a full two months after the initial mass protests before publishing any reports. After more than a month of relentless assault, the blackout tactic returns, with little or no mention of Falun Gong in the media after the year 2000, and words related to the group quickly deleted from Internet chat rooms and blocked on search engines.

From a broader perspective, the Falun Gong coverage is also notable for its more persuasive overtones, contrasting sharply with the more coercive, authoritarian sound of previous media campaigns. Perhaps best exemplifying this trend is the frequent use of testimonials, a form seldom seen in the past, that seem designed to bring the issue down to the common level by showing ordinary readers how lives of the group's followers often end in tragedy or disaster. These testimonials, which read like a stern warning from a parent to a child, are accompanied by similarly paternalistic editorials and other articles explaining to readers why the government outlawed the group and has labeled it an "evil cult." Other reports explain that at the end of the day, the banning of Falun Gong was necessary for maintaining social stability, again driving home the fact that the campaign was launched for the good of society above all else.

Chapter 10

A Bombing in Belgrade and Anti-Japanese Marches

The Nationalism Card

Chinese demonstrators hurl stones at the British embassy in Beijing on May 9, 1999, in protest against NATO's missile attack on the Chinese embassy in Belgrade. Beijing encouraged similar demonstrations throughout the country after the bombing to show its displeasure, but later clamped down after the situation showed signs of getting out of control.

Photo Credit: Reuters/OTHK

As China continued its transformation to a market economy in the 1990s, two important things started to happen. On the everyday level, living standards began to rise sharply, producing new feelings of national pride for many Chinese after more than a century of humiliation at the hands of the colonial powers and three decades of economic and social turmoil under early Communist Party rule. At the same time, China's opening to the outside world was making the average Chinese more aware of his status compared with other countries, resulting in a strong admiration for the West previously discussed in the chapter on the Tiananmen Square movement.

The Communist Party was quick to showcase its achievements to feed the strong demand for positive stories spotlighting China's progress for a new generation of nationalistic Chinese, and made liberal use of the media to that end. At the same time, the government, alarmed and perhaps feeling threatened by the admiration for the West, also embarked on a broader campaign, subtle at times but also quite loud and obvious at others, of discreditation, using the media whenever it could to highlight shortcomings of Western nations and portray them as bullies trying to hold China back.

Instances of the fanning of nationalistic pride and selective bashing of Western countries have been relatively frequent in the Chinese media after the Tiananmen Square movement, with two illustrating the point well. The first came in 1999, when the accidental NATO bombing of the Chinese embassy in Yugoslavia at the start of the Kosovo war led to massive anti-Western demonstrations throughout China. The second came six years later, in 2005, when Japan's attempt to win a place on the United Nations Security Council and its approval of a controversial textbook downplaying the country's aggression in World War II resulted in a series of similar demonstrations outside the Japanese embassy in Beijing and Japanese consulates throughout the country. In both cases, the massive demonstrations were not only tolerated but actually encouraged by the government, which made extensive use of the media to fan anti-foreign sentiment, and in the latter case allowed ordinary citizens to use cell phone texting and the Internet to organize mass movements at the grassroots level.

Government use of nationalism is hardly unique to China, and in fact is often used by other countries to rally citizens around common causes, especially in wartime. What was different in China's case is that the nationalism card went largely unused for several decades after the Korean War of 1950–1953, as China shut itself off from the outside world and embarked on domestically focused campaigns like the Great Leap Forward and the Cultural Revolution. With the advent of reform and China's growing prosperity starting in the 1980s and accelerating into the 1990s, the government found that it was once again possible to tap into a growing sense of national pride to rally people around its various agenda items.

The new nationalism dovetailed nicely with the Propaganda Ministry's separate strategy of focusing on good news to showcase Party achievements, as such news made people feel good not only about the Party but also about being Chinese. As a result of this positive focus, we see an explosion of news and events to showcase Party achievements and stoke national pride starting in the 1990s, culminating with the Beijing Olympics of 2008 and the Shanghai World Expo of 2010. Another area that gets big play is technological achievements, with a special emphasis on China's fast-growing space program, which gets massive national media attention with the achievement of every new milestone.

In my years in China during this period, it seemed like barely a year would go by without one city or another holding a major event, most often sporting extravaganzas complete with elaborate opening and closing ceremonies. Such events, which included the Asian Games of 2010 in Guangzhou, and the Universiade Games of 2011 in Shenzhen, were always widely televised and heavily covered in the Chinese media, with reporters under strict instructions to tell only positive stories and showcase local accomplishments. Reporters who covered the Beijing Olympics and Asian games in Guangzhou told me they were repeatedly told that no negative news was allowed from such events, a tactic that will be discussed in greater detail in the upcoming chapter on the Olympics.

The Party found that such nationalism not only fed the strong appetite for positive stories about its achievements, but was also useful for diverting attention from its own shortcomings. Some have said that the huge anti–US demonstrations in May 1999 after the bombing of China's Yugoslav embassy by NATO planes were a convenient way to divert public attention from the 10th anniversary of the Tiananmen Square crackdown. The Party also used such nationalism to divert attention from the failure of socialism in the early 1990s, a period when growing national pride culminated in the 1996 publication of the bestselling book, *China Can Say No,* pointing out that China could and should stand up to the bullying tactics of the West.

Concurrent with the rise in nationalism, the average Chinese was rapidly learning about the outside world through several channels, including a growing number of foreign visitors to the country, increasing numbers of Chinese traveling and studying abroad, and the flood of pirated movies and TV shows that became common with the advent of CDs and DVDs. Having lived in China through much of this period, I can personally attest to the massive change in perception of foreigners that took place over this time. For me, the change was most obvious in the sharp drop in the "staring squad" phenomenon—the term I use for the groups of gaping Chinese that used to form on the streets and in shops behind the backs of unsuspecting foreigners, clamoring for a closer look at what must have seemed to them like aliens. Such squads were common even in major cities like Shanghai and Beijing in the 1980s, as people got their first look at real-life foreigners after going their entire lives with little or no exposure to the outside world. But by 2000, these squads had largely disappeared, and foreigners can now travel nearly anywhere in China—down to the smallest village—without being stared at like Martians.

The arrival of so much outside influence provided a challenge to China due to the blind admiration that I've mentioned before. To counter that, the government found it could often double up the nationalism card with selective anti-foreign campaigns that could rally ordinary Chinese to a common cause centered on an outside bully, bringing that country down a notch in the eyes of the average Chinese while also often diverting attention from problems at home.

Anti-foreign campaigns can take several forms in the Chinese media, including the frequently used portrayal of China as a victim of outside aggression or disrespect. This victimization tactic comes easily to China, given its very real status as the victim of bullying by the West and Japan during the hundred years of humiliation from the Opium Wars of the 1840s through the Communist victory of 1949. The Communists made liberal use of the victim approach during the Korean War, when the media painted the United States and West in general as bullies trying to take advantage of China under its new Communist leadership. The victim approach has become more subtle in recent years, with the media often making lower-key moves to discredit the West in the eyes of the general public.

From my own perspective as a journalist, a major product of this subtle campaign to discredit the West is the broader feeling among average Chinese today that the foreign media are inherently biased against their country. To be fair, Western media do tend to write more negative stories about China than positive ones, as most foreign journalists will openly acknowledge. But most of us would also point out that the Western media in general have a built-in similar bias toward the negative in general, including in their home countries, as such news often attracts the most readers. Any observer would quickly note that the Western predilection for negative news runs completely opposite to the state-controlled Chinese media's government-mandated bias toward the positive.

Regardless of the reason, the popular Chinese belief that the Western media are out to report negative news on China is common today, and the domestic media never fail to seize on this suspicion whenever they embark on anti-foreign campaigns. Such suspicion is part of the broader phenomenon that has many Chinese believe that the West is somehow in a greater conspiracy to hold their country back, which again is subtly encouraged by the government and media. The government seized on such suspicion in its "peaceful evolution" campaign, previously discussed in the chapter on the Tiananmen Square movement, which saw the media go on at length about a greater Western conspiracy to quietly undermine Communist governments throughout the world during the fall of communism in the 1990s. President Jiang Zemin himself even warned in a 1994 speech that the international community was engaged in a plot to westernize China, while also trying to keep the country from growing strong.

Fanning national pride while bashing foreign governments, as we saw in the Yugoslav embassy bombing of 1999 and the anti-Japan demonstrations of 2005, is usually a clear case of win-win for Beijing. From the government's perspective, such tactics allow everyone to feel good about being Chinese and about the state of the nation in general, helping to bolster its own credibility. At the same time, such tactics also send a clear message to the foreigners being attacked, not only expressing Beijing's displeasure but implying the potential for a much broader backlash by angry mobs of Chinese, who, in both of the above-mentioned cases, were allowed to engage in violent demonstrations against foreign targets, hurling objects at embassies and consulates, and burning and looting property connected to the country under attack.

Putting out the Flames

The government did discover that the situation wasn't completely win-win when some of the anti-foreign activities got out of hand, resulting in sharp reversals that often saw the media go from fanning the flames of nationalism to suddenly issuing stern warnings to Chinese citizens to stop their activities or risk serious consequences. These sharp reversals show up as an on-again-off-again effect in the media, which sees traditional newspapers and broadcasters run stories and commentaries to inflame the masses, only to suddenly slam on the brakes with stern warnings and news blackouts when things get out of hand. The potential for loss of control has led the government to use the anti-foreign card in the media less frequently in major diplomatic flare-ups today, and to tone down its campaigns when it does so. Still, it also realizes such campaigns are useful for letting the masses vent their frustration over issues at home, and it also knows that such negative sentiment is quickly forgotten by most ordinary people within months or sometimes even weeks of a major event.

One exemplary case reflecting the current tempered approach to foreign flare-ups came in 2010, when a disgruntled former policeman in the Philippines kidnapped a bus full of Hong Kong tourists, ending in a botched rescue that left eight of the tourists dead and many others wounded. Anti-Philippine sentiment quickly grew in Hong Kong afterward, and then spread to China with reports of gross incompetence, cover-ups, and a failure by the Philippine authorities to provide quick and reasonable explanations. When the situation began to spin out of control, the government quickly directed all media to keep in line with official statements from the Foreign Ministry and report more positively on the rescue attempt. As a result, anti-Filipino sentiment quickly faded, and the situation soon returned to normal.

New media also play a prominent role as a major new force for spreading information and become a key government tool at around the time of the Yugoslavia and Japan incidents, a topic that will be more deeply discussed in a later chapter. Cell phone use was already on the rise at the time of the Yugoslav bombing, and was even more widespread by the time of the anti-Japanese protests, allowing Chinese urbanites to send out mass messages over their phones to mobilize hundreds or even thousands to attend hastily organized rallies. The Internet was also an important force in the anti-Japanese movement, first helping to fan discussion and fuel outrage, and later serving as a tool for planning demonstrations.

The government would later also use these new media to supplement traditional newspapers and broadcasters to help bring unruly situations back under control. At the height of the anti-Japan movement, cell phone users in many provinces received threatening text messages from local police in the run-up to a series of new protests being planned for May 1, 2005, warning them that any such demonstrations were illegal and strictly forbidden. Not surprisingly, the demonstrations quickly ended after those warnings, complementing similar messages in the traditional media.

In terms of what actually happened, the Yugoslav embassy bombing was quite straightforward. NATO began bombing the Yugoslav capital, Belgrade, in early May 1999, opening a brief war that would ultimately result in the independence of the Kosovo region. On May 7, US planes, acting as part of the NATO offensive, accidentally bombed the Chinese embassy in Belgrade, killing three journalists and injuring

20 others. China immediately condemned the bombing, and a series of demonstrations throughout the country broke out afterward, culminating with the May 9 gathering of over 100,000 people outside the US embassy in what essentially became a siege of the compound. It was one of the largest mass demonstrations since the Tiananmen Square movement, and would see the embassy stoned and smeared with paint by angry demonstrators while the police stood by and did little or nothing.

During and after the incident, a number of rumors would emerge, including one that the Chinese in Belgrade were using their embassy to help Yugoslavia track NATO missiles being used to shell the city. Other reports would emerge that China had bussed in large numbers of people from nearby universities and the surrounding suburbs to beef up the demonstrations at home, and then later bussed them back and gave them hot dinners and possibly other remuneration. Most of the protests were loud and bordered on the violent, but they were also quite short-lived.

In terms of media reports, the *People's Daily* made only a small mention of the NATO bombing in its May 8 edition, the day after the Belgrade embassy was hit, in a brief front-page story saying that NATO had started bombing Yugoslavia. It's possible the embassy bombing occurred too late to make it into that edition, or that newspaper staff simply held back to wait for guidance from the central government on how to report the incident. Regardless of the reason for this brief delay, the story suddenly blows up to consume the newspaper's entire front page on the next day, May 9, with nearly every article devoted to the subject. The coverage includes a large photo of a protest held on the previous day, May 8, with people holding signs that read "Strongly Denounce American Hegemony." Other stories detail protests outside Beijing, including one outside the US consulate in Shanghai. The liberal use of photos in the coverage is particularly striking, including shots of the victims in Belgrade and demonstrations throughout China, providing a more visceral element and further fanning public fury.

The show of outrage on May 9 continues on the inside pages of the *People's Daily*, with page-three stories about China's protests to the UN, photos of bloodied victims, and a cartoon of China punching back at NATO. Additional stories include statements from Hong Kong and Macau, in a throwback to the strategy of older days where support from sources outside China proper was added to create a feeling of consensus and universal outrage at this kind of injustice. On this first day of coverage and the days that follow, a new stable of buzzwords will also start to emerge, including protests against American and NATO "hegemony" and words connected to China's "dignity" and "pride" and the "insults" that the bombing represented.

The saturation coverage continues on May 10, with angry remarks from future President Hu Jintao on the front page of the *People's Daily*, followed by reports of mass protests throughout China, including one with a photo of militant-looking students in the central city of Nanchang. For anyone who had yet to pick up on the anti-foreign and nationalistic messages, there's an unequivocal editorial at the bottom of the front page on that day, proclaiming "The People of China Cannot Be Insulted," which also plays to the China-as-victim theme. Another good show of the victim mentality comes in a second editorial, headlined "It's Not Easy to Violate the Dignity of China." The previous day's statements from Hong Kong and Macau were also joined on this day by similar expressions of outrage from other world leaders and demonstrations outside China, building on the consensus theme. One story on this day also plays to the human element, simply headlined "A Teary Mother's Day," describing how one of the Chinese victims was a mother whose children wouldn't get to celebrate the upcoming Mother's Day with her.

The anti-foreign coverage continues the next day, May 11, now four days after the actual bombing, though in a noteworthy shift all mention and photos of domestic demonstrations suddenly disappear from the *People's Daily*. Instead, the coverage becomes mostly diplomatic, featuring one article on President Jiang Zemin calling Russian leader Boris Yeltsin to complain, while another has high-ranking official Li Ruihuan canceling a meeting with a South Korean counterpart. An additional report has China suspending all military exchanges with the United States. This move to diplomatic stories and the disappearance of more inflammatory reports of demonstrations seems to be Beijing's way of saying it wanted to maintain the pressure through diplomatic gestures, but also needed to keep its own domestic situation from getting out of hand. Apart from these diplomatic stories, the coverage on this date is largely confined to editorials and other forms of criticism by groups and individuals, again part of the move to a more measured approach and away from more inflammatory reports.

This new shift in media coverage focusing on diplomacy and criticism essentially becomes the norm for the rest of the reporting period, as Beijing attempted to tone things down after giving the Chinese people a chance to vent their anger and show off their nationalism. The abrupt end of grassroots coverage from this point was yet another use of the classic blackout tactic, which in this case was the government's way of saying: "We've given you your chance to show your outrage, now it's time to move on."

By May 14, it was clear that the government wanted to wrap up public discussion of the matter, as a front-page story features top Chinese leaders welcoming back staff from the Belgrade embassy. A rare sign of the anti-foreign frenzy of the past few days also occurs in a report headlined "Media Spokesman for the National Tourism Bureau Points Out That Citizens of the United States and Other NATO Countries Will Have Their Safety Guaranteed When Traveling to China," and denies that any Americans were hurt in the demonstrations. A final sign of the cooling of tensions comes the following day, May 15, when the *People's Daily* features a front-page story of President Jiang Zemin on a phone call with US President Bill Clinton, in which Clinton apologizes for the bombing. The story was largely gone from the top headlines by May 18, 11 days after the bombing, with only a single front-page report on the re-raising of the Chinese flag at the Belgrade embassy. And thus, just as quickly and violently as it started, the intensive anti-foreign coverage, where both the government and general public could express their outrage, suddenly disappeared less than two weeks later, replaced by a more conciliatory tone as the coverage entered the off-again phase.

One reporter who was working in Shanghai at the time said he was able to contact his own source at the Belgrade embassy shortly after the bombing and write a story for his paper, reflecting the relative freedom already by then that saw many media allowed to report their own stories, even on bigger global topics. But he also noted that independent reporting for a big event like that could take place only until central authorities had issued their directives on how to cast stories, which back then would usually come within a day or two and now often comes within hours of the occurrence of big news events. From that point on, he said, everyone had to follow the official Party line.

He also noted that China's apparent initial hesitation at how to react, followed by its strong denunciations and anti-foreign campaign, may have resulted from a popular perception that the government was being too weak and should have retaliated more forcefully right after the bombing. He said the bussing in of large numbers of people from schools and suburbs to participate in mass demonstrations was actually a tactic from the Mao era, when the government often used such protests as a way to show its dissatisfaction to the rest of the world in cases like the entry of the United States into the Korean War.

Japan: A Case of Old Resentments

The anti-Japanese demonstrations six years later in 2005 were somewhat more complicated, as they were far more decentralized and fragmented, occurring in many cities over several weeks, and were mostly organized at the grassroots level as the government stood aside and let ordinary people take the lead. Two external developments were credited with stoking the demonstrations. One was Japan's previously mentioned bid for a permanent seat on the UN Security Council, which China vehemently opposed, partly to protect its own status as Asia's sole permanent member of the council and also due to deep lingering mistrust due to Japan's invasion of China during World War II. This mistrust runs quite deep in Chinese society, creating negative feelings that the government can easily draw upon whenever it wants to whip up anti-Japanese sentiment. The other development that fueled the 2005 demonstrations was Japan's approval of a new school textbook that many felt downplayed its World War II aggression. This kind of news that sees right-wing Japanese occasionally play down their country's responsibility for World War II atrocities is a recurrent flashpoint, not only for Sino–Japan relations, but also for many Asian countries that suffered at the hands of the Japanese.

Japan's UN lobbying, combined with the textbook issue, led to widespread outrage in China starting in the latter half of March 2005, with millions of people signing online petitions opposing a permanent

Japanese seat on the Security Council. Those petitions were allowed to circulate on the web with little or no interference from central government censors, reflecting Beijing's tacit support as most of the nation's leading web sites joined in the effort. After the initial wave of online activity, demonstrations started breaking out across the country, usually outside the Japanese embassy, consulates, or other Japanese targets, starting with protests on April 2 and 3 in the cities of Chengdu and Shenzhen. A major protest took place on April 9 in Beijing as the movement gained momentum and showed early signs of getting out of control.

On April 9, the Foreign Ministry urged people to remain rational and behave in a lawful manner, even as more protests took place in southern Guangdong province, where thousands threw eggs and other objects at the Japanese consulate in the provincial capital of Guangzhou. On April 10, Japan lodged a formal protest against these happenings, but activity still continued after that, with a major protest on April 16 in Shanghai that saw people throwing paint and objects at the Japanese consulate, and looting nearby Japanese shops. In most instances, all of these things were happening under the watchful eyes of local police, who stood by to keep situations under control but did little or nothing to stop the hurling of objects and looting.

After the movement showed no signs of slowing and more protests were planned, in the third week of April the government finally decided enough was enough and started strictly prohibiting new demonstrations with the threat of stiff punishment. Nearly all the activities quickly came to an end after that, with the movement finished by the end of April.

Within the pages of the *People's Daily*, the first report related to the movement appeared on March 15 on page seven, with a short article on the textbook controversy quoting a Japanese official justifying the use of the book. Separately but not coincidentally, the paper's front page on this day was dedicated to the closing of the National People's Congress in Beijing, the annual session of China's legislature that runs for the first few weeks of March each year. During this high-profile annual event, domestic media coverage is strictly devoted to the government, the Party, and their agendas for the year ahead, and negative news is strictly prohibited—a factor that is critical to understanding why China initially hushed up the SARS epidemic of 2003, which will be discussed in the next chapter. But in 2005, the fact that the National

People's Congress was over meant that news not directly related to the government's broader agenda for the year ahead was once again allowable, which perhaps explains the timing of this first appearance of a story on an issue that led to the anti-Japan movement.

After this first mention of the textbook controversy, the anti-Japan theme disappears from the *People's Daily* for the next five days, only to reappear on March 22, with Japan's bid for a permanent seat at the Security Council. Even at this point, the paper is careful to back its way into the story with a non-front-page story on a South Korean newspaper's objections, headlined "South Korea's Dong-A Ilbo Notes the Voice of Public Opinion: Japan Is Unqualified for a Place on the UN Security Council." The anti-Japan theme continues the following day on a different subject, with a report on a group suing the country for using them as human guinea pigs for medical research during World War II.

More anti-Japan rhetoric pops up periodically in the next two weeks on a range of issues, including not only Japan's bid for a Security Council seat, but also unrelated issues like a sovereignty dispute between China and Japan over a chain of unpopulated islands; and the dismissal in a Japanese court of a lawsuit by a group of Chinese women who were used as "comfort women" during the war. Clearly, Chinese propaganda officials have taken a sudden interest in printing anything anti-Japanese that they can find in their bid to stir up negative public sentiment in response to the Security Council bid.

While I believe the Security Council issue was the main factor behind this quiet campaign, the central government and media finally zeroed in on the more visceral textbook issue to bring the cause into focus. With little warning, the textbook issue vaults back into the headlines of the *People's Daily* on April 6, now more than three weeks after the first trickle of rhetoric began, with word that the book has been officially approved for use in schools. Coverage that day leads off with a lengthy article calling the book "dangerous," followed by an official objection by the Chinese Foreign Ministry, an editorial, and a cartoon of four Japanese scholars each holding up a separate word that together read "Deny Aggression."

While the official *People's Daily* remained mostly diplomatic in its coverage of the issue in the days and weeks ahead, confining itself to government objections and the occasional editorial, other newspapers were allowed to take a far more populist approach. One such paper, the popular Beijing-based *Youth Daily*, ran a series of articles on April 6 condemning Japan for trying to downplay its aggression, and was generally more aggressive in reporting on the anti-Japan movement that would break out in the weeks ahead. While the *People's Daily* remained mostly quiet for the next few days, the *Youth Daily* continued reporting on the matter with stories on dissatisfaction among Chinese and chilling relations between Japan and South Korea. This sort of backseat treatment by a big official media outfit like the *People's Daily* was consistent with the government's general approach throughout this period. It frequently uses this kind of approach in more subtle cases of perceived slights against China, letting central sources stand back and maintain a mantle of diplomacy while local media and individuals are allowed to assume the role of rabble rousers to stir up negative public sentiment. In fact, most reports on the front pages of the *People's Daily* during this early period of the protests had nothing at all to do with Japan, and were instead focused on a trip by Premier Wen Jiabao to India. Yet, despite its more aggressive reporting style, the *Youth Daily* also remains mum on the subject of the actual protests that had begun springing up throughout China by this time, indicating the central government had probably embarked upon one of its old-style blackouts for this part of the story, perhaps learning its lesson from the earlier Belgrade experience.

Signs that the situation was possibly getting out of control appear around the middle of the month, even though traditional media in China had still never reported on any of the mass protests. An April 14 *Youth Daily* article seems aimed at trying to soothe public outrage by saying Japan's foreign minister will come to China to jointly research and analyze historical events. That is followed the next day by more conciliatory articles in the *People's Daily*, one quoting a Japanese official saying there have been some difficulties in Sino–Japan relations over the past two years, but expressing hope that things will develop in an atmosphere of mutual respect. Another cites a Chinese Foreign Ministry spokesperson saying Japanese media reports of Chinese students being harmed while studying in Japan are incorrect.

I can personally attest that the situation was quickly spiraling out of control following a massive protest outside the Japanese consulate in Shanghai, which I witnessed on April 16, when thousands of people surrounded the building and hurled paint and rocks, as angry protesters burned and ransacked nearby Japanese restaurants and burned Japanese cars.

The government's concern over the direction of events shows up in the media at this time, with inflammatory articles and even conciliatory ones quickly disappearing from the headlines completely, replaced with more stern and even menacing ones warning the public to calm down, even though no actual reports on the protests had ever appeared to date.

In this tenser environment, the old public announcement format suddenly reappears in the papers, as the government returns to this older way of issuing broader messages with no room for discussion. One of the first such announcements for Shanghai appears in the locally popular *Xinmin Evening News* on April 16, the day of the big protest in the city. It appears as a simple boxed item on the front page with no headline, simply saying the city's police expect everyone to behave rationally, follow the law, and protect social stability. It also points out that the Shanghai police have not issued any permits to hold demonstrations, in an unsubtle warning that the demonstration that day was illegal. The media were now speaking with a single voice by this sensitive time, with another Shanghai newspaper also containing the same message in an identically worded announcement.

The ominous reports continue into the next day, including the introduction of the "few bad seeds" approach seen during the Tiananmen Square movement, used to downplay the populist nature of the protests by blaming the trouble on a handful of rabble rousers. The volume of articles on the matter drops dramatically after that, with a return to the conciliatory approach for the few stories that do appear on the subject as the government hopes that things will calm down on their own. As part of this approach, the *Youth Daily* in an April 22 report from Xinhua makes one of the few actual references to the marches, citing a police spokesperson saying the outrage is understandable and the majority of people who took part were law-abiding citizens. But it also notes that a handful of troublemakers broke the law, in an indirect way of saying "Enough of this."

When the indirect message doesn't work, as a new round of protests are planned in Shanghai and possibly other cities, the papers once again go back to their menacing tone for a couple of days to end the movement once and for all. I remember watching a stark TV warning the day before a planned Shanghai protest, telling people not to attend the event being planned for the third week in April. The Shanghai-based *Liberation Daily* is equally definitive in its April 25 edition, running another public announcement–style front-page item stating there will be no tolerance for people who break the law. That same edition contains a headline proclaiming "Protesting Japanese Goods Is Not 'Loving China.'" The media fall silent on the matter after that, as any planned demonstrations are scuttled and the government proclaims the matter unofficially closed for further discussion.

As with Falun Gong, most of the reporters I talked to said they weren't allowed to report on the actual protests throughout the movement, although their papers were allowed to write locally based reports on other anti-Japanese themes. One reporter commented that since the matter involved foreign relations, newspapers had to be careful about what they used and, when writing anything original, stick to the official tone being carried by reports in Xinhua, *People's Daily*, and other central media. Many said they had personally witnessed rallies in their hometowns, but as individuals, and in no capacity as reporters. One reporter said his paper held a meeting the afternoon before one of the demonstrations in his city, where everyone was told to stay away from the event, underscoring the official Party line that these marches were to be strictly organized at the grassroots level with no official backing by the traditional state-owned media.

At the end of the day, the Yugoslav embassy bombing and anti-Japanese demonstrations shared a common theme that saw the government use both to whip up national pride and anti-foreign sentiment, achieving those aims through a combination of intense coverage followed by blackouts when officials decided enough was enough. From the government's perspective, both instances also provided valuable lessons in the danger of using media to promote national pride by tapping anti-foreign sentiment, as this approach in each case led to unrest that quickly snowballed out of control, with restoration of order possible only through harsh measures that included the threat of arrest.

From a media perspective, both events used a hybrid of older tactics, combined with some newer ones that have come to characterize the modern Chinese media landscape, where central control remains the main goal but original reporting is also tolerated, both at the official and grassroots levels. In both cases, the government fanned the flames of nationalism and anti-foreign sentiment with liberal coverage of events in the early stages, only to fall back on older blackout tactics when situations got out of hand.

The embassy bombing saw the use of such tried-and-tested tactics as guerilla coverage, albeit only briefly, as well as the introduction of buzz-words like "hegemony" to drive home the outrage that China wanted to express. The anti-Japan demonstrations saw more sparing use of many of the conventional methods, although the public announcement format popped up toward the end when the government was trying to bring the situation under control. Many of the older tactics would appear less and less frequently with the passage of years, with some now completely retired. But to this day the nationalistic and anti-foreign cards remain effective weapons in the media's bag of tricks for showcasing the Party's accomplishments, distracting people from negative news, and keeping admiration for developed countries in check.

Chapter 11

SARS

Don't Spoil Our Party

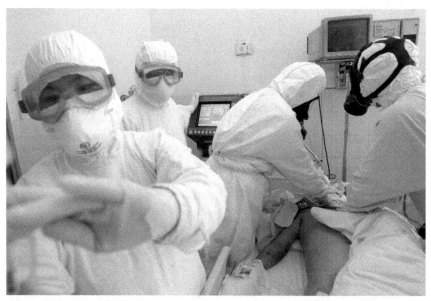

Chinese doctors and nurses wear protective suits as they tend to a SARS patient at a hospital in Beijing, May 1, 2003. China initially downplayed the SARS epidemic, but later became more open in its reporting under intense international pressure after the disease spread to Hong Kong and a number of other countries and regions.

Photo Credit: Reuters/OTHK

C ommon knowledge says that timing is everything, and China seemed to take that wisdom to heart in its handling of the Severe Acute Respiratory Syndrome (SARS) crisis of 2003. The outbreak lasted from November 2002 to July 2003, which saw the nation's media engaged in a massive cover-up for several months before finally coming clean on the matter. It would be an oversimplification to say that any single factor was behind the cover-up and news blackout that lasted from the beginning of the outbreak in November 2002 until the following April, even as a panic-fueled epidemic raged in adjacent Hong Kong and around the world. But the timing of the outbreak right in the middle of a landmark change of the guard in China's top leadership was probably the single issue most responsible for the delay, which experts would later say may have cost hundreds of people their lives due to lack of knowledge and advance warning about the disease.

To understand what was happening on the political stage in 2002, one needs to look at China's government since 1949, where top positions were almost always filled by top Communist Party officials, and distinctions between the Party itself and the government are poorly defined. For most of the nation's first three decades, when Mao reigned supreme, the selection process for government officials and terms of office was poorly defined and often not defined at all. Most of the highest officials were selected by Mao himself, either explicitly or through others acting with his backing. During that time, people came into and out of power mostly with the ebb and flow of political movements, again often with Mao's direct or indirect backing.

After Mao's death in 1976, the old system continued for more than a decade when Deng Xiaoping became the new kingmaker, personally selecting many of the country's top leaders even after he gave up all of his own official titles. But after Deng's death in 1997, a consensus evolved that a more stable form of government was needed at the top, even though the selection process for officials from the top on down remained largely opaque and driven by internal Party politics. With that in mind, the Party officially rolled out a new system of five-year terms for the nation's two top government posts starting in 2002 and 2003 with the selection of Hu Jintao as president and Wen Jiabao as premier, in what outsiders called China's first planned and peaceful transition of power under Communist rule. That system remains in effect today, with both Hu Jintao and Wen Jiabao stepping down after two terms to hand over their positions to two new leaders, Xi Jinping and Le Keqiang, who look likely to also serve 10 years in office before again yielding power to the next generation of leaders.

In the previous chapter on the anti-Japan demonstrations of 2005, I discussed how the National People's Congress, the meeting of China's legislature for the first few weeks of March each year, is a time when media may report only on good news, with a special focus on the Party, the government, and their agendas for the year ahead. From late 2002 and into the first three months of 2003, the good-news-only mantra was louder than usual, as the Party and government prepared to embark on their landmark leadership change that would result in the formal installation of a new president and premier for the next decade. Against that backdrop, it's not difficult to see how the outbreak of a major new disease like SARS would be viewed as not only a major distraction, but also a downbeat, bad-news story that would draw attention from the Party's biggest achievement to date in the slow process of political reform. Thus, some would say that the blackout on any discussion of SARS, both by government and medical officials and in nearly all media, was in no small part due to issues of timing.

A number of smaller elements also came to play in the media's treatment of SARS, including its near blackout that lasted almost four months after the start of the epidemic. One of those was also related to timing, in this case the timing of the Chinese New Year, which usually falls in late January or early February. In 2003, the Lunar New Year fell on February 1, right in between the original outbreak of the disease during the previous November in southern Guangdong province and the beginning of the National People's Congress in early March. While the focus on positive news is a general mantra for the Chinese media throughout the year, the imperative becomes even greater during the Lunar New Year, which is China's most important holiday that often sees family members travel for hundreds or even thousands of miles for annual hometown reunions, similar to Christmas in the West. During that time, negative news is severely frowned upon in the media and the focus remains on upbeat matters, national unity, and social harmony in general. Anything negative that does make it into the news is often given a positive spin, such as stories of local officials coming to the rescue of the thousands of people who are inevitably waylaid each year by snowstorms and other problems during the massive homecoming season.

Related to these factors of timing in the initial news blackout was the very real possibility that central officials were largely unaware of the outbreak for the first two months or more after the first appearance of SARS. Looking back at the way events unfolded, it appears that for the first two or three months of the outbreak local officials in Guangdong may have decided they could handle the situation on their own, in part due to the tradition of trying to downplay local bad news. In Chapter 4, one reporter described how the *neican* system of generating internal intelligence reports for central leaders was designed in part to find out what was really happening on the ground when local authorities tried to hide problems in their territory. In the case of the SARS crisis, the first Xinhua *neican* report on the outbreak apparently didn't reach Beijing until February 9, after which the central government made its first official report on the disease to the World Health Organization two days later. That timing would suggest that local authorities did indeed try—and succeed—in covering up the crisis, leaving top leaders in Beijing largely unaware of the existence of SARS before early February, or more than two months into the outbreak.

One final, broader factor behind the cover-up and media blackout was China's history of classifying just about any sort of major negative news as a "state secret." This classification could apply to just about anything sensitive in the first four decades of Communist rule, and was often used liberally for a wide range of matters—from major industrial accidents to the aftermath of natural disasters and other acts of nature beyond the government's control. A major earthquake in 1976 that left more than 200,000 dead in the city of Tangshan, about 100 miles from Beijing, was classified as one such secret for years after it happened, with little or no discussion, or other references allowed in the media or other public forums. The government would also determine whether other major disasters—be they natural or manmade—qualified as state secrets, with the result that most people often remained ignorant of major accidents and other negative incidents even when they happened in their own backyard. With that kind of tradition of secrecy, it's not difficult to imagine why something as new and unusual as SARS— with the potential to not only kill but also create mass panic—might be treated like a state secret by anxious government leaders.

More broadly, the whole state secret concept is closely tied to systemic problems with a Chinese political structure that sees most officials, from government to health and regulatory officials, more interested in their own political advancement than anything else. Many will try to hush up negative developments on their turf, often under the nebulous mantle that such matters are "state secrets," for fear their careers will suffer if they ultimately have to take the blame for such bad news.

One final factor that probably also played into China's reluctance to be more forthcoming on SARS was historical, as reflected by the country's old nickname of the "sick man of Asia" during the Hundred Years of Humiliation from the 19th to the first half of the 20th century, when China suffered one defeat after another at the hands of the colonial powers. As a true illness originating in China, SARS clearly had the power to dredge up memories of this period of history that most Chinese would prefer to forget. Whereas the previously mentioned reluctance by local officials to notify Beijing for the first few months of the outbreak was mostly due to the big leadership change and Lunar New Year holiday, memories of the sick-man image must also have played a part at a deeper psychological level.

Within the media, the mantra for "good news only" was clearly the biggest theme during the SARS period. This huge desire to avoid anything negative resulted in arguably one of the longest news blackouts in modern Chinese history, with word of the epidemic effectively barred from the press during its first four months, despite numerous signs of what was happening, especially outside China. Along related lines, another media theme was the positive spin that pervaded coverage when reporting finally did begin, reflecting a broader government directive to accentuate the positive. Despite the destructive nature of the disease and mortality rates that would reach as high as 10 percent, the media were told to focus their reports on what the government was doing to protect and cure victims, and what it was doing to educate the public to help prevent the spread of the disease.

The prevention effort included numerous educational campaigns, including one to raise awareness of the dangers of eating wild game, after wild animals were identified as the likely source of the disease. I was based in Hong Kong at that time, working for Reuters, and remember a trip I made into Guangdong to one such wild-game restaurant, called the Big Nose, where gloomy staff told me their business had dropped to zero during that time. Consumption of wild game dropped considerably after the epidemic and remains low to this date, testifying to the effectiveness of such government media campaigns that emphasized, among other things, sanitation and avoidance of eating wild game to prevent the spread of diseases.

Cracks in the Monolithic Façade

One other major theme to come out during SARS was the emergence of cracks in the façade of a state-run media machine that had previously been monolithic in the unity of its coverage, often down to the wording of articles themselves. In the new era of increasing independence for many newer media, the SARS period would see the start of an almost-defiant form of reporting in some bigger publications that have become much more assertive and independent than in the past. In the case of SARS, some media in Guangdong province were reportedly much more aggressive in covering SARS than those in other regions, even though early signals coming from Beijing were for muted or minimal coverage. One of the most aggressive in this case was the Southern Media Group, which has emerged as a major independent voice in China's media landscape today, writing stories that consistently irk both provincial and central propaganda officials.

In terms of actual events, the SARS outbreak began in November 2002, near the city of Foshan, not far from Guangzhou, the capital of

Guangdong province. Experts still aren't completely sure where the disease came from, but many now believe it originated in wild game consumed by humans, with the masked civet often cited as one of the most likely sources. The epidemic quietly spread through nearby towns and villages in its first three months, infecting 300 and killing at least five by the time Xinhua sent its first *neican* internal report to Beijing on February 9, 2003.

After issuing that first *neican* on SARS, Xinhua would go on to write more than a thousand additional internal reports on the disease, along with 2,700 public ones. Yet, even though the first *neican* went out on February 9 and was followed two days later by China's official confirmation to the World Health Organization (WHO), the country didn't allow widespread reporting on the matter in the domestic media until early April, including several hastily organized press conferences early in the month, where officials formally answered questions for the first time in a public forum.

Experts would later say that the outbreak peaked in Guangdong in the first two weeks of February, with new infections occurring at the rate of about 24.5 cases per day, as nearly 700 people came down with the disease and 28 died. As a resident of Hong Kong at that time, I remember that rumors of a strange new disease were already percolating through the grapevine by then, spread through the strong social networks between Hong Kongers and their many friends and relatives in nearby Guangdong. Those rumors resulted in a brief run on vinegar in local grocery stores after more rumors spread saying that vinegar could prevent or cure the mysterious disease.

Anyone who lived through the epidemic knows that despite the long blackout, China was finally forced to come clean on SARS under a huge amount of international pressure after the disease spread from Guangdong to Hong Kong, and from there infected people as far away as Singapore, the United States, and Canada. That foreign pressure was the direct result of the country's rapid opening up to the outside world starting in the 1980s, creating a new range of unfamiliar situations for a central government used to having complete control over the flow of information for anything that happened within its borders. China also faced big pressure from internal whistle-blowers, most notably a doctor named Jiang Yanyong, who forced the government to stop downplaying the situation and disclose the full magnitude of the outbreak.

More broadly speaking, the huge amount of overseas capital that had poured into China since the 1980s also led many foreign investors to demand details on what was happening, as many worried about the safety of the billions of dollars they had pumped into the country. Panicked about what was happening and with little information from official sources, many of the largest foreign-owned factories turned into massive fortresses at the height of the epidemic, with none of the thousands of employees who lived and worked in these gated compounds allowed to leave for weeks and even months during the crisis.

Facing all that pressure from outsiders, especially from worried officials at the World Health Organization, on February 11, 2003, China finally told the WHO about SARS, which at the time was still commonly referred to simply as atypical pneumonia. Once the word became official, the WHO eventually renamed the disease as SARS and embarked on a global campaign to better understand it and educate the public about the new disease.

After peaking in Guangdong in early February, SARS would go on to spread to Hong Kong, where it peaked in March. From there it spread to a number of other major Chinese cities and other countries, with Hong Kong, Singapore, Taiwan, and Canada the worst hit outside of mainland China, and Beijing the worst hit domestically. In the end, the disease would infect more than 8,000 people globally in more than 20 countries worldwide, killing nearly 10 percent of all those it infected. The largest number killed were in China, where 349 people died, followed by 299 in Hong Kong. While it made global headlines in 2003, the disease itself died a quiet death in the summer of that year, disappearing, never to return, the following year despite big concerns that it might reemerge in the next flu season.

After the epidemic ended in the summer of 2003, top European Union health official David Byrne would criticize China for making the epidemic worse by its failure to openly discuss the situation from the beginning. The World Health Organization's David Heymann would make similar comments later to a US Senate committee.

The subject of SARS remains a sensitive matter to this day, with the media seldom reporting on the disease or writing about the epidemic. Reflecting just how sensitive it is, rumors that a new outbreak had occurred at a military hospital in central China's Hebei province in 2012—nearly a decade after the original epidemic—prompted a quick denial from the government, as it sought to quash suspicions of a new cover-up. One man who said on his web site that the disease was a reappearance of SARS was quickly sentenced to two years in a "labor reeducation facility," and was officially branded in the media as a rumor monger whose actions had threatened social order.

Media coverage of SARS in the *People's Daily* can be divided into two distinct phases, one before the National People's Congress of March 2003, the annual meeting of China's legislature, and the other afterward. Following the media blackout from when the disease first appeared in November 2002 until early February the following year, the first phase of actual reporting began on February 12, 2003, when the *People's Daily* carried its first report in a small item that mentioned the disease. Coverage continued for the rest of February, but was limited to a few small stories on days scattered throughout the month. Nearly all mention of the disease then suddenly disappeared for most of March during the National People's Congress, although a trickle of articles did reappear late in the month after the congress had ended. April marked the start of the second phase of coverage, with much more comprehensive reporting starting on April 3 and running through the end of the epidemic.

The first report of the disease in the February 12 edition of the *People's Daily* set the tone for the rest of the month, with coverage limited to a brief, three-paragraph story that seems almost like an afterthought, appearing three days after central leaders received their own initial briefing through the first Xinhua *neican*. This first article, in which the disease was still being called atypical pneumonia, appeared at the bottom of page two and also came from Xinhua with the headline "Atypical Pneumonia Appears in Parts of Guangdong, Experts Point Out Only Prevention Is Necessary, No Need for Panic." It went on to say that 305 cases had been documented in the province so far, and five deaths had occurred. Symptoms were described for the disease, which was said to be contagious but controllable through preventative measures.

This article and all of the ones that followed in February contained little or no context in terms of when SARS first appeared and whether it had spread beyond Guangdong. This lack of background initially seems like a way to downplay the seriousness of the situation, but in hindsight could perhaps also indicate that Xinhua reporters and even central leaders themselves lacked access to the locally based doctors and other health officials who could answer such questions at this stage of the epidemic, as many of those with deeper knowledge of the situation were reportedly told by other Guangdong officials not to talk about it with any outsiders for the first few months of the outbreak.

After the first article, another one appeared three days later in the February 15 edition, setting a hopscotch-style pattern that would see two more reports occur four days after that on February 19 and February 20, before the story went into hibernation during the National People's Congress, not to appear again until late March. Like the first report, the second mention of SARS on February 15 was placed in an unassuming position at the bottom of page two of the *People's Daily*, again in a brief Xinhua story headlined "Controls Against Guangdong's Atypical Pneumonia Proving Effective, Most Patients Recovering Completely and Leaving the Hospital." The story, which pointed out that 80 percent of infected people had left the hospital, seems to have been the government's way of saying that the problem was under control. The report included little other information in the way of new statistics or other background about the disease.

After February 15 the story briefly disappears from the *People's Daily* as coverage during the next two days was devoted to the appointment of Hu Jintao and Wen Jiabao as the new Communist Party secretary and premier, respectively. The story reappears on February 19, this time sinking even further inside the paper to a highly clinical editorial-style report on page 5, analyzing the actual virus and discussing how to treat and prevent it, with little or no actual news on developments in the outbreak. This relegation to the back page continued with the newspaper's final story on the subject before the start of the National People's Congress, appearing on February 20 in an article on page 11. If the previous clinical article marked a trend toward a more oblique approach to coverage, this final article was even more obscure, discussing a resident in the Guangdong city of Panyu who had been fined the equivalent of nearly $1,000 for killing and eating a masked civet. It's unclear to me whether this story was even directly related to SARS, although the running of such a regional story in a national newspaper

like the *People's Daily* on a subject that would later be so clearly tied to
the spread of SARS seems too closely linked to be coincidence.

After this February 20 report, SARS disappears from the *People's
Daily*, which for most of March was preoccupied with coverage of
the National People's Congress. Ironically, that month would mark the
peaking of the crisis in Hong Kong and the spread of the disease
around the world. Despite all of that, the *People's Daily* remained steadfast in its devotion to political coverage in Beijing for the first three
weeks of the month, in an old-style news blackout, even as many
throughout China were aware of what was happening thanks to the
relatively pervasive presence of the Internet and cell phone text messaging by then.

The first and only mention of the epidemic in March came on the
20th day of the month, just after the congress had ended. It was made in
a locally written *People's Daily* article that didn't even make it into the
newspaper's front section but rather appeared on the front of the East
China section for stories on Shanghai and the Yangtze River Delta area.
This article said there had been no reports of SARS in Shanghai and a
couple of other major nearby cities, in what looks to me like a safe way
to back into the subject by reporting from an unaffected region while
reemphasizing that the disease was under control and posed no danger. More significantly, this report also contained the first mention of
the epidemic raging outside China, citing unnamed other reports saying that cases had occurred in Hong Kong and Singapore, and that their
numbers were growing.

Two more short articles appeared on the inside pages of the
People's Daily on April 3 and April 4 before the blackout on more
comprehensive reporting was finally lifted. The April 4 story contained some of the first new information released by China at one
of its first official press conferences on the subject, where a health
official revealed that the outbreak had begun three to four months
before. The sense of frustration that many reporters at the press conference must have felt at the lack of information to date is on display
when the official also defends China's initial failure to tell the World
Health Organization about the disease, saying it was not required
to do so under the WHO's rules because the new disease had never
been legally defined as contagious.

Breaking Open the Coverage

The first major report on the subject, launching what I earlier described as the second phase of coverage, appears in the April 5 edition of the *People's Daily*, though again still on page two, in a watershed day as China shifted to a new policy of openness on the subject. The big story that day was an edited transcript from the earlier press conference by the country's health minister, which forms the centerpiece of three articles on SARS that took up nearly all of page two. The headline of the main story underscores that from this point onward China would be quick and forthcoming in providing information on the latest developments, with the health minister saying that relevant government agencies needed to "establish and perfect" their reporting mechanisms.

I personally attended a smaller press conference in Guangzhou on April 8, which was a bit like something from *The Twilight Zone* in the way that it came together. My editor called me to his office the afternoon of the day before, told me he had just been told the event would take place early the next morning, and asked did I want to go. At that point we knew very little about what was happening in China, despite the proximity of Guangdong to Hong Kong. Still, the risks seemed acceptable enough that I agreed to go, starting a hasty but strange odyssey that saw me get a visa to China in record time, and then cross the border in the early evening, where I and another international correspondent hired a car to drive us to Guangzhou. We literally had no idea what we would find when we reached the city, the epicenter of the disease, and were surprised on our arrival to see that everything looked perfectly normal. We went on to attend the press conference the next morning, where health officials said the disease had peaked months ago in the area, explaining the relative return to normal by our arrival. The next day the local government bent over backward to answer all of our questions, taking me to a local children's hospital to talk to health officials there about how the disease had affected children, and giving me a newly published book on SARS containing graphic pictures from the hospitals where people were treated at the height of the crisis.

From this point forward multiple stories on SARS appeared in the *People's Daily* each day, most often still on the inside pages but also occasionally on the front page, usually in connection with stories on top leaders discussing the subject. This period saw a steady stream of updates on the number of cases and development of the disease, though the newspaper clearly focuses on more positive elements like prevention and cures, along with words of reassurance from top officials that everyone was being treated and the epidemic was under control. Good examples of the positive spin include an article based on an interview with a recovered victim on April 9; a photo of two patients, still in their hospital clothes, who were up and about with smiles on their faces, accompanied by the headline "SARS Can Be Prevented"; and stories on top government leaders meeting with outside officials to show that they were working together to bring the crisis under control. From this point onward, SARS finally began receiving the coverage it deserved as a global news story. That level of reporting would continue until the disease finally subsided with the arrival of summer.

Two major themes emerged from reporters I talked with who worked through the SARS period. One was the frustration they felt at being unable to report on the epidemic despite the obvious signs of it all around them. The other was a lack of awareness about the magnitude of the epidemic, which led many simply not to pay the matter much attention until after the central government became more forthcoming about it.

A Shanghai-based reporter in the former group noted that bans on writing about contagious diseases actually date back to the Maoist era. He said he and his colleagues were also well aware of the broader ban on negative reports during the National People's Congress, and that few reporters would have bothered to pitch or write stories on SARS at the time because they knew that they would never be published. Deciding to take a chance despite the odds against him, he wrote a lengthy report on the disease, including a discussion of the methods being used to try to control it and on the people who had died. Not surprisingly, the report was rejected by the Shanghai city authorities, who even then still had the right to approve or veto articles on such a sensitive topic. The reporter said he wasn't too surprised or even disappointed at the rejection, as he knew the odds were already heavily against him, though he did throw the article in his supervisor's face on hearing that it would never be published.

Another reporter in central China said that he and his colleagues had learned about SARS through cell phone text messages from friends in neighboring Guangdong. Around the same time, he said, everyone received a Propaganda Ministry directive forbidding the publication of articles on the subject, saying such reports could influence social stability. In the end, the domestic media were finally allowed to report on the subject after newly installed President Hu Jintao and Premier Wen Jiaobao came out and openly discussed the subject after the end of the National People's Congress. Even so, everyone was under strict orders to write only upbeat reports, including how seriously the government was treating the matter and what it was doing to tackle the disease, he said.

Two other reporters I interviewed said they were largely unaware of how grave the situation was until leaders in Beijing finally gave the green light for in-depth reporting. One was even based in Guangdong, not far from the disease's epicenter, showing just how effectively local officials kept the matter quiet by quickly centralizing victims in a small number of hospitals and then strictly instructing doctors and other health officials not to discuss the situation with anyone. This reporter commented that many people in the area knew that something was going on by Chinese New Year in early February of that year, but everyone assumed the situation wasn't that serious since they had heard nothing to indicate otherwise. He said it wasn't until March that people learned that some patients had actually died from SARS, although even then newspapers were barred from writing major reports on the situation until after the end of the National People's Congress.

One other Beijing reporter with links to the *neican* system said that if SARS had occurred in the 1950s or 1960s, it most likely would have been handled only through internal reports with no mention ever made in the public media. He added that this kind of case would usually fall under the supervision of a specific government office, in this case the health department, which would run the show independently without bothering central leaders. It was only after the huge foreign pressure that top leaders finally realized the gravity of the situation and got directly involved, including allowing more open public discussion, he said.

From the perspective of the media, SARS saw some traditional tactics from previous decades used in newspapers and broadcasts, but also marked a watershed by showing that Chinese society had opened up too much for the practice of many other traditional tactics. The biggest theme, which continues to this day, is the directive for all media to focus on positive news in general, and to accentuate the positive when the telling of bad news is unavoidable. This emphasis contrasts sharply with that of the West, where media tend to focus on conflict, often leading to the Chinese perception that the foreign media have a bias against their country. The case of SARS also demonstrates that the good-news-only theme is especially imperative during big events like the National People's Congress and the Beijing Olympics, which are designed to showcase the government's achievements and focus on its agenda.

At the same time, SARS represented one of Beijing's final attempts to keep a major global news event out of the domestic media. The eventual abortion of the early news blackout is significant because it showed central leaders that such blackouts were no longer feasible due to China's growing integration with the outside world. Related to this trend is the rise of new media, most notably cell phone text messaging and increasingly the Internet, which allow for real-time sharing of news and information from anywhere in the world. This makes the suppression of big news often difficult or impossible, and even undesirable, since such news vacuums often cause rumors to sprout and quickly spread. More broadly, SARS was also a watershed event in the government's concept of "state secrets," with many matters once classified as highly confidential now becoming fair game for reporting by the mainstream media. At the end of the day, SARS was not only a lethal disease in human terms, but also marked the death knell for one of the government's oldest media tools, namely the carefully timed release or outright withholding of information that allowed it to manage public perceptions.

Chapter 12

The Beijing Olympics and Sichuan Earthquake

Rallying Points

Chinese celebrate as the countdown of the last 1,000 days to the 2008 Olympic Games begins in front of an official countdown clock in China. The games received huge coverage in China's media, spotlighting not only the nation's athletic prowess but also its huge economic strides since the launch of market reforms in the 1980s.

Photo Credit: Reuters/OTHK

I f the Belgrade bombing of 1999 and anti-Japanese movement of 2005 were about whipping up anti-foreign sentiment to bolster Chinese nationalism, then the 2008 Beijing Olympics represented another approach to playing on Chinese nationalism to advance the Party's agenda. Rather than thrash the foreigners, the Chinese media turned their spotlight inward during this massive event and used it to showcase the nation's huge progress over the past two decades, taking any opportunity to show the Chinese public that progress, especially when it came in the form of praise from foreigners. Of course, nothing ever goes completely according to script, and such a high-profile event in Beijing would become a natural lightning rod for numerous protest groups to draw attention to China's shortcomings.

But the biggest unscripted event of all would come completely out of the blue when a magnitude 8.0 earthquake hit a remote area of Sichuan province on May 12, just three months before the Olympics, leaving tens of thousands dead and hundreds of thousands more injured. Compounding an already-bad situation, the collapse of numerous schools during the quake, killing thousands of students as they attended classes, would lead to accusations that this manmade element of the disaster was the direct result of shoddy construction due to official corruption.

This chapter will look at the media coverage for these two very different events, which both occurred around the same time. While the two were very different in their basic premises, they shared the common theme of the government mobilizing the media to rally people around a common cause, one in a time of crisis and the other in a highly scripted debutante-style event to celebrate China's coming out on the global stage.

In terms of context, the big story behind the Olympics was China's amazing growth, which saw its economy expand by about 10 percent each year for much of the 1990s and the first decade of the 21st century, lifting millions of people out of poverty. Just two years after the curtain closed on the Olympics, China would officially surpass Japan in 2010 to become the world's second-biggest economy behind only the United States—an amazing feat for a country that barely made it into the ranks of the 10 largest economies just 20 years earlier. In many ways the Olympics were a celebration of that growth story, with China splashing out billions of dollars on new state-of-the-art stadiums and infrastructure to host the games. That spending spree would later lead to criticism in some of the country's more independent media and also in social media on the Internet. But in the run-up to the games the buzz was mostly positive—and indeed most media were under strict orders to write only upbeat stories—as the nation literally counted down the days to the start of the event in carefully updated countdown clocks that sprouted up all over the country.

The rapid economic development was a cause of national pride and celebration for many, but the Sichuan earthquake, along with Olympic-related protests and even a few terrorist attacks, would also remind everyone that numerous growing pains had come with the fast growth. Protests and terror attacks would highlight the fact that many of China's ethnic minorities still felt they were second-class citizens, despite Beijing's claims that many were treated better than the majority ethnic Han Chinese. The Sichuan earthquake would also cast a painful spotlight on the millions of Chinese still living in peasant-like conditions in the countryside, revealing the less-affluent side of a nation where economic development had brought huge new wealth to some while many others remained in poverty.

To truly understand the significance of the Olympics for China, one needs to delve beyond the actual games and look at the tradition of sports in Communist China, and indeed the Communist world in general during the Cold War. At a clear economic disadvantage to the more affluent West in the years after World War II, many Eastern Bloc countries quickly realized they could still stir up national pride by winning medals at big global sporting events. From a very practical point of view, the investment needed to select and cultivate the elite super-athletes who would bring home the medals was relatively small, requiring only living and training costs.

This emphasis on sports helped to produce the consistently strong showings at the Olympics and other major sporting events by the Soviet Union and its Eastern Bloc allies during most of the Cold War. Many of these countries developed highly specialized systems to cultivate their athletes from an early age by sending them to special training schools and then treating them as national heroes when they won major events.

China didn't participate very much in global sporting events during Mao's lifetime, largely because most of the world's industrial nations recognized the Nationalist government in Taiwan as the representative of China and therefore refused to allow participation from mainland teams claiming to represent the country. All of that changed after the United Nations shifted its recognition to the Communist government in Beijing in 1971, with the result that the mainland could send teams to global sporting events as the sole representative of China. When that happened, Chinese leaders would quickly turn to the Soviet-style system of elite schools to begin training super-athletes to bolster national pride at home and show off the nation's growing clout on the global stage.

The system and its single-mindedness are a regular source of scrutiny for Western media, which like to point out its many shortcomings. Reports frequently mention the clinical way in which children are recruited for the system and taken from their homes at very early ages based on their body types and coordination. The vast majority of those who enter the system never succeed, leaving many with few or no marketable skills when they are ultimately forced to leave a network that has nurtured them for all of their lives.

One poignant case became a source for national introspection in 2011, when a Beijing resident spotted a man performing tricks on the street for money, whom he recognized as Zhang Shangwu, a former world-class gymnast. The person took a photo and posted it on Weibo, China's equivalent of Twitter, touching off a national debate on how the nation often failed to take care of former athletes who couldn't find work after their sporting careers. In Zhang's case, he was forced to retire after suffering an injury in 2003. With little education beyond his athletic training, Zhang had turned to crime and was arrested for stealing equipment from a sports school in 2007.

Whereas Zhang's story touched off a national debate, stories of other athletes who failed to make the global cut seldom make it into the headlines. By comparison, athletes who bring home world championship medals are worshipped as national heroes, receiving all kinds of government perks and rewards, and also earning increasingly big money through endorsement deals from both the private sector and China's big state-run companies.

Related to the cultivation of athletes, Beijing has increasingly realized over the past two decades that big sporting events themselves provide a good bang for the buck in terms of trumpeting government accomplishments and rallying people around positive, patriotic causes. Since successfully hosting the Asian Games in 1990, Beijing has embraced the staging of big shows, especially sporting competitions, by allowing a growing number of cities to host their own major events, often taking a spare-no-expense approach to building the new stadiums and infrastructure needed for such shows. Opening and closing ceremonies for these events have become extravaganzas in their own right, complete with parades, dances, and other activities designed to highlight the accomplishments of the host city, the Communist Party, and Chinese culture in general. Such events are often dominated by Chinese athletes, again providing a platform to showcase the country's athletic achievements. Most of these sport fests receive abundant media coverage, especially from central state TV and Xinhua, with local media also strongly encouraged to write about these positive stories.

The earthquake in Sichuan was obviously quite unlike these major staged events that easily lent themselves to feel-good stories. But even before the earthquake, as early as the 1990s, Chinese propaganda officials had already begun to discover the value of giving the media broad access to cover natural disasters. In 1998, when major floods occurred on the Yangtze River, the government noticed that media coverage of such disasters allowed it to showcase relief efforts that helped local people to cope and kept bad situations from becoming worse. When more flooding occurred on the Yangtze in 2011, the government again encouraged reporting on the disaster, with a special focus on the positive role in limiting the impact played by the controversial Three Gorges Dam, China's biggest engineering project.

The government now openly encourages reporting of smaller floods and other natural disasters, which inevitably occur each year in a country of China's size. At the same time, it is also careful to monitor news reports to make sure that the messages remain positive, and it quickly steps in to stamp out darker overtones, for example, when government corruption or negligence is uncovered. Beijing's attitude has become one of increasing confidence in its ability to handle natural disasters, but clearly an element of insecurity remains as reflected by its hypersensitivity to showing any form of weakness.

In terms of media themes, the Olympics was clearly an extravaganza for spotlighting achievements and prosperity. This theme was expressed repeatedly in every conceivable way in the coverage of the games, from stories on champion athletes of humble origins to ones on the advances in China's roads and telecom networks that made the holding of this huge event possible. The promotion of sports in general was also a major theme during this period, as part of the government's focus on more abstract issues like strength and good health, helping to further distance modern China from the sick-man image of the pre-Communist era.

While accomplishment, prosperity, progress, and health were all in the spotlight, reporting on any bad news in connection with the games, including accidents, disturbances created by construction, and over-spending and other waste, was strongly frowned upon. Nearly all of the reporters I talked to told me they were explicitly instructed to avoid any negative reports related to the Olympics, and that similar orders routinely go out around other big events like the National People's Congress, the annual meeting of China's legislature in Beijing. The good-news-only mantra gets even stronger just before and during such events, with negative news in any form, even if it's completely unrelated to the event, being strongly discouraged.

One story involving a young performer who was abruptly cut from the opening ceremony just before the games began became popular fodder for foreign media, which saw it as reflecting Beijing's overzealous desire to put on the perfect show, even though the story was largely banned from domestic coverage. In that instance, a seven-year-old girl named Yang Peiyi, who was originally set to sing at the opening ceremony, was dismissed just days before the event after a senior Party member reportedly saw her at a rehearsal and decided that her chubby face and crooked teeth might give a less-than-perfect impression. Sympathetic comments from ordinary Chinese on the Internet were quickly deleted, and the subject became largely taboo for both official and new media as the games began. The carefully orchestrated avoidance of nearly anything negative in the run-up to and during the Olympics would later lead many outsiders to comment that coverage of the games in China's domestic media felt more like the telling of a children's fairytale than a real-world event.

Resurrecting the Laundry List

While many of the older media themes and devices from the Mao era were largely discarded by the time of the Olympics, one that did continue to appear was the old "laundry list" style of reporting from earlier days. We saw such list-style reporting in the Nixon trip of 1972, where many stories were often nothing more than long compilations of the names of Party and government officials who attended a particular event, reflecting who was in charge in order of importance. During the Olympics this older format was on display with the publication of a steady stream of short reports, especially just before the opening ceremony, of each and every foreign government leader or dignitary who had come from abroad to attend the event. Another throwback to earlier days also came as central media like Xinhua and the *People's Daily* revived the older practice of carrying stories that were simply reprints of other material, such as speeches by top leaders and song lyrics.

The Sichuan earthquake was also notable for several media themes, most importantly extensive coverage of a natural disaster to spotlight the government's rescue and recovery work. In the days after the quake, I remember being mesmerized by the steady stream of reports on TV and in the papers on a number of lakes that had formed as a result of damming by avalanches, and how army engineers were working around the clock to relieve the pressure before these makeshift dams burst and destroyed towns below them that were already heavily damaged. These and other reports of people being pulled from the wreckage and relief supplies coming in over difficult routes after main arteries were destroyed flooded the newspapers for weeks after the quake, rallying the nation around the recovery effort.

While the government found most of the earthquake coverage to its liking, the media's relatively free hand in writing about the disaster would reinforce how difficult it now was for central officials to manage major news as they did in the past through heavy-handed tactics like media blackouts. If the SARS epidemic of 2003 demonstrated the difficulty of maintaining such blackouts in the face of a major story, the Sichuan earthquake drove home that point for propaganda officials accustomed to telling the media what they could and couldn't cover. The earthquake proved once and for all that traditional media blackouts were no longer an option in the Internet age, although the government continues to use this tactic for smaller, localized events such as crimes, corruption, and industrial accidents and pollution.

Chronologically speaking, China's history of trying to host the Olympics dates back to 1993, when the country made its first bid for the 2000 games. Australia would ultimately win the right to host those games, resulting in huge disappointment for many Chinese. The country's luck would change eight years later, in 2001, when Beijing tried again and this time was picked to host the 2008 Olympics. The city then embarked on a multibillion-dollar spending and construction spree that most modern Olympic hosts must undertake, building an Olympic village complete with the Bird's Nest stadium that would come to symbolize the games.

Most major preparations were complete and the Torch Relay was underway in the spring of 2008 when the Sichuan earthquake struck on May 12, just three months before the opening ceremony. State data would later put the death toll at 70,000, with another 375,000 injured. An intensive rescue effort lasting weeks would ensue, capturing most media attention during that time and kicking off a recovery effort that continues to this day. But as the Olympics drew nearer, attention would shift back to the big event in Beijing, with the spotlight firmly fixed on the city when the games formally began on August 8, 2008.

Since the Olympics were continually in the Chinese media in the years building up to the event, I will focus my analysis on a few key moments, including the announcement in 2001 that Beijing would be the host and on the days leading up to and including the opening ceremony.

Given the intense level of domestic media coverage, I have chosen to focus on several major themes from this time rather than what was written on any single day. In a divergence from previous chapters, I have also focused my look at the Olympics on reports in Xinhua's English-language news service. The reasoning for this is two-pronged. Whereas Olympics articles in the English service were certainly abundant, their volume was nowhere near that in the domestic Chinese-language media, helping to tune out some of the background noise and focus on the bigger picture. At the same time, a look at the English-language coverage gives a sense of how China wanted the rest of the world to see it, since the Olympics was akin to a global coming-out party for the nation and Xinhua's English service is the government's primary mouthpiece for foreign readers.

In looking at coverage of the Olympics and Sichuan earthquake, I will start with the latter, followed by a broader look at Olympic media themes to try to stick as closely as possible to the order of real-world events. Before taking a detailed look at the earthquake, it is important to realize that due to its obviously unscripted nature the government had no way to plan how it would approach media coverage of such a catastrophic event, which came right as Olympic buzz was rising to fever pitch. As a result, one detects a certain hesitancy in the earliest reports from big state media, as central leaders considered how they wanted to spin this event and what kind of coverage to allow. All the reporters I talked to told similar stories that reflected the government's initial indecision as well as its final approach.

In the days right after the quake, most reporters who came to Sichuan were quickly ordered by on-site propaganda and other officials to return to their home bases and use only the official Xinhua reports for their coverage. But in an age where the media were used to taking more risks, many reporters refused to go back. Instead they continued to make their way to the hardest-hit areas to do their own reporting. Government officials finally realized there was nothing they could do to block this younger and bolder group of reporters from their mission, and soon stopped issuing threats. As the first few days of reporting went by, propaganda officials then began to realize that allowing wider access to disaster scenes for both domestic and foreign media was actually working to its advantage, as most of the earliest reports focused on the massive rescue effort. As that happened, the government not only backed down from its original stance of trying to keep reporters out of the region but actually encouraged them to come, and even provided limited assistance after their arrival.

Looking at the actual coverage, May 12, 2008, the day of the quake, was just another day in the *People's Daily*. The top story was about building beautiful villages, another commemorated the newspaper's 60th anniversary, and a third story was about a government leader meeting with his counterpart from Slovenia. The first earthquake story appeared the next day, May 13, with a headline at the top right of the front page reporting a magnitude-7.8 earthquake had hit Sichuan. The story describes what President Hu Jintao and Premier Wen Jiabao were doing to address the disaster, including Wen's departure to the quake zone to personally assist in the rescue effort. The other main story, also in the lead position on page one, described the central committee of the Communist Party holding an emergency meeting on the situation, and a photo of Wen at the scene is also featured. But in what some Westerners might consider an unusual decision, nearly half of the front page coverage that day was focused on other matters, all involving the activities of other high-level leaders engaged in a range of meetings with officials from the United States, Slovenia, and Guinea-Bissau. I attribute this odd mix of articles in part to the *People's Daily's* tendency to focus on anything involving Party and government leaders, but also to the previously discussed uncertainty on how to handle coverage of this massive event—the biggest natural disaster to hit China in the post-1978 Reform era.

That indecision is also reflected on page two of the May 13 *People's Daily*, which contained no mention of the earthquake but rather listed 16 major achievements of the Communist Party, in what appeared to be part of an ongoing series in the lead-up to the Olympics. The earthquake didn't reappear until page four, where the two top stories again featured Premier Wen. It wasn't until page five that the paper devoted itself completely to the disaster, with seven articles on the topic, in what looks like the kind of coverage one would expect throughout a major Western newspaper following such a disaster. After page five, mention of the earthquake disappeared for the rest of the May 13 edition, which returned to prewritten stories on topics such as the 30th anniversary of economic reform and other economic and social news. From a practical standpoint, this somewhat-schizophrenic coverage probably reflected the reality that the newspaper may have simply lacked the reporting resources to fill an entire edition with earthquake coverage and was doing its best under the circumstances. But my sense is that this odd mix of disaster coverage with business-as-usual stories also reflected the hesitancy and indecision that many of the paper's editors were feeling about how exactly they should report on the disaster.

The focus sharpened a bit the next day, May 14, with the entire top of the front page dedicated to the earthquake-related activities of President Hu and Premier Wen, the country's top two government officials. The broader coverage paints Hu as the man in charge of the operations from Beijing. Among other things, the paper reports Hu has mobilized 50,000 troops to assist in the rescue work and has also taken a sympathy call from US President George Bush. Meantime, Wen was the man in the field, visiting victims and assisting in the rescue effort, with coverage of him touring the disaster zone and comforting crying children. By this time, propaganda officials must have realized that coverage of the rescue effort could be a potent force in shaping public opinion, putting the Party's power, determination, and compassion all on display, while the disaster itself could rally the people of China together to address this national calamity. With opinions still possibly divided on what level of coverage was most appropriate, the bottom of page one that day was still taken up mostly with accounts of other top officials engaged in various unrelated foreign affairs.

On this second day after the quake, most of the inside pages of the front section were now devoted to earthquake coverage, with some interesting older media formats appearing, though only for this single day. Page two contained one of the older-style umbrella banners at the top of the page, calling on everyone to "Be of one heart, unified in purpose, move forward in the face of adversity, and remain steadfast in the face of repeated obstacles." Another older format reappeared on page three, in the form of a long list of international leaders who sent their sympathies and offered assistance. Interestingly, the banner format would disappear after this first day and the use of the list format would also drop off sharply, unlike an earlier era when such items would have appeared for several more days as part of the old guerilla coverage. Perhaps by now leaders had realized the true magnitude of the disaster and no longer felt compelled to use these older tactics to raise the government's profile in the eyes of readers.

Coverage of the quake filled the first five pages of the *People's Daily*'s May 14 issue, after which the story was mostly absent except for a few more articles on page nine. While Olympics coverage was side-lined during this time, one story, on the Torch Relay making its way through China as it headed toward Beijing, did manage to make a low-profile appearance on that day, on page eight.

This pattern of coverage would continue for the next few days, with increasing focus on the disaster and a spotlight on the actions of top leaders and the Party as other news faded into the background. By May 15, the *People's Daily* had even included a box at the bottom of the front page with a list of many quake-related stories on the inside pages, in a nod to the public's strong demand for news on the disaster that state-run media could now provide as more reporters and rescuers arrived on the scene. Playing to this demand, the number of photos from the quake scene also grew in the following days, with images slanted toward positive elements like victims being cared for and rescuers hard at work, along with the usual photos of top leaders meeting victims. In a sign of the growing openness toward disaster coverage, the *People's Daily*'s May 15 edition even carried a report on all of the foreign media arriving in Sichuan to cover the quake. This day also included a report containing one of the first casualty counts, stating that nearly 15,000 people had been killed or injured—a sharp reversal from the situation with the Tangshan earthquake of 1976, when that kind of information was still considered a state secret.

In addition to President Hu and Premier Wen, the words of a growing number of other high officials commenting on the disaster would be published in the *People's Daily* for the duration of the earthquake reporting period. Numerous reports also would appear on the many government and Party-level meetings that took place in response to the disaster—items that probably wouldn't have qualified as news in the West, but were designed to show how the Party was taking action. Finally, articles would also focus on the People's Liberation Army, which was spearheading the rescue effort on the ground, reflecting the Party's recurrent efforts to build positive sentiment toward the military, which had suffered after the Tiananmen crackdown of 1989. My look at this period ends on May 17, five days after the quake, when President Hu officially traveled to the region for his first visit, solidifying the pattern of coverage for weeks to come.

Two younger reporters I talked to said they first started to realize the magnitude of the situation shortly after the quake when they received calls from contacts in Sichuan on the afternoon of May 12. Both said their papers immediately started sending reporters to the scene without waiting for guidance from Beijing, resulting in a wide array of reports in regional media over the first few days. About three or four days after the quake, the Propaganda Ministry finally put out an order to stop sending people, saying the presence of so many reporters could compromise the rescue effort. But by then it was largely too late to stop the flow, as so many reporters were already in the area and no one wanted to leave. Then, in a sharp reversal, propaganda authorities changed their stance two or three days later, telling the media to send more people and report even more on the rescue effort.

One reporter said that most reporters understood that propaganda officials wanted them to report only on positive elements of the story, most notably the massive rescue effort. While many of the initial stories were indeed positive, a growing number of negative stories also began to crop up within days from these regional reporters, many involving the previously mentioned collapse of numerous schools due to suspected shoddy construction, resulting in the deaths of thousands of children. While officials initially tolerated these negative reports, they finally intervened and ordered everyone to stop writing such stories after the first couple of weeks, and started encouraging people to return home soon afterward. This reporter said Beijing adopted a relatively open attitude toward the media during this time, possibly because so much international attention was already focused on China due to the upcoming Olympics. Given that attention, leaders didn't want to risk engaging in any heavy-handed actions that might compromise the nation's multibillion-dollar coming-out party that had been years in the making.

Coverage of the earthquake recovery would continue for much of the next couple of months, although stories on the Olympics would make a quiet comeback and would once again become the focus of attention in July as the nation turned back to this feel-good story of national accomplishment. Again, rather than focus on coverage from individual days in the run-up to the August 8 opening ceremony, my analysis will look at several of the major themes in the media during this period of intense Olympic coverage starting from late July 2008 and running through the opening ceremony.

Proud to Be Chinese

The biggest of these themes is one I call "proud to be Chinese." This theme covers many of the articles with patriotic overtones, which were designed to make people feel good about themselves through feel-good stories about their country and its accomplishments under Communist Party leadership, both in connection with the country's ability to stage the Olympics and also in a broader economic sense. Xinhua's original English-language headline when China was first awarded the games in 2001, "Beijing Wins Honor to Host 2008 Olympics," nicely captured the tone by showing both the honor that the Chinese felt at being selected, as well as the pride that they should feel for their ability to host such a big event. In effect, this headline indirectly referenced the huge strides that China had made, which brought the nation to the point where it could stage what is arguably one of the world's top regularly scheduled global events.

Closer to the event, Xinhua would also carry a steady stream of stories focused on how far China had come, with headlines like "Scholar: Gathering of World Leaders for Olympics Shows Positive View of China" and "Survey Says Beijing Olympics Set to Improve West's View of China." Many of these articles drew heavily on the inference that China's staging of the Olympics had put it in the exclusive company of an elite group of similarly prosperous countries that had both the resources and global respect to stage such an event. The national pride theme also came across clearly on opening night, which Xinhua declared as "China's Night of Joy, Pride as Olympics Ceremony Captures World." The story went on to lead with an image of exuberant Chinese cheering throughout the country, from their homes, outdoors in front of big screens at public venues, and even in the remotest villages, as the momentous event kicked off.

The second major theme, linked closely to the show of national-ism, was of praise and acknowledgment from developed countries for China's achievements. One of the biggest displays of this theme came in the days before the opening ceremony, with the previously mentioned laundry list of scores of top government officials arriving from around the world. This second theme also included numerous stories showing how the rest of the world was paying special attention to the Beijing Olympics, confirming the country's place of importance on the world stage. Two headlines focused specifically on coverage from the United States, with one August 7 headline pointing out that NBC, the TV net-work that was broadcasting the games in the United States, was pro-viding "unprecedented" broadcasts of these particular games. A headline two days later, the day after the opening ceremony, followed in a similar vein, noting that "Olympic Opening Coverage Has Best Ratings, NBC Says," again confirming the importance of these particular games in the eyes of Americans.

The US acknowledgment of the importance of the games appeared again that same day in two other stories. One was a simple report sum-marizing a *Los Angeles Times* article about the pride the Chinese felt at watching the opening ceremonies in Beijing. The other, head-lined "NASDAQ Puts up Celebration Message on Beijing Olympics," described the stock exchange's congratulatory message that was flashed on its tower in Times Square, again showing that one of the world's top financial markets was also paying its respects to the games. For any-one who hadn't picked up on the theme, yet another Xinhua headline that same day provided a list-style roundup of how other world media reported on the opening ceremony, with glowing reports ranging from media in Japan, South Korea, and Thailand in Asia, to the *Wall Street Journal* and *New York Times* in the United States and the BBC in Britain.

Another theme from the coverage saw a range of articles focused on China's actual accomplishments, typified by a July 14 headline not-ing "Olympic Games to Advance Modernization in China." One other theme was what I like to call "no news is too small," which saw items that would never qualify for coverage under normal circumstances tak-ing on much greater importance because they involved someone saying something Olympic-related. Included in this theme were the previ-ously mentioned many individual stories of foreign dignitaries arriving for the opening ceremony. Another headline typical of these reports was a standalone interview on August 8, the day of the opening ceremony, with the president of Vanuatu, a small Pacific island nation, proclaiming in a headline, "China Doing Wonderful Job in Preparing for Olympics: Vanuatuan President." One final theme saw a return to some older practices from the Maoist era, which included not only lists of dignitaries but also the full text of speeches and even songs as standalone stories. In the former category was the text of a toast by President Hu at a welcoming luncheon on August 8 while the latter included a piece that was simply the lyrics of the official Olympic theme song, "You and Me," in a throwback to the Cultural Revolution when song lyrics and music were often printed in the newspapers as well.

One reporter from south China said his newspaper sent a team of about 20 reporters and editors to the games, a large contingent for most regional papers of that size, reflecting not only the importance of the games domestically but also the fact that central leaders wanted the event well covered. He said that for much of 2008, the Propaganda Ministry put out periodic guidelines about what would be happening in the coming weeks and months, and what to focus on, though many reporters never saw those reports. Still, everyone knew that only positive stories were allowed.

He also noted that when an American who had come to see the games was stabbed to death at Beijing's landmark Drum Tower in an apparently random attack the day after the opening ceremony, no Chinese media reported on it, even though the story received relatively wide coverage in the West. There was no specific ban on covering the crime, he said, but no one wanted to report on an incident that looked relatively random and was in sharp contrast to the upbeat note of the rest of the coverage. Similarly, when a nationally renowned star Chinese hurdler had to pull out of the games at the last minute due to an injury, in a huge disappointment for the country, this reporter said his paper wrote extensively about the news, but again put a more positive spin on it, saying it was natural for athletes to sustain that kind of injury.

Another reporter in central China said he and his colleagues were strictly forbidden from reporting on the negative effects of China's rapid industrialization, such as pollution and industrial accidents, in the month before the games. He also personally observed that many areas on the Torch Relay in China were being sealed off from most media and all outsiders, and considered proposing a story on the subject. But after more consideration he decided not to even try, as such a negative story was most likely to be vetoed from the start. By comparison, he said, even the smallest matters had to be reported when they involved some of the themes mentioned above, such as economic achievement and visits by foreign dignitaries. In one instance, a couple of African leaders came through their area, and their visit received full coverage in his paper. He said he was also pressured to write a story at one point on how the Olympics would help China's economic development, based on a government report, even though he didn't believe it was true. Another reporter in Shanghai said he and his colleagues were instructed not to make China look too proud in their coverage, and to avoid writing about negative aspects of general public behavior such as spitting and the city's unruly traffic.

A couple of reporters I talked to did say that a certain amount of negative reporting was eventually allowed, though mostly after the games were over and the world's attention was no longer on China. One negative subject that often came up was wasteful spending, as publications discussed the billions of dollars used to build massive stadiums and venues that would most likely end up as white elephants. He said the government probably saw such articles as part of a postscript public debate on whether the Olympics were worth their huge cost, and whether the country should hold similar mass events in the future.

Thus ended a go-go time for China and its fast-evolving media, which would report on two major global events within the relatively short time frame of four months in 2008. The overriding media theme during this period was the focus on the positive, specifically on China's huge economic achievements in the case of the Olympics, and on how the government and military assisted victims of the worst natural disaster in three decades in the case of the Sichuan earthquake. This emphasis on the positive remains a central mantra for the Chinese media to this day, with censors quick to clamp down on anyone who reports too extensively on negative issues like crime, social unrest, or pollution. This focus on the positive has become a central part of Chinese perceptions of the media, and often leads to the view by many Chinese that Western media are somehow out to get China because of their preference for focusing on more negative news.

Closely coupled with the positive theme was the growing use of nationalism in coverage of both the Sichuan earthquake and the Olympics. In the former, the catastrophic event became a rallying point for all Chinese to throw their support behind the efforts of the government's army-led rescue effort. In the latter, people could rally around the Olympics as a display of China's rapid economic development. In both cases, the media were instructed to focus on the positive to make people feel good about being Chinese, which would translate to positive feelings about the government and their country. Any negative reports that might detract from those feelings were strongly discouraged, though some reports of corruption were allowed during the Sichuan quake and reports of overspending during the Olympics were tolerated after the games. If Mao's love of movements was the central theme in China's media through the 1970s, then this nationalistic theme centered on growing economic achievement is probably the biggest theme in the past 30 years.

From a more nuts-and-bolts perspective, the Chinese media had become much less homogenized by the time of the Olympics than was the case in the country's early years, although propaganda officials still exercised a broader form of control. As such, many of the old media tools and tactics like guerilla coverage, banners, and buzzwords had largely disappeared by this time, though catchphrases surrounding older issues such as Tibetan independence and the Falun Gong spiritual movement were still being used. The earthquake saw the Propaganda Ministry try to exert some of its old centralized control over the situation by at first discouraging reporters from going, only to later relent when it realized the positive value of reporting on rescue efforts. The Olympics would also see the use of a few older reporting tactics, most notably the publication of speeches by major leaders and even song lyrics, and the use of list-style reports to make a particular point, in this case how many important world leaders were attending the event. On the whole, the Sichuan earthquake and Olympics offered a glimpse of one of the most diverse Chinese media landscapes today in terms of actual reporting and relative independence of individual publications, even if the Propaganda Ministry's hand remained firmly on the "positive" switch.

Chapter 13

Google in China

Editorializing

A man places flowers on the Google logo at its China headquarters building in Beijing in March 2010. Google shuttered its China-based search service that year and moved it to Hong Kong after a high-profile spat with Beijing over China's strict self-censorship policies for all media.

Photo Credit: Reuters/OTHK

T he story of Google in China, or more precisely its abrupt pullout from the market in early 2010, differs from other events described in this book in that domestic media reported the tale largely through editorials rather than straight news. In order to understand the story and the choice of editorials to tell it, one first has to look at the broader development of the Internet and other new media in China, and the different dynamic between the government and these newcomers compared with traditional media.

For its first 50 years in power, the Communist Party exercised strict direct oversight of all newspapers, magazines, and TV stations through strong Party connections, including powerful internal Party secretaries at all media. But the same is far less true for new media like the Internet, which are dominated by a field of young, entrepreneurial companies with names like Sina, NetEase, and Sohu, nearly all of which were founded by people born during or after the 1970s, many of them educated abroad and with few formal Party connections.

China's leaders committed early on to the development of the nation's mobile networks and Internet, realizing that connectivity would be critical for the kind of modern society they hoped to build. Accordingly, the nation embarked on a huge spending spree on telecommunications infrastructure in the 1990s that continues to this day, in the process creating the world's biggest cellular and Internet markets. Today, around three quarters of Chinese now have mobile phones, and about half of the country's 1.3 billion people now surf the Internet. For someone like me, who lived in China during the 1980s, when having a phone in your home was a privilege reserved for the highest government officials, the change is truly remarkable.

Despite its commitment to developing these new media, China has remained highly sensitive about those same media's potential to become breeding grounds for discontent and unsavory activities like pornography. That paranoia, combined with the government's traditional tendency for heavy oversight, led Beijing to create a massive system to regulate and control these new media through a web of direct and indirect channels.

At the center of that web is a huge array of regulations governing everything from who can set up web sites to how to register them and the content that can go on them. To date, the government has created and implemented more than 60 laws pertaining to the Internet, a huge number for a medium whose commercial use dates back less than 20 years. At the same time, at least a dozen government departments now oversee the web, controlling everything from the telecom infrastructure at its core to the content that can go on sites and who is allowed to set up sites at all. Even Xinhua has even gotten in on the act, monitoring many popular web sites and compiling bulletins for central leaders on the latest online sentiment, somewhat akin to the old *neican* system of internal reports compiled by reporters for leaders' eyes only.

One exemplary case reflecting the heavy government oversight made national headlines in 2009, when two departments with overlapping regulatory responsibilities got into a turf war over a simple licensing dispute involving a popular online game. The case highlighted both the bureaucracy that has taken over the Internet, as well as the importance of good government relations. Such good relations with regulators and other officials are critical for any company doing business in China today, but especially for new media firms due to the high degree of oversight they receive.

In this web of oversight, news sites are an especially sensitive area. Whereas most Internet site operators can open shop with relatively little red tape, news sites must go through the Office of Foreign Propaganda or the State Council information office. What's more, the vast majority may provide news only from official sources, most notably Xinhua, with only a few rare exceptions. In reality many of these sites still post news from other nonofficial sources with little or no consequence, operating in the gray area where many newer media now do business. But they do so at their own peril, and risk big penalties or shutdown if any particular regulator decides to take action against them.

For those sites that make it past the rules and regulators, China has set up one final roadblock to try to maintain control over these newer media, using sophisticated software commonly known in foreign circles as "The Great Firewall of China" to filter out and block sensitive content. China can do this because no one in the country can access the web except through a handful of state-controlled Internet service providers, all of which run the latest filtering software on their systems. The firewall itself is officially administered by the Public Security Bureau, whose main role is to block access to web pages and sites on sensitive subjects like the Falun Gong spiritual movement and Tibetan independence.

Some estimate that more than a half million global web sites are officially blocked in China, running the range from more obvious ones to those that don't appear to have any controversial subject, such as Facebook and Twitter, both of which have been blocked since 2009. While some sites are permanently blocked, others are blocked only periodically when they post sensitive material. One acquaintance who oversees a popular news web site run by a major Western newspaper said he is frequently blocked whenever he publishes articles on sensitive subjects such as corruption. The government never provides any warnings or explanations when it puts up such roadblocks, creating the very real uncertainty for site operators that the blockage could last for weeks or even permanently, making everyone think twice about posting anything controversial.

To avoid being blocked or shut down by the censors, most major web operators have devoted huge resources to making sure that controversial content stays off their sites. Social networking sites are the most vulnerable, and often have huge teams whose main purpose is to actively police user-generated messages and other content for sensitive material and immediately remove it when it appears. In their eagerness to target anything even remotely sensitive, these internal online police are often quick to delete many items that don't really seem controversial at all. I was the victim of one such removal when I posted an item on one of my blogs about a controversial new real-name registration requirement for users of Twitter-like microblogging services. The new system was being widely publicized by Beijing in a campaign to crack down on rumor mongering, but was sensitive among the general public due to its Big Brother overtones. My post was removed within

24 hours and replaced by a simple message notifying me and apologizing for the removal.

Other vulnerable groups are ones that rely heavily on user-generated content, such as online video sites like YouTube, which itself is blocked in China. Even uncontroversial sites focused on areas like e-commerce and online travel have to watch out, as many also host internal message boards where users can rate and discuss products and services that can end up with sensitive material. The burden is especially heavy for online search engines like Google, who must heavily police themselves to keep any controversial subjects from ever appearing in their results. This produces the strange outcome that searches on terms like "Dalai Lama" or "Falun Gong," which should technically return millions of results, often produce only a handful of results or none at all for China-based search engines. It was this requirement for strict self-policing and censoring, which was at once onerous and more importantly contravened its dedication to free speech, that ultimately led Google to decide to shutter its China-based web site in 2010.

While the government tries its best to maintain control over the Internet and new media in general, it also realizes that any controls inevitably have their limits in a world where hundreds of millions of web surfers can publish their latest thoughts whenever they want on a wide range of sites. As a result, the rise of the Internet has resulted in an unprecedented plurality on China's media scene unlike anything seen in the pre-online age, reflecting the broader trend that has also seen the government broadly relax its strict oversight of traditional media while still reserving the right to set the main tones and punish anyone who strays too far from the Party line.

A microcosm of the current state of plurality is contained in Weibo, the hugely popular Twitter-like microblogging service that took off in China after the original Twitter was blocked in 2009. Weibo now boasts more than 300 million registered users, from celebrities to famous brands and ordinary Joes, who write their latest thoughts on everything from what they ate for breakfast to the latest social issues. Like Twitter, Weibo allows any registered user to monitor any of the system's other millions of users and view all their postings over any Internet connection. Thus the most popular celebrities might have tens or even hundreds of thousands of followers, known on the site as *fensi* or fans.

Even people with much smaller followings of dozens or hundreds of fans can quickly get big audiences if they post sensitive material, which is often retransferred again and again by interested viewers to all of their own respective followers. Weibo and others like it use software to closely monitor individual messages for sensitive keywords, then delete them when objectionable material is found.

When Issues Go Viral

The use of such software makes it easy to muzzle individuals who like to discuss sensitive issues, as their accounts can be quickly disabled and their posts deleted. But it becomes much harder to control for major issues that find their way into the spotlight and go viral, taking on a life of their own. One recent notable case occurred in 2011, involving a young woman named Guo Meimei, who touched off a national debate on corruption and waste at nonprofit organizations after she boasted on her Weibo account of a lavish lifestyle while claiming to work for a unit of the China Red Cross. That case was less controversial than issues directly related to the Party and government, but it was still somewhat sensitive, as many similar nonprofit organizations have close ties to the state and the attacks raised questions about wasteful spending in general. But in the end the Guo Meimei debate was largely allowed to continue uncensored, as the government felt it was far enough removed from the issue of the role and nature of charities in society, and the discussion was creating a healthy public debate.

Another case that sparked a huge national debate, which was previously discussed in Chapter 2, occurred when two high-speed rail trains collided in 2011, leaving more than 30 dead and about 200 injured. That case elicited a government response that was far less tolerant. That accident quickly became the subject of millions of Weibo microblog posts, made even more visceral with the inclusion of graphic pictures of twisted wreckage alongside. Unlike the Guo Meimei case, however, the high-speed rail crash had much closer ties to the government, which was in the midst of a multibillion-dollar spending campaign to build a massive national high-speed rail network. Many questioned the government's rapid construction of the network, saying that safety had taken a back seat to the government's eagerness to quickly build up the system. Talk of cover-ups also quickly mushroomed, as word circulated that rail officials had wanted to remove the wreckage from the tracks within hours of the accident rather than leaving the scene intact for a more thorough investigation. In the end the government let the debate continue for a while, before finally lowering the boom when it decided enough was enough. That approach in general reflects a more recent pattern that has seen Beijing tolerate debate on less politically sensitive matters for brief periods in all forms of media, new and traditional, before stepping in to officially end things when it feels that negative sentiment is getting out of control.

This more recent pattern of relative tolerance itself reflects a growing division within the government on how to handle the media. A clear conservative camp still exists, with many of its strongest backers in the Propaganda Ministry. At the same time, a more progressive camp has emerged, including a generation of many younger, more confident Party brass who think that China's media should operate more like their Western counterparts. Such reformists think a freer media could benefit the government and broader society by shining a spotlight on trouble spots, much the way the media do in the West. In a high-profile move reflecting the rise of this more open faction, a group of two dozen influential former leaders, including names from Xinhua and the *People's Daily*, sent a letter to the standing committee of the National People's Congress in 2010 calling for freedom of the press and an end to censorship. With so many competing forces on China's media landscape, it's easy to see how debates on the level of control can crop up often, and how inconsistencies often occur as individuals and government agencies jostle to exercise jurisdiction over their private and often-overlapping patches.

From the media perspective, the debate around Google's sudden decision to shutter its China search engine in 2010 may have taken place during a more open time for reporting, but sensitivity over the core issue of censorship meant the Party still called all the shots in terms of setting the tone and dictating the broader coverage. The government's tool of choice in the largely one-sided media debate over Google's surprise withdrawal was the editorial—a widely used format throughout modern Chinese history that, as noted in an earlier chapter, reached a zenith during the Cultural Revolution. While most of the events detailed in this book were told through traditional news stories, the tale of Google's blowup with Beijing was told almost exclusively through editorials appearing in much of the traditional Chinese media. By taking such an approach for a straight news story that made global headlines elsewhere, the government seemed to be saying the whole dispute was simply a matter of opinion, with the heavy implication that its own view was the right one and that Google was being a crybaby for refusing to play by the rules of its host country. Such an approach also downplayed the importance of the story, relegating it to a matter not even worthy of being labeled as news, but rather a difference of opinion.

More broadly speaking, the government has developed an interesting approach to editorials over the years, encouraging the media to write them locally as a form of limited public debate. In the case of Google, the local media were allowed to write their own editorials, though most probably understood they had to closely follow the Party line from Beijing. But in a growing number of cases, the government also allows more freedom in editorial writing when it wants to gauge public opinion on certain topics. One good example occurred in 2009, when an obscure Chinese company made a bid for the insolvent gas-guzzling Hummer brand being sold by General Motors. In that case a wide range of editorials appeared in many regional media on the subject, producing an eventual consensus that the deal made little sense. Not surprisingly, the government ended up vetoing the purchase months later.

The Google case also shines a spotlight on the whole issue of self-censorship, as Google's distaste for self-censoring its own search results in China lay at the heart of its decision to leave the market. In that self-censored world, everyone—from ordinary web surfers to site operators—knows what is and isn't acceptable for discussion. Chinese media have to put up with such self-censorship because China is their only market and they have no other choice; but foreign media like Google face a much tougher choice since they often come to China for its big potential, even if much of that potential lies in the future and they have to abide by tough self-censorship rules that go against their core principles of free speech in the meantime.

One final minor theme from this case is how the media almost became a de facto mouthpiece for the Chinese government on the issue. Throughout the Google debate, China made few public comments on

the matter, discussing it only at regular government ministry news conferences for foreign reporters. Instead, the government stepped back and
let the media do most of the talking to echo what the Party wanted
to say, making it into a one-way debate and shaping it into a discourse
around a difference of opinion rather than censorship or human rights.

To put the event in the proper context, one also needs to look at
the history of Google in China. The company was already one of the
nation's most popular search engines dating back to the early 2000s,
through a Chinese version of its main Google.com site based outside
China. It formally won a license to operate in China in 2005, setting
up its main office in Beijing and launching a new China-based service
at the web address of Google.cn. Almost immediately, the company
came under fire from human rights and freedom of speech advocates in
the West, who accused it of self-censoring its China site. In fact, every
Internet company doing business in China, be it domestic or foreign,
must also actively self-police its content and eliminate results on sensitive
topics as required by Chinese law, or risk being blocked or even closed
down. Other big Western names that practiced similar self-censorship
included Yahoo, which purchased China's then-leading search engine
in 2003, and Microsoft, which launched a Chinese version of its Bing
search engine in 2009.

But Google, because of its size, US connections, and central principle to "don't be evil," received much greater scrutiny from the Western
media for its willingness to play by China's rules. As a result, some of
its officials were called along with executives from other major Internet
companies to testify at a US congressional hearing on the matter in
2006, resulting in a great deal of negative publicity not only for Google
but for many of the other US Internet firms active in China.

Google remained a reluctant self-censor in China throughout its
brief tenure there, continuing to abide by Chinese rules as it also steadily
lost its dominant market position to a local up-and-comer named Baidu,
which now controls the lion's share of China's online search market.
As its market share was dwindling, Google on January 12, 2010, abruptly
announced that it was seriously considering pulling out of China, citing the broader issue of censorship as well as a major hacking attack that
appeared to have come from the country. After a brief period of intense
publicity right after the high-profile announcement, Google largely

went quiet as it presumably tried to negotiate a better deal for itself with Beijing that would ease up some of the censorship rules.

No reports ever came out on what actually took place behind the scenes during that time, but whatever discussions took place—if any—clearly didn't produce the compromise that Google was seeking. In the end, the company abruptly shuttered the search service on its Google.cn site in late March 2010, and moved it to Hong Kong, where Beijing's stiff self-censorship rules didn't apply.

Despite relocating the actual search engine to Hong Kong, Google still maintained its Google.cn site with a message informing visitors of the move and links to the new site. That maintained presence, albeit small, would be the source of one final confrontation with Beijing during the dispute, which would see China threaten not to renew Google's license for the site in late June 2010. Again, no reports ever emerged about what took place behind the scenes after that, but the two sides apparently resolved their differences and China officially renewed the license in early July 2010. The search site remains active to this day, although only as a placeholder with links to the Google Hong Kong search site.

For my analysis of Google coverage, I looked mostly at the *Youth Daily*, a popular Beijing newspaper whose target audience of young readers is especially applicable to the Internet, which in China is dominated by users under the age of 30. The newspaper had zero coverage of the blowup for the first full week after Google's original announcement, in a classic news blackout most likely ordered by Beijing while leaders figured out how to respond to the unexpected development, both in terms of policy and media coverage.

On January 13, 2010, the day after Google first voiced its unhappiness with the status quo, the *Youth Daily* carried no direct mention of the story but did contain another report on page seven related to a different controversy involving a group of authors that has accused Google of copyright violations. In this case the article stated that Google had postponed the latest round of talks with the authors to settle the ongoing dispute. Google was earlier involved in a similar, much higher profile controversy in the United States, and indeed copyright cases involving the Internet are so common that it's unclear whether this story had any relationship at all to the latest conflict with Beijing.

Breaking the Silence: "China's Internet Is Open"

The first direct reference to the controversy did not appear until January 18, nearly a week after the matter made headlines in the rest of the world, in an editorial in the inside pages that would come to characterize most of the *Youth Daily*'s coverage. This first editorial appears in the newspaper's law and society section on page six, under the headline "China's Internet Is Open." The piece defended China's approach to the Internet, with no mention of the Google controversy until well into the editorial. When the Google matter was finally raised, the editorial was critical of the company's China site for containing material that violates authors' copyrights, a reference to the earlier controversy, as well as links to pornography. The next day followed with another critical editorial on page two, this time headlined "When Google Coughs, America Speaks Out," a reference to the fact that the US government quickly came to Google's defense in the matter. Adding to the dismissive tone of China's reporting on the issue, this editorial included an interesting mini-banner above it with the words "Freezing Topic," which was probably a reference to the frosty relations between both China and Google, and China and the United States, that resulted from the controversy. In a bit of wordplay, this banner can also be read as "Cold Topic," a takeoff on the similar Chinese expression for hot topics, conveying the author's view that the controversy was a non-story that Google was using as a publicity stunt.

After these first two editorials, the *Youth Daily* adhered to its view that this news was a non-story by going five more days before mentioning it again on January 24. This time, the story suddenly jumped onto the front page as the pressure was mounting on China from the rest of the world. And this time the news came in the form of a regular story from Xinhua, which didn't address the censorship controversy directly but instead focused on Google's other stated reason for its threat to withdraw, namely the discovery of a major hacking attack that most likely came from China. When Google first disclosed this attack at the time of its original announcement, its pronouncement strongly suggested that the government may have been partly or fully behind the action, as it appeared to come from a school campus. This January 24 article directly addressed this part of the story with the headline "China Is the

Country that Suffers the Most from Hacker Attacks." It made no reference to the censorship issue and simply referred to the broader controversy as the "Google incident." In the story, an official from China's Internet emergency response center pointed out that Google had yet to provide his agency with any concrete details of the attack. The story also pointed readers to a related story showing that Baidu, Google's chief rival in China, had also come under a major hacking attack at around the same time.

In addition to this front-page story on January 24, the *Youth Daily* continued with its use of editorials in a page-two item headlined "Internet Freedom: A Pretext for the US Government's Advantage." As in the past, the tone of this editorial was both defensive and dismissive, accusing the United States of preaching Internet openness through cases like the Google controversy when doing so works to its advantage.

The string of editorials continued for the next few days, largely in the same vein of belittling and downplaying the controversy, accusing the United States of seeking political gain and creating a broader feel that Google was just a crybaby throwing a temper tantrum because it couldn't dominate China like it had most other major markets. A January 26 editorial along those lines came with the headline "A Dejected Google Bows Out After Finishing its Noisy Performance," reflecting Beijing's growing confidence in the matter as Chinese public opinion started to move squarely in its desired direction. In a throwback to an older media tactic, another story on January 27, now two weeks after the original controversy broke, cited high-profile foreigners outside China speaking on the subject in a way that seemed to vindicate Beijing's stance. In this instance, the article reprinted comments from a US media interview with Microsoft's Bill Gates, in which he said that the Internet in China must be allowed to develop and become an engine for free speech. In the article, Gates, whose Microsoft has invested years and massive resources to build up its China business, also noted that anyone who does business in another country must observe that country's laws—a clear reference to the fact that Google knew it would have to self-censor when it made its initial decision to enter China.

From this point in the story I jump ahead two months to Google's announcement in late March 2010 that it was formally withdrawing from the China search market, after failing to reach a compromise with Beijing. The *Youth Daily* carried its first report on the decision on March 24, this time shortly after Google announced its formal withdrawal. By now, the paper's confidence had grown to the point where it seemed that editorials were no longer needed to tell the story, which appeared on the front page with two articles, both of which downplayed the political significance of the decision. One cited an Internet regulatory official saying China would refuse to let commercial issues become politicized, again painting Google as the sore loser that simply couldn't compete in China and thus took cover under the politically charged excuse of censorship. The second article was similar, quoting a Foreign Ministry spokesman saying the decision was a commercial matter that should not be dragged into Sino–US relations. Unlike previous editorials, which were penned by *Youth Daily* writers, these two articles were both reprints from Xinhua, which had become the only source for any formal news stories on the matter. From this point on, the conflict disappeared from the pages of the *Youth Daily*, which by now had determined the matter was clearly a non-story.

As one final note, I also looked at the *Liberation Daily*, Shanghai's major Party newspaper catering to a more mainstream and older audience, to see how it covered the story. The *Liberation Daily* gave even less ink to its coverage than the *Youth Daily*, not mentioning it at all until January 20, or a day after the *Youth Daily*'s first direct reference and a full week after the controversy erupted. Even then, the *Liberation Daily* mentioned the controversy merely in a brief item from its News Summaries section, saying recent comments from Google CEO Eric Schmidt might indicate the company was softening its stance on leaving China.

One Shanghai-based journalist working for a major domestic business newspaper said that from a reporting perspective, the Google controversy unfolded much the way that many sensitive stories now do in China. He said his paper wrote several of its own major stories the day after Google made its initial announcement, which it ran on the newspaper's front page, looking at it more from a diplomatic than a purely business perspective. After that first day, he said, all media were instructed not to report further on the subject until receiving guidance from the Propaganda Ministry, which had been blindsided by the development just like everyone else. This reporter said that he and many of his media peers were surprised by the confrontational, high-profile way that Google handled the matter, forcing China to come up with its own strong response and making any form of compromise difficult. In the end, no one was allowed to write on the subject until Xinhua issued its first reports, reflecting the government's decision to spin the issue as Google's attempt to politicize a commercial decision. That pause while everyone waited for Xinhua explained the weeklong delay before the story appeared in less-aggressive publications like the *Liberation Daily* and even the *Youth Daily*. It's hard to say what actually went on inside individual publications without knowing any reporters there, but my sense from talking to ordinary Chinese was that many honestly believed that Google was indeed crying foul simply because it couldn't compete in China and that its high-profile withdrawal was largely a political smokescreen. If that was the case, then much of the reporting at the *Youth Daily* and other publications probably reflected their real view that Google's withdrawal was a non-story, as they bought into the Party line coming from Beijing.

Another reporter at a less-aggressive newspaper in south China said his editors mostly used the Xinhua reports and gave the story relatively light coverage. One other reporter in a smaller market in central China said that many people in that city couldn't see what all the fuss was about, reflecting the acceptance by many Chinese that sensitive topics usually will be censored, and again reinforcing a general feeling that the whole controversy was perhaps in fact a non-story. He said that most people ultimately saw the controversy as politically motivated, with the result that no one seemed to care too much.

At the end of the day, the Google controversy in China highlights the rise of new media there, with Beijing still holding a firm grip on the big picture while allowing limited public debate. On the one hand, the conflict underscores how China's media have become a much more diverse and varied group of voices that can air their own views to a certain extent in terms of the scope and depth of their coverage on specific issues. On the other hand, it also shows how even in the Internet age Beijing continues to set the tone on sensitive stories, using its old system of phone calls and memos to senior editors at major media to shut down coverage of certain topics and then later decide on the tone of coverage.

In the case of Google, the central government's decision was clear when it finally came about a week after the news broke. It set out to

paint the controversy as a purely commercial matter, with Google trying to hide that fact by appealing to the US government and freedom
of speech advocates to draw attention away from its inability to compete
with local rivals.

At the more nitty-gritty level, the Google tale started off with a
classic news blackout, as Beijing considered how to respond, including
how it wanted to spin the story. In the end, the government decided
to tell the media tale through editorials, a tried-and-tested format that
permits closely guided public discussion while downplaying the significance of the matter through the limited use of actual news stories.
Today's Chinese media have made growing use of this editorializing tactic to treat similar stories on sensitive subjects, especially ones involving outside criticism on issues like human rights and limitations on free
speech. By taking such an approach, the government can at once address
these kinds of sensitive matters and provide its side of the story, while
also downplaying them by saying that they don't even qualify as news.

Afterword

'm calling this brief appendix an afterword rather than a formal conclusion to reflect the fact that the Chinese media, like their counterparts throughout the world, are evolving very quickly and therefore
are very much a work in progress. As such, it would be foolish to try
to conclude anything about this dynamic and increasingly diverse force
that to a large extent still retains its original role of delivering the Party's
important messages of the day to the average Chinese. But even that
central role has shown signs of change in recent years, with the rise
of new media and a younger generation of reporters and publications
increasingly willing to push the envelope beyond the Party line.

A good metaphor would be to liken China's media to a single
body in its early days, with the Party as the brain directly controlling all
movements of the arms and legs, representing the various media. In the
past decade, that model has been replaced by one that looks more like
a symphony orchestra, with Beijing as the conductor waving its baton
while individual musicians are allowed some room to interpret the
music in their own way. One person I interviewed described the transformation in an earlier chapter of this book, saying the Chinese media
in their first few decades were like a person tied to a chair in a locked

room. In the past decade, the ropes have been removed but the person remains locked in the room.

There's no question that China has relaxed its grip on the broader media in recent years, though how far and how fast it is prepared to go following a major leadership change in 2012 and 2013 is anyone's guess. Whereas less-sensitive areas of the media like TV shows and Internet social networking sites have seen relaxed government oversight in recent years, the more sensitive news sector remains a touchy area and could continue to be so for years to come.

The year 2012 was a seminal one in many ways, marked by a series of major new initiatives that sent a clear message that Beijing wanted the media to become more market focused and create products that people wanted. Equally important, the allowance of a number of major foreign players into the market, ending years of informal prohibition, also signaled that Beijing was less concerned about maintaining direct ownership over every element of the media.

The year began with the announcement that China would allow significantly more foreign films into its theaters, relaxing a cap that had limited the number to 20 for more than a decade. Not long afterward, big Western media names, including Disney, DreamWorks Animation, and the QVC Shopping Network, announced new joint ventures to develop programs and launch channels in the market one after the other.

And in perhaps the most symbolic move, the web site of none other than the *People's Daily*, the ultimate symbol of the Party's voice, made a landmark initial public offering by listing its shares on the Shanghai Stock Exchange in May. That act above all others seemed to be China's way of telling everyone that it was determined to build world-class media, and that market forces and foreign expertise were welcome as part of that campaign. Beijing had already rolled out the welcome mat several years earlier for a number of other foreign media, including Reuters and the *Wall Street Journal*, allowing them to set up their own Chinese-language financial news web sites.

But all that said, financial news is far less controversial than reporting on politics and sensitive social trends, and clearly animation and home shopping are even less so. When it comes to more traditional news, China likes to keep its hands much more directly on the levers of power to control the messages being delivered. Foreigners are still largely excluded from this area, and even private Chinese investors, with a few exceptions, are mostly forbidden from operating news sites without direct ownership by government entities.

Although the news is still largely off limits for anyone outside the government's sphere of influence, it could be just a matter of time before that, too, changes. I'm relatively confident that the change will come at some point, as evidenced by my decision to teach in one of China's top journalism programs, where many of the students are enthusiastic, and eager to go out and write investigative and analytical reports on the latest social trends and other hot issues. At the same time, they know there are limitations on what they can do, which has led more than a few to drop their journalistic aspirations in favor of more practical careers.

At the end of the day, China may have no choice but to liberalize its news media and allow more independent voices as it discovers the difficulties of controlling the message in an increasingly pluralistic new media world where just about anyone can express his or her views on the Internet. It won't give up its control without at least some resistance, and any final transformation to a truly Western style of media with many independent voices will come—if it ever does—only after a lot of debate and soul searching.

About the Author

Doug Young is an associate professor in the journalism department at China's Fudan University in Shanghai. He has worked in the media for nearly two decades, half of that in China, where he has witnessed the massive changes that have taken place in the country since the earliest days of the reform era in the 1980s. Most recently he worked for Reuters from 2000 to 2010 covering the China story out of the Shanghai, Hong Kong, and Taipei bureaus. Before that he worked as a journalist in Los Angeles. He is a native of Washington, D.C., and received his bachelor's degree in geology from Yale University and a master's degree in Asian studies from Columbia University. In addition to his current jobs as teacher and author, he also comments on the latest China company news and industry trends on his personal blog at www.youngchinabiz.com.

Index